URBAN FLOW

ILR Press, AN IMPRINT OF CORNELL UNIVERSITY PRESS • ITHACA AND LONDON

URBAN FLOW

BIKE MESSENGERS AND THE CITY

JEFFREY L. KIDDER

First published 2011 by Cornell University Press

Printed in the United States of America

Library of Congress Cataloging-in-Publication Data

Kidder, Jeffrey L. (Jeffrey Lowell), 1977–
   Urban flow : bike messengers and the city / Jeffrey L. Kidder.
      p. cm.
   Includes bibliographical references and index.
   ISBN 978-0-8014-4992-5 (cloth : alk. paper)
   1. Bicycle messengers—United States—Social conditions.
   2. Sociology, Urban—United States.   I. Title.
      HE9753.K53   2011
      388.3'472—dc22   2011004994

Cornell University Press strives to use environmentally responsible suppliers and materials to the fullest extent possible in the publishing of its books. Such materials include vegetable-based, low-VOC inks and acid-free papers that are recycled, totally chlorine-free, or partly composed of nonwood fibers. For further information, visit our website at www.cornellpress.cornell.edu.

Cloth printing   10 9 8 7 6 5 4 3 2 1

Photo credits: 1–7, 9–14, 17, 19–23: Keri Wiginton; 8, 15–16, 18: Kenton Hoppas

For K.E.W., C.B.K., and S.E.C.

CONTENTS

ACKNOWLEDGMENTS

First and foremost, I am indebted to all the messengers who let me into their lives, and those who took the time to discuss the occupation and the subculture with me. Without the friendships of those I had the honor to meet while on the road there would have been nothing to write. I am especially indebted to Jacky Hoang, Kenton Hoppas, Jason Kleinmann, and Matt Nascimento for their help along the way. Josh Korby and Mike Morell of 4 Star Courier Collective were kind enough to take some time out of a busy (and rainy) day to make sure there was a suitable photograph for the book's cover (that, unfortunately, did not make the final edit). This list should be much, much longer, but there are too many names to mention them all. So let me just say to everyone hustling to make that dollar: keep the rubber side down, and ride safe.

I had the good fortune of having numerous people help me turn a jumble of ideas into something comprehensible. Patrick Badgley, Rick Biernacki, Jim Dowd, Michael Hanson, Robert Horwitz, Josia Lamberto-Egan, Isaac Martin, Christena Turner, and Keri Wiginton all read and commented on various parts of the manuscript (in many different stages of completion and/or disarray). Regretfully, the final product does not fully reflect all the wonderful advice they provided. Offering far more than editorial advice, Christena, Isaac, and Jim, along with Kwai Ng, were wellsprings of guidance throughout the many years of this project, and I cannot thank them enough. Further, without the support of Fran Benson, ILR's editorial director, this manuscript might never have seen the light of day. I am also appreciative of the careful reading and constructive criticism provided by ILR's editors and anonymous reviewers.

Several sections of this book were previously published in different forms, and I would like to thank the various publishers for their permission to reuse parts of those articles here. Chapter 4 is derived from "'It's the job I love': Bike Messengers and Edgework," *Sociological Forum* 21 (2006): 31–54. Chapter 5 is derived from "Bike Messengers and the Really Real: Effervescence, Reflexivity, and Postmodern Identity," *Symbolic Interaction* 29 (2006): 349–71. Chapter 6 is derived from "Appropriating the City: Space, Theory, and Bike Messengers," *Theory and Society* 38 (2009): 307–28. Chapter 7 is a reworking of "Style and Action: A Decoding of Bike Messenger Symbols," *Journal of Contemporary Ethnography* 34 (2005): 344–67.

Last, but certainly not least, Keri Wiginton, my wife, is responsible for most of the wonderful photographs in this book. For years now I've goaded her into lugging around cameras and gear whenever we were visiting a city populated with bike messengers. She also had to indulge my tenacious approach to finishing this project—often at the expense of far more fun ways to spend a Saturday night. I am forever indebted to her for the patience and support she's given me.

URBAN FLOW

INTRODUCTION
The Lure of Delivery

It was just after dark in Claremont Park, in the Bronx, on Saturday, August 24, 2002. I was dressed in a mock-up of a New York Yankees baseball jersey, with my face painted yellow and red. Five other guys were dressed just like me. We were a comic-book caricature of a street gang, and we called ourselves the Furies. Standing around us were eighty-four other equally fictional gangs: the Bloody Marys, the Cutters, the Electric Vikings, the South Side Slashers, and more. In total, almost six hundred oddly dressed men and women were in Claremont Park that night. We all had bicycles, and many of us were bike messengers. Not just New York bike messengers, but messengers from across the country and around the world: Boston, Chicago, London, Philadelphia, Tokyo, Toronto (to name just a few places). The event was called the Warriors Fun Ride. It was part bicycle race, part scavenger hunt, and all party.

The "fun ride" was a tribute to the 1979 cult classic *The Warriors*—a film depicting a not-so-futuristic New York City overrun by hordes of street gangs, all wearing ridiculous uniforms. The movie's "heroes" are a gang from Coney Island, the Warriors, who must fight their way back to Brooklyn from the Bronx. As in the movie, the goal of the fun ride was to make it to Coney Island. However, before arriving at the finish, each "gang" had to make it to checkpoints scattered across the city. At these checkpoints, there was some sort of challenge or task to be completed. One checkpoint, for example, involved a game of handball. At another checkpoint, one member of each team had to get a real tattoo. Teams received points based on their arrival time at each checkpoint and their success at completing each challenge. Additional points could also be earned by finding answers to various trivia questions about the city. To answer these questions riders needed to travel to specific places to find, for example, the exact inscription on a statue or the number of flag-poles in a park. Beyond the checkpoints and trivia questions, there were also mandatory party stops with food, beer, and more illicit types of in-toxication. These were stops where many of the racers, less interested in the actual competition, stayed well past the required time. Just as in the movie, the event was organized so the finishers arrived at Coney Island at dawn. Fifty-two of the original eighty-five teams stuck with it to the end.

A Glimpse into the Messenger Subculture

I had been working as a messenger for about three months, and the Warriors was my first messenger event. I had first heard about the War-riors from Jason, whom I had met months before as I haplessly looked for the service entrance to a building. Days later I ran into him on the Williamsburg Bridge, where he formally introduced himself. It was a pat-tern I would see repeated over and over again. If you were a messenger new to the city, Jason would make an effort not only to say hello, but to invite you to a bar or a party where you could meet more messengers. At the time, Jason already had five years of messenger experience. He had started working in D.C. and had moved to New York a few years back. It was thanks to Jason that from my very beginnings in New York, I was able to meet many veteran couriers and alleycat organizers—including the people responsible for putting on the Warriors Fun Ride.

Jason was in his late 20s, and, beneath his warmth and congenial-ity, he was rather intimidating. Stocky and strong, he was not afraid to assert himself physically whenever he deemed necessary, and alcohol—which he (like most messengers) was quite fond of—increased this necessity. We were riding together one evening when a cab cut us off. Jason's expression turned to stone. He spat on the cab's windshield and stared the driver down. I was shocked (and impressed) with his display of violent intent. Apparently the cabbie was too. He yielded to us, we rode on through the intersection in front of him, and Jason transformed back into the smiling companion he had been just seconds before. Jason was also quick-witted, well read, and a world traveler. His thoughtfully liberal politics continually contrasted with his otherwise gruff working-class masculinity.

However, even if I hadn't met Jason or the other people who orga-nized the Warriors, it would have been impossible to not know about the upcoming event. While a lot of what messengers do in their free time is thoroughly underground—you need to know the right people to hear the word—this was not the case with the Warriors. As the day of the ride approached, couriers I did not know would talk to me about it in elevators. One messenger even chased me down in traffic to make sure I knew about it. The Thursday before, new faces started appearing in Tompkins Square Park. Tompkins has been an after-hours meeting place for decades, and the out-of-town messengers knew it was *the* place to meet other bike couriers. Excited about the coming event, more than the usual share of local couriers also made a point to swing by the park.

By Friday, Tompkins was bursting with messengers. The Cutters, from San Francisco, were already in their uniforms. They wore ripped jean vests, the backs painted, motorcycle-gang style, with straight razors and brass knuckles. As is the case with many messengers, the stripped-down, scratched, and stickered look of their bicycles concealed (from the lay ob-server, at least) that their machines were actually worth thousands of dol-lars. The Cutters rode around the park performing wheelies and other, far more complicated bicycle tricks. More messengers joined in a friendly game of one-upmanship. It was like dueling banjos, but on bikes. The San Francisco messengers were the only couriers I had seen come close to matching the skill of Salvador, a New York messenger renowned for his tricks. I once watched Salvador ride his bike seated on the handlebars, facing backward, for blocks on end—while negotiating his way through a mass of other cyclists. During the actual Warriors ride, Salvador astounded onlookers at one of the checkpoints by bunny hopping his bike over sev-eral people lying on the ground.

Friday was officially the day to preregister for the event, but, more importantly, it was a time to socialize. Many of the out-of-town couriers were already friends with New York messengers, having met many times before at courier events held around the world. Others were meeting people for the first time. Many messengers came to New York not even knowing where they would stay, but all found places. Hospitality for trav-eling messengers is universal. Some messengers actually financed their trip by staying for weeks after the Warriors. They worked for New York courier companies in order to save up enough money to return home. To put it another way, these messengers, living not much better than hand to mouth, came to New York with barely any money, and they had no choice but to find work so they could eventually make their way home.

Saturday, as my team rode from Brooklyn to the Bronx, we crossed paths with numerous other gangs also on their way to Claremont Park. It seemed as though the entire city was filled with out-of-place Halloween revelers—on bikes. Claremont Park was simply out of control. Standing on a park bench and speaking through a bullhorn, Squid, one of the event organizers, advised the crowd that the event was to be more of a "fun ride" and less of a "race." He told us to focus on having fun, rather than competing. He also attempted to explain that scoring for prizes would be based not only on time, but also on answering the trivia questions. With these words said, and a smattering of referential quotes from the film ("Can you dig it?" "Come out and play," ad nauseam), the competition started. Despite Squid's advice to the contrary, for many the Warriors was very much a race. However, messengers have a very particular way of racing. For example, a countdown started the Warriors. It began with "three," but before the word "two" had a chance to leave the organizer's lips the riders were already off.

From a legal standpoint, there was nothing official or sanctioned about Saturday night. No governmental agencies were informed of the event—certainly not the police. Most importantly, there was no set racecourse. There were only set destinations. It was each team's responsibility to find the best way to get there. Indeed, that was the primary challenge of the event. It was understood that, in order to get from checkpoint to checkpoint, riders would do *whatever* they deemed necessary to shave time off their route. There were very few rules, and traffic laws were *completely* ignored. People were darting in and out of cars and swerving in front of buses. This is completely typical behavior for bike messengers, but for those unaccustomed to such "urban cycling" it undoubtedly looked like suicidal pandemonium. Adding to the chaos, as if on cue, rain began to pour from the heavens as our nearly six hundred souls swarmed through the streets of the Bronx.

Hours later, at one of the mandatory party stops in Brooklyn, hundreds of cyclists filled an entire block of a run-down warehouse district. Nearly dry again from the earlier storm, we ate free burgers, hot dogs, and veggie burgers and drank beer donated by Pabst (without a doubt, the most cherished sponsorship the event organizers were able to procure). At one point, a lone police car attempted to make its way through the throng of people. No one moved. The cop turned on his siren. Still, no one moved. He used his loudspeaker to tell us to disperse. The crowd just ignored him. Another command rang out from his car, this time followed by the threat of arrest. Slowly, the crowd shifted just enough for the car to pass. For whatever reason, the cop backed down from the challenge, and the party went on. At this point, for most of the teams, the original vigor had long since waned. For the teams that did not finish, most called it quits here. Not because the ride had failed to be fun—rather, the exact opposite. The event was so enjoyable, many people figured, why push oneself further? Fun had already been had in copious amounts.

As for the rest of us, though, we rode on. A few teams still had their eyes on the prize. The gang that would go on to win were the Banditos—a group of New York messengers composed largely of Mexican immigrants known for their punk-rock style and defiantly hedonistic attitude. My team, though, now riding with a Chicago gang modeled after the *Saturday Night Live* skit the Super Fans (famous for gorging on bratwurst and toasting "da Bears"), had no qualms about taking the rest of the night slowly. But, even riding slowly, we still ignored traffic regulations. Somewhere in between Williamsburg, Brooklyn, and Coney Island, we spent half an hour trying to find a bodega to sell us beer in the wee hours of Sunday morning (which is against the law). I was the only member of our combined group to believe it was humanly possible to complete the ride without further libations. Clearly, I was insane, and finally a storekeeper took pity on our plight and consented that no law should inhibit the group's inebriation.

Though I arrived at Coney Island completely sober (I was a distinct minority), I was so tired that the morning exists only as a shadowy blur in my mind. I must also admit that my field notes are of only marginal use. Some people stripped down and swam in the Atlantic. There was a final showdown between the teams in a tug-of-war match. Our baseball-themed gang was pitted against a hockey-themed gang from Toronto. We lost. Exhausted, we took the train back to Brooklyn, and I got a few hours' sleep before heading up to Socrates Sculpture Park, in Queens, for the awards ceremony. This was the one and only part of the weekend that, in fact, had a city permit. Among the various awards given out were best overall gang, best coed gang, best female gang, and best out-of-town gang (since local knowledge is an extreme advantage in such an event). Awards were also given for best costume, neatest manifest, best crash, etc. The prizes included two tickets to Copenhagen for the Cycle Messenger World Championships (one rider from the best overall gang and one from the best female gang), a thousand dollars cash (for the best gang costume), as well as a bicycle, a bike frame, and various cycling components.

I was already enjoying my time working as a messenger, but after the Warriors Fun Ride, I became even more enthralled with the job and its surrounding subculture. I met interesting people (from all over the world), I saw crazy things (from cool bicycles and unbelievable bike tricks to drunken mayhem), and all the while I was also pushing my own comfort level in how I could ride as an urban cyclist. Because of all these things, I had an incredible amount of fun during the Warriors. And, because of these things, I also knew I had made the right choice in deciding to undertake a research project on bike couriers.

Bike Messengers and Sociological Study

Bike messengers are paid to deliver time-sensitive items (e.g., court filings) in congested urban areas. In 1993, an article in the *Toronto Star* claimed: "They live the life you may have dreamed of but never had the courage or foolish disregard to try....The life of the bicycle courier...You have a primal dream about it....You go to the parties the straights never hear about....You have the kind of sex they would give their fortune for. And you don't wear a tie, either." A decade later, the *Seattle Times* printed some equally compelling comments: "In case you haven't been in the urban core of any major American city for the past few decades, bike messengers are those toned, tattooed daredevils who cut through exhaust and traffic all day long delivering just about anything that will fit in their shoulder bags." Both of these articles reproduce a typical strand in popular culture: the bike messenger as folk hero. In fact, in the mid-1980s, a writer for *New York Magazine* observed: "They are becoming folk heroes—the pony-express riders of the eighties. The bicycle messenger might even be regarded by some as the ultimate urban man—tough, resourceful, self-contained, riding against the odds the city stacks against everybody." A columnist for the *Washington Post* captured the other side of public sentiment, proclaiming: "In my gentler moments, I've called them law-flouting, obscenity-spewing, bath-needing, wild-riding, pedestrian-smashing madmen." Twelve years later, the same condemnation was expressed in an editorial in the *New York Times:* "Some of these boys look good in tights, but most are maniacal and dangerous.... Getting hit by a bike messenger is a true New York experience."[1]

"What's the Lure of Delivering Packages?"

To those not living in major metropolitan areas (especially, major metropolitan areas with primary transportation infrastructure constructed before the suburban housing boom following World War II), bike messengers sound quaint at best. Often the concept just sounds silly. Every now and again, I am asked (always by someone who has never spent substantial time in such cities), "But what do they deliver?" followed by a chuckle. However, as the small sampling of newspaper articles above shows, for those living in larger, older cities—Boston, Chicago, New York, San Francisco, Washington, D.C.—as well as a few newer ones, bike messengers are a source of cultural fascination. Even to the casual observer, bike messengers appear to be part of an interesting, but obscure, subculture.

When I was working as a messenger in Seattle, a businessman in an elevator asked me: "What's the lure of delivering packages? I see a lot of people doing it, and they seem to love it." And love it they do. I cannot count the number of times I have heard messengers describe their occupation as "the best job ever." The businessman's question, "What's the lure of delivering packages?" should be enough to make anyone stop and ponder—most certainly a sociologist. Really, what is the allure?

When I worked at Sprint Courier in New York, my average daily wage was $63 (for the days that I did work). I had no health care, no paid holidays, and no sick leave. When I was injured or when my bicycle was broken, I had no income. I was in multiple accidents with motor vehicles and pedestrians, thankfully nothing serious, but this had more to do with luck than skill. In order to deliver packages in a timely manner I regularly broke traffic laws, and racked up hundreds of dollars in citations. And I, not my company, was responsible for paying them. Moreover, I had to endure working in the rain and snow. I put up with irate drivers and condescending clients on a daily basis. *What is the allure?*

How does this job, which sounds downright awful when described this way, result in an internationally attended, all-night race/party through the city (complete with commemorative tattoos)? Or, to put the question somewhat differently, how does a low-end service job (rife with danger and for minimal material compensation) produce so much attachment that people want to throw parties celebrating it? To quote an advertisement (which ran in a desktop-published magazine produced by New York couriers) for an upcoming race in Philadelphia: "Come join us in Philadelphia this September to remember Tom and all the other messengers who have fallen [i.e., died while working]—as well as to celebrate being a bike messenger, the best job you'll ever have."[2]

Meaning and Identity in Contemporary Times

A vast cross section of literature tells us that work is no longer the primary source of self-identity. Of course, there are exceptions. Medical doctors and military officers, for example, see themselves through their chosen occupation.[3] And, certainly, religious officials are expected to have virtually no separation between their "work selves" and their "real selves." These occupations (along with lawyers) are what could be considered the classic professions. They require a high degree of formal training and present strict barriers to entry. They also involve creative decision-making, personal responsibility, and an uncertainty of outcomes. That is, in these jobs individuals are charged with making choices in which the final results are unknown.

Sociologist Robert Dubin contends that because of the challenges they offer their practitioners, these occupations can become central life interests.[4] The job tasks themselves can be a source of individual satisfaction, and the occupation tends to be an integral part of identity. In a word, the work has the possibility of being *meaningful*. Central life interests, whether they are vocational or avocational, are how individuals realize their authentic selves. They are activities that actors are not forced into (out of necessity or obligation) but seek (out of personal desire). For example, a soldier may march through the woods only because he is ordered to, but an outdoor enthusiast needs no such external motivation.

For Dubin, work is rarely a central life interest anymore, and this should come as no surprise. How can fry cooks, janitors, or data-entry assistants feel challenged by their paid labor? It is difficult (if not impossible) to imagine these jobs as central life interests. Really, much of the work done in contemporary societies is boring and unsatisfying.[5] This is not to say such jobs are not important. They are, and all of us depend on them getting done. After all, someone must collect the city's garbage and organize the courthouse files. However, the tasks are usually menial and lacking in personal fulfillment. We can contrast this, of course, with the sort of activities in which people find intrinsic purpose.[6] Unfortunately, few people are paid for the latter, and most must use the former to finance their avocational central life interests.

The success of movies like *American Beauty* and *Fight Club,* as well as the television series *The Office,* highlights the disconnection many people feel between their occupation and personally meaningful action.[7] And this, of course, is an observation social theorist Max Weber made long ago. In his characteristically dramatic prose he noted: "The idea of duty in one's calling prowls about in our lives like the ghost of dead religious beliefs.... For of the last stage of this cultural development, it might well be truly said: 'Specialists without spirit, sensualists without heart; this nullity imagines that it has attained a level of civilization never before achieved.'"[8] It is a grim picture, and, even worse, with only the ghost of a calling prowling in the background of our lives, the dissatisfaction many of us find in our paid labor throws into question the meaningfulness of life itself.

In fact, sociology as a discipline was born from a concern that industrial capitalism not only alters work relations (by moving the locus of production from the field and the home to the factory and the office) but also challenges the very foundations of society. This fear is at the heart of German sociologist Ferdinand Tönnies's classic distinction between traditional community and modern society (what he famously refers to as *Gemeinschaft* and *Gesellschaft*).[9] His value-driven contrast between tradition and modernity is repeated throughout sociology's earliest writings. Speaking about capitalism, for example, Karl Marx states: "Constant revolutionising of production, uninterrupted disturbances of all social conditions, everlasting uncertainty and agitation distinguish the bourgeois epoch from all earlier ones.... All that is solid melts into air, all that is holy is profaned." Weber, writing of rationalization, claims: "Culture's every step forward seems condemned to lead to an ever more devastating senselessness." Lamenting the egoism and anomie of industrial organization, French sociologist Émile Durkheim contends that the modern individual is "unable to escape the agonizing and exasperating question: to what purpose?"[10]

In other words, sociology is built on the assumption that meaning was, in earlier times, simpler. Now, though, it is assumed to be problematic. Or, if meaning was always problematic (as some postmodern critics have asserted), now it is *more* of a problem. As British theorist Anthony Giddens argues, modernity brings with it a radical emphasis on reflexivity.[11] That is, we live in a world where we feel compelled to constantly question our beliefs and values. We do not merely accept things as they are (or appear); we reflect, ruminate, fret, and worry.

But what then of the lure of delivering packages? As we have already seen (and as I will develop more as the book progresses), messengers are devoted to their labor as if it was a calling. To use Weber's words again, couriers inject both spirit and heart into their labor. However, their devotion does not come from an ideological connection to their economic function, and messengers do not celebrate their role in commerce. To the contrary, we will see that couriers are lured to deliveries *in spite* of their clients' needs. Why, then, do messengers conflate their work selves and their authentic selves? Why does the job provide such a profound sense of meaning?

To answer these questions (i.e., to explain the lure of delivering packages) is to contradict what Weber saw as an inevitable march toward senselessness. That is, modernity may be defined by the dynamics of the free market; it is coldly rational and often anomic. But if riding a bicycle around the city dropping off packages can produce deep affiliations with one's labor (to the point that some people travel around the world for events like the Warriors—doing for free what they would otherwise be paid for), then assigning purpose to one's life is not so agonizing or exasperating. Of course, there is nothing novel about this claim. It is a well-known fact that most people, regardless of their circumstances, find meaning in their lives. The mystery, therefore, is not *that* we find meaning, but *why* we do and *how* we do.

One of Marx and Weber's lasting legacies is a set of theoretical propositions insisting that life in the *Gesellschaft* should be anything but fulfilling. Intellectuals on both sides of the Seine (metaphorically, as well as literally) have grappled with this matter. At the most basic level, the Left accuses the masses of false consciousness (e.g., finding satisfaction in wearing designer clothing and lusting after expensive automobiles), while the Right belittles the individual for finding satisfaction in the mediocrity of the masses (e.g., supporting social welfare programs over the competition of the marketplace). Beyond the political implications of this debate is a question about where meaning resides. It is a question about what actions should be seen as authentic, and what should constitute a person's identity.

Such matters *far* exceed what can be accomplished in this book. I do, however, propose to make a small contribution to this much larger question. Specifically, analyzing the bike messengers' subculture allows us to see how a low-wage service job—an occupation far more analogous to fry cooking, janitorial work, and data entry than the classic professions—can generate authentic action and a strong sense of identity. In explaining why and how this is possible, a previously divergent set of social theories must be synthesized, and in this synthesis I hope to sharpen the sociological tools with which researchers can dissect the old, but pervasive problem of meaning. In other words, in looking at why and how there is a lure in delivering packages, sociologists (and those willing to think sociologically) gain greater insight into the human condition. As I will briefly detail below, and then elaborate in much greater detail in the chapters that follow, the answer to *why* there is a lure in delivering packages comes from emotions generated in practice, and *how* this is achieved comes from locating these practices in material space.

Emotions and Space

What distinguishes messengering from most service jobs is the incorporation of play into the workday, and play is the starting point for unraveling the puzzle of the messenger subculture. According to Stanley Aronowitz, a sociologist and former union organizer, "[Play is] the one human activity within capitalist society that is noninstrumental—that is produced for its own sake."[12] To address play is to bring emotions into the analysis. By definition, play is an activity entered into only for the intrinsic rewards of participation. While people can give discursive accounts of the games they play, play itself has no purpose beyond the emotional satisfaction it gives the individual. As we will see in chapter 4, it is the emotional involvement required in making deliveries from which the subculture sprouts. In a word, unlike most paid labor, urban cycling can be fun.

Durkheim was the first sociologist to appreciate the relevance of emotions. Unfortunately, the significance of this appreciation is often overlooked—especially outside the study of religion. For Durkheim, religion is not a system of ideas; cognitive logic is ancillary to its function. Which is to say, the written content of religious doctrines does not fully encapsulate the meaning of a religion, nor is it the primary basis of religious faith. At its heart, religion is a series of social celebrations that "make us act and help us live."[13] Religion's true power comes from ecstatic rituals generating what Durkheim called collective effervescence. Moreover, he believed that effervescence-producing rituals were the basis not just of religion, but of *all* social organization.

The emotional charge of collective effervescence is part of what sociologist Kenneth Allan calls affect-meaning.[14] It is the *felt* reality of culture. Affect-meaning is generated through action and is nondiscursive. That is, it has a corporeal quality distinct and separate from the rationalized logic of discourse. It is the discursive dimensions of existence that receive the most attention in sociology. Social scientists are generally attuned to asking people what they think, and wary of efforts to grasp how they feel. But culture is not simply a set of meanings people carry in their heads.[15] Rather, culture is largely emotive; it is knowledge we carry (first and foremost) in our bodies. As such, affect-meaning *feels* undoubtedly real. It is what we typically describe as coming from our "heart." Such an expression is shorthand for capturing beliefs that transcend any simple translation into words. The importance of this realness for the creation and perpetuation of the messenger subculture will be addressed in chapter 5. There we will see that the play of courier work is intensified and ultimately sanctified in the ritual of messenger races.

Because emotions are lived through the body, the generation of affect-meaning always happens in a *physical* place. Which is to say, culture is emplaced.[16] Such a point is beyond obvious, but the implications of this are systematically ignored in sociological analysis. This is a problem, because the built environment is part and parcel of the social world. And this is not simply because the built environment is constructed by people. Just as important, once we have constructed our material surroundings, they exert their influence back onto us—prescribing and proscribing what we can (or should) do within them.[17] A key aim of this book, therefore, is to explain how the lure of delivering packages involves more than affect-meaning. My argument is equally about the city as a built environment and its relationship to the messenger subculture. Acknowledging the role of emotional experience in identity formation is an important component, but we must also understand the sociological significance of space.[18]

As should already be apparent, messengering is a strictly urban phenomenon. The city, however, is not simply a stage in which social action occurs. Instead, the city must be brought *into* the analysis. To borrow from sociologist Thomas Gieryn, the city is "an agentic player in the game."[19] Which is to say, the material environment is a medium that is produced and reproduced through social practices. As we will see in chapter 6, in making their deliveries, messengers manipulate the space of the city—the play of work and the effervescence of rituals only happen through a unique use of space. It is this appropriation of the urban environment that generates the lived emotions of messenger practice. I call these place-based and corporeally felt activities the *affective appropriation of space.*

Rethinking Cultural Analysis

The point of this book—the sociological puzzle I want to solve—is why messengers find meaning in a seemingly menial occupation. As Fannin, a Seattle messenger and artist, admitted, "That's like basically what the job is: errand boy." Which leads to the question, why have couriers constructed and maintained such a vibrant subculture that, to a large degree, emulates their work?[20] To be succinct, I will assert that there is no messenger subculture beyond the affective appropriation of space, and that messenger identity (i.e., the meanings that couriers ascribe to the world) is inseparable from an analysis of emotions and the physical environment.

To this end, chapter 7 provides what I call a practice-based semiotic analysis of messenger style. Courier style, of course, is "pregnant with significance."[21] It is intimately tied to how messengers view themselves. The primary argument of this book is that there is an astounding homology between the affective spatial practices of bike couriers and their style. That is, the objects of cultural analysis—practices, symbols, and values—are integrated and constituted *through* emotions and space. In other words, I am claiming that in order to solve the puzzle of the messenger subculture, emotion and space must be given explanatory priority. Overtly cognitive and aspatial sociological theories fail to grasp the courier's world, and misrepresent the significance of why messengers love their jobs.

In looking at the messenger subculture, there is a larger political question to be addressed. To argue that lived emotions are an important part of cultural analysis is not terribly controversial. However, with the second step—the inclusion of space—new and grander issues come into focus. Messengers do not merely generate emotions as they use space; they generate emotional ties as they *manipulate* space and the norms that govern its use. This is why I focus on the affective *appropriation* of space and not simply the affective *use* of space. Every individual, of course, uses spaces in every moment of his or her existence, but because the material world has a taken-for-granted quality to it, spatial structures reify social structures. In other words, the built environment makes the ordering of things appear as the nature of things.[22] However, this process is never completely totalizing. Taken-for-granted conceptions of space can be appropriated in unintended ways. This is what French writer Michel de Certeau calls tactics—"the ingenious ways in which the weak make use of the strong."[23] He believes that it is these small, everyday manipulations of the existing order that liberate individuals from the crushing conformity of rationalized societies.

As will be made clear in chapters 4 and 6, messengers work in an occupation that requires tactics. To understand the lure of delivering packages, then, is to rethink the conditions of human liberation and the role of cultural practices within it. The liberty I am discussing here is not liberation from capital, or from gender or racial oppression. It is liberation from an overly reified existence. That is, it is liberation from choices that seem predetermined—from the false transparency of a pre-ordered world. In a word, it is liberation from alienation. Looking at how messengers appropriate the urban environment highlights the joys and thrills that can be achieved in small tactics that alter, even if only momentarily, the dominant order. Just as Henri Lefebvre, the iconoclastic French Marxist, cherishes the carnivalesque festival for its subversion of power,[24] in the messenger's affective spatial appropriation, individuals briefly regain control of their life through the creative and spontaneous use of the urban environment.

Of course, in many ways, this sort of liberty is exceedingly small. It offers no respite from economic demands and social inequality. This matter will be more thoroughly addressed in the conclusion, but I want to propose that by analyzing the messenger lifestyle through emotions and space (not simply through aspatial questions of cognition), we not only come to understand why the subculture is significant to its members; we also see glimpses of what is required for all of us if we want to step outside the iron cage of rationality.

A Note on Data and Method

Before starting, a few words about my research are necessary. The data for this book were gathered over three years of participant observation spread over the course of five years. From June 2002 to June 2003, I worked as a bike messenger in New York City. From August 2006 through May 2007, I worked as a bike messenger in Seattle. In between these two extended periods of fieldwork, I regularly participated in messenger events and sporadically worked as a bike courier in San Diego. Additionally, I traveled to Atlanta, Boston, Chicago, Milwaukee, Philadelphia, San Francisco, and Washington, D.C., to discuss messenger work and life with local couriers.

In New York, I worked for two companies, Sprint Courier and Dragonfly Courier.[25] Sprint was one of New York's largest messenger companies, employing over one hundred bikers, in addition to a fleet of trucks and walkers. I worked at Sprint for seven months. Dragonfly Courier, by contrast, consisted of just two bikers. I worked at Dragonfly for five months. For Sprint and Dragonfly I was dispatched to pick up any number of odd things. I once delivered a shopping bag full of family portraits for actress Kathleen Turner; I couriered a blood sample from someone's home to the Red Cross. In Seattle, I worked for Choice Legal Services (CLS). CLS not only carried out deliveries but also provided a wide array of legal work from process service to research and investigation. With over ten riders, CLS was large by Seattle's standards. With minor exceptions, CLS's bike couriers dealt only with legal documents going to and from law firms and courthouses. In San Diego, I worked for Aloha Bicycle Courier, an all-purpose bike messenger company. Aloha never had more than three riders on the road at any one time.

At each place, working as a messenger, or being able to introduce myself as a former messenger, gave me entry into the social world. Couriers can come off as a rather indifferent lot. If you are an outsider and you walk up to a messenger lounging in between deliveries, you will likely be greeted with a blank stare, if not a grimace. But if you tell the messenger you're an out-of-town courier, the tenor of the interaction immediately changes. I have experienced this social transformation countless times. Guarded hostility quickly melts away to reveal familial warmth. It is not uncommon to be invited out for drinks or told of an upcoming party within minutes of an introduction, and it is this nonwork socializing that is essential. These are the occasions when messengers discuss, contest, and represent their subculture. In nearly every social situation, couriers freely discussed various aspects of messenger life. Thus, engaging couriers about their social world was remarkably easy and unobtrusive.

In this book, I rely primarily on informal discussions and questions asked *in the moment* of activity, or soon after. Not only is this a less obtrusive form of data collection, but respondents are less likely to distort their actions or self-consciously manage their image when not awkwardly forced into an interview. Not only have I asked couriers to describe what being a messenger is like; I have also experienced it myself. This emic approach gives me firsthand knowledge and allows me to converse with messengers as an insider. Surveys and interviews—removed from the nuances of the lifeworld and devoid of personal relationships—result in caricatures of social groups.[26] In addition to active participation, informal discussions, and formal interviews, I supplement my ethnographic work with historical and contemporary documentation. However, it should be made clear that my data come, first and foremost, from participant observation; quotations from other sources are used only to reinforce my findings.

To protect the identities of some my respondents, I use a mixture of pseudonyms and real names. All messengers with whom I had recurring contact were informed of my research, and all were supportive of the project. Some, however, after reading earlier drafts of this manuscript, asked, out of modesty or embarrassment, to have their identities concealed.[27] Of course, given the number of couriers with whom I interacted—often just in passing—not all could be approached to give informed consent. In these cases I have generally decided to err on the side of caution and use pseudonyms. Of course, there are exceptions, such as when I quote from other sources, or when I discuss well-known facts about couriers who have become public figures through their exposure in various media outlets.

THE JOB

Bike messengers provide on-demand delivery. During normal business hours (usually eight in the morning to six at night), messengers will deliver any item (with obvious limits to physical size) anywhere within the downtown core of a city and its surrounding area in a short span of time. Many companies offer early-morning and late-night service, and many even provide longer-distance delivery. Some Seattle messengers, for example, make regular runs to Bellevue, Washington (over ten miles from downtown Seattle). Size and weight are also negotiable. Although it is rare, some companies use cargo bikes that allow them to deliver hundreds of pounds in one trip. Even without a cargo bike, a messenger can fit at least one banker's box (i.e., a standard-size filing box) in her bag and balance one to two more on her handlebars. Most bike messenger companies offer options ranging from same-day service to deliveries completed in fifteen minutes. It is this "on-demand" aspect of messengering that distinguishes it from the services offered by the U.S. Postal Service, DHL, FedEx and UPS (all of which follow set schedules and routes). FedEx, for example, can deliver a package from New York to Los Angeles by tomorrow, but only a bike messenger can get something from midtown to downtown by lunchtime.

The Historical Context of Bike Messengers

Since their invention, bicycles have been used to make deliveries. At the turn of the twentieth century, telegraph companies like Western Union had "bicycle boys" working in every major U.S. city. Even UPS got its start on two wheels. While the automobile and urban sprawl drastically reduced the comparative efficiency of bicycle delivery, Western Union continued using bikes well into the mid-1900s. In 1962, for example, it was Western Union bicyclists who mediated the missile crisis by delivering encoded messages from the Soviet embassy in Washington, D.C., to the White House.[1] In fact, pedal-powered couriers never entirely disappeared from the occupational landscape, but for decades the job appeared to be nearly extinct. Then, at the end of the twentieth century, there was a major resurgence. In New York, for example, a handful of bike couriers working for the film industry in the 1970s surged to several thousand by the mid-1980s.[2]

Telegraph Bicycle Boys and the Postindustrial Bike Courier

The resurrection of bicycle delivery can only be understood within the context of global economic restructuring. As historian and geographer Gregory Downey shows, bicycle boys were a by-product of the first wave of industrial urbanism in the United States.[3] These bikers provided the first and last steps in a nationwide system of communication by physically picking up telegrams from their original destinations and delivering them to their final destinations. The telegrams themselves were transmitted across the country through wires, but the transmission and reception points were telegraph stations. It was the bicycle boys, therefore, who connected the telegraph with its users. In addition to intercity telegraphs, the boys relayed intracity messages. Thus early messengers were part of a complex flow of information. Even as the telephone became more common, bicycle boys served as errand runners and temporary workers for the telegraph companies' clients. By the early 1940s, however, telephones and cars made the bicycle boys' occupation largely redundant.

Today's bike couriers are not industrial, but postindustrial messengers. That is, the bike messenger revival is a by-product of globalized international finance. Like their predecessors, bike messengers provide a crucial link between information nodes—a link that cannot currently be connected electronically. The biggest difference between the past century's

Figure 1. New York messenger riding a cargo bike

bicycle boy and the contemporary bike messenger relates to their economic functions and their relations with employers and clients. That is, today's messengers service a new economic niche, and their labor relations are drastically different from those of the bicycle boys of the past.

Keeping the Global City Rolling

Since the 1980s, finance has superseded manufacturing as the backbone of the world economy.[4] Capital is now highly mobilized and continually shifting around the world. The best way to understand this is to contrast the relative stability of Fordism (named after the business model developed by Henry Ford) with contemporary production models. From the mid-1900s through the 1960s, industrial production in the United States and Western Europe was premised on a unionized blue-collar work-force laboring in relatively stable factory locations. One can think here of the heyday of manufacturing in places like Detroit. Since the 1970s, however, advances in communication, production, and shipping technologies have reduced the cost of operating factories in far-off locations. Geographer David Harvey refers to this new production model as flexible accumulation, and its consequences for cities like Detroit are well known.[5] Many industries are no longer wedded to specific locations and move from country to country to exploit cheaper labor and less stringent environmental regulations. This reorganization of the economy can be characterized by the term *globalization*. The global mobility of capital also comes with new forms of urban concentration.[6]

Even as industrial production shifts around the globe, management of the worldwide economy has remained relatively stable. While their factories move, transnational corporations have continued to locate their the headquarters in select cities, including London, New York, and Tokyo.[7] Such "global cities" are the control nodes of the worldwide economic system. One should not assume, however, that these cities are populated only by high-powered button-pushers ensconced in glass skyscrapers—a popular image that even the most cursory glance shows to be horribly myopic. Sociologist Saskia Sassen corrects such a one-sided view by emphasizing how the process of globalization requires the agglomeration of *services* utilized by international financial firms. That is to say, global cities are still sites for low-wage production, but it is production increasingly oriented to the management function of cities, not to traditional factory labor. According to Sassen, the companies ancillary to transnational trade cluster within central business districts. Their services include everything from financial and legal management to storage and cleaning. Sassen refers to these companies as producer services. Global cities, therefore, are not just the location of corporate headquarters. Even more importantly, they are the location for the producer services used by international corporations in the management of their worldwide operations.[8]

In recent years, advances in global telecommunications have created a lot of excitement about a "death of distance."[9] Without a doubt, the world has become a much smaller place. Regardless, telephones, the Internet, and video conferencing have not dissolved the significance of place. Physical proximity still improves communication within firms and facilitates contact between firms, and companies are willing to pay astronomically high rents for this access.[10] The advertising industry provides an excellent illustration of why urban centralization still exists, and why postindustrial production still requires bike messengers. Advertising agencies, photographers, graphic designers, postproduction companies, magazine publishers, clothing designers, fabric manufacturers, and printers are all part of a vast network (which spirals out into other networks as well). A photographer requires a dress for a photo shoot. The clothing designer requires fabric from a manufacturer. Obviously, these things cannot be e-mailed. Once developed (or in the case of digital photography, once the image has been toned), the photograph is sent on to the graphic designer. The designer, advertising agency, and printer are equally connected. Calibrating computer monitors and printers across different offices (using different software and different machines) is highly problematic. So photographs and other color-sensitive items are generally not sent electronically. People within the network must be given a hard-copy proof in order to verify the exact colors being reproduced, and advertisers and their clients can be very specific about the exact color being reproduced.

In places like New York, there are countless networks of this kind. Within the networks, proofs in various stages of development are constantly circulating from firm to firm, and bike messengers are the ones providing the actual connections. The bulk of Dragonfly's deliveries, for example, came from just one of these networks. Dragonfly primarily serviced a graphic-design firm, the three ad agencies it worked with, its postproduction company, and a printing company. Five days a week, nine hours a day, information that could not be e-mailed or faxed flowed between these firms via bike messengers. Thus bicycle delivery—"the fastest known way through the morass of Manhattan traffic"[11]—is an essential (if not somewhat paradoxical) aspect of the information age. Similarly, legal firms comprise another major network for messenger service. This network, however, it is a bit simpler: opposing counsels and courthouses. Like the advertising industry, legal work involves a continual flow of documents circulating throughout the city. In this case, though, it is the need for personal signatures on documents and the desire to have physical proof of delivery that hamper the transition to full digitalization.

There are significant similarities and differences between bike messengering now and messengering in the past. Telegraph companies used bicycles because it was the most efficient option. Companies today also use bike messengers because it is the most efficient option. At the same time, technology has advanced, and the economy has shifted. In both cases, messengers deliver what cannot be sent via electrical currents, but contemporary bike messengers do not deliver some kind of postmodern

Figure 2. Messenger riding next to a bus in New York's Times Square

letters via bicycle (thus making them futuristic telegraph messengers). They use old technologies to aid the entirely new processes of the global city. In other words, it is not only high-tech button-pushers driving the new economy. Even in the most prosperous of urban centers, low-tech, unskilled, and informal labor is still required for the postindustrial production of the global system, and bike messengers are part of this.

A Python Squeezing Its Prey

Just as technological changes reduced and eventually replaced telegraph messengers, new forms of telecommunication coupled with the financial contractions of the late 1980s, late 1990s, and late 2000s have (again and again) reduced the need for bike deliveries. While the advertising industry is an example of why bike couriers are still useful, it should be apparent that much of what messengers were delivering in the early 1980s can now be digitized. In the early 1990s the fax machine reigned. Now the Internet has become increasingly useful for relaying data. In fact, messengers today are delivering little more than the table scraps remaining from the grand conversion to virtual data. For example, Breakaway Courier Systems, one of New York's largest messenger companies, claims that from 2001 to 2006 they cut over 60 percent of their riders.[12] Nevertheless, the messenger industry continues to survive in the new millennium. It is estimated that there are around one thousand bicycle messengers still working in New York City; by contrast, when I worked there the estimate was double that. There are hundreds of messengers working in Chicago, San Francisco, and Washington, D.C. Even after the dot-com fallout in the late 1990s, there were over sixty messengers working in Seattle's small downtown core. However, this number was much larger in years past. Boston and Philadelphia have comparable numbers to Seattle. Smaller cities (with proportionally small central business districts) like Atlanta, Milwaukee and San Diego maintain messenger populations under twenty.[13]

Beyond what I have already described, architectural blueprints, court filings and other legal documents, film, medicine, and model portfolios either cannot currently be digitized or, if they can be, as in the case of court filings, are preferred by many clients in hard-copy form. For legal work, couriers are given duplicate copies of what they are delivering. These "conform copies" are stamped on delivery, thereby providing proof that the court or opposing counsel received the documents. In the not-too-distant future, however, much of this will change. The courts of King County, where Seattle is located, actually made e-filing mandatory in 2009—which is why their messenger population has recently contracted yet again. As Robert Koch, the president of Breakaway notes, "There is a slow erosion in the business because of the growth of digital documents....It's like a python squeezing its prey."[14] Likewise, the manager of a Seattle legal messenger firm bluntly informed me in 2006: "Five years from now what we do will be gone." To this end, the manager was trying to find new services for bicycle delivery. Among the possibilities is a shift away from deliverables for the legal industry to the delivery of unalterably tangible consumer goods, such as cigarettes, clothes, food, and medicine. This model was vigorously, but unsuccessfully, attempted by a nationwide courier company called Kozmo.com in the late 1990s.

And You Don't Wear a Tie Either

In solving the puzzle of the messenger subculture, in understanding the lure of delivering packages, much of this book will focus on the issue of labor relations (at least indirectly). For now, in explaining how postindustrial messengers differ from the bicycle boys of old, two simple points should be made. First, in the heyday of the telegraph, the messengers were literally boys. Hiring young workers allowed companies to severely suppress wages.[15] Second, and more importantly for my argument, the telegraph companies were obsessed with control. Western Union believed its riders required supervision and surveillance. This was not only a matter of profits, but of moral fortitude. Further, Western Union considered uniformed and cordial riders integral to their business strategy.

Contemporary messenger companies have little interest in their riders' appearance or demeanor. Small messenger companies purposely reject efforts to make rules, save making deliveries on time and getting a signature to verify the delivery. Larger companies like Sprint and CLS do provide their new employees with handbooks filled with rules, but it is understood that these formal regulations will be routinely disregarded. My first day at Sprint, for example, I was told that to work for the company I needed a helmet. The company sold helmets along with other messenger supplies at a discount. The manager asked me if I wanted to buy a helmet. I told him no, and he made no effort to verify if I had brought my own. I had not. Further, after I declined to buy a helmet, he informed me: "You have to wear a helmet, but it's not like we're going to be out on the streets checking to see if you're wearing one." That was the one and only time rules were ever brought up with me, aside, of course, from the one cardinal rule: deliver packages on time. Some messenger companies require their riders to wear company-issued shirts or use company-issued bags. These practices, however, are both rare and roundly criticized by messengers, so many of whom are attracted to the occupation by the lack of workplace control.

Messenger companies and their clients have come to expect that the men and women who deliver packages by bicycle will have an edgy, if not grubby or menacing, appearance. And it is interesting to contrast the accepted appearance of the bike messenger with the fully uniformed garb of almost all other types of delivery personnel. Many clients like how messengers look,[16] and smaller companies often play up their "alternative" image. At Aloha, Kenton went through a period of wearing tacky Hawaiian shirts with clashing ties (all of which were incongruent with his Dickies shorts and bicycle helmet). Ian, the owner of Dragonfly, constantly swore over my radio because he felt that his crass demeanor only

Figure 3. Ian, former owner of Dragonfly Courier

further endeared him to his clients. While I am no prude when it comes to language, Ian, barking profanity over the radio as I stood in elevators and offices, often left me blushing with embarrassment. One of Ian's favorite tactics was a pornographic alteration of the phonetic alphabet. When confirming delivery signatures, even when he heard the receiver's name correctly, he would ask for a verification of the spelling: "Was that Chuck with a C? C as in cunt?"

Of course, not every client likes this sort of behavior, but most have come to accept the iconoclasm of messenger style as a matter of fact. The point here is that the contemporary bike courier is thoroughly distinguishable from the bicycle boy. While the latter was part of industrial business (complete with Fordist methods of labor relations), the former is postindustrial. Contemporary bike messengers are postindustrial not only in economic function, but also in the shift away from moralizing control to the embrace of otherness. That is, not only do contemporary messengers deliver different things (with different purposes) from the bicycle boys, they are allowed to deliver them differently. The notion of standardizing and regulating the worker seems irrelevant, if not contradictory, to the business at hand.

Working as a Messenger

Bike couriers work for messenger companies. Firms requiring deliveries contact messenger companies. Most firms have accounts with specific companies. Beyond simplifying bookkeeping, having specific accounts allows firms to negotiate individual deals with their delivery companies, reducing the actual amount they pay for services.

The Basic Structure of the Occupation

In terms of services, messenger companies offer several delivery-time options: same day, two hour, one hour, half hour, and fifteen minutes. The cost of each delivery is based on the client's requested time frame and the distance covered. Messenger companies divide the city into zones, and every zone a rider must cross in making his or her run increases the charge. Companies also charge extra for large or heavy items. Alternatively, firms that consistently send out a high volume of jobs may choose to hire their own in-house riders. In-house staff bypasses the need for the messenger company altogether, but it is rare.

The biggest variation in the occupation's structure is whether the messenger company pays a piece rate or an hourly wage and whether it considers its riders independent contractors or employees. A piece rate versus an hourly wage (in theory, at least) drastically alters an employee's relationship to her labor. A commission rider is paid only when actually making a delivery. An hourly rider is paid regardless. From the company's perspective, a piece rate provides a strong incentive for the rider to perform and absolves the management of financial responsibility for riders when they are not generating profit. Messengers tend to look at the issue in terms of compensation. The piece-rate system compensates riders for harder deliveries; an hourly wage does not. However, as we will see in chapter 4, messenger behavior on the job (i.e., how *motivated* they are to perform their labor) extends far beyond monetary compensation for their efforts.

Figure 4. Matt bringing a package into his company's office

Companies consider their hourly riders employees, unless, like many messengers, they work off the books. Commission riders are often listed as independent contractors. The legality of such a listing is certainly debatable. Riders do not generally have enough control over the terms of their labor to qualify for such a designation. Government agencies (e.g., the IRS and Social Security Administration) have, at various times, vigorously policed the industry, levying substantial fines for improperly listing riders as independent contractors.[17] According to the IRS, a payer for the services of an independent contractor can control or direct only the result of work performed, not the method or means of its accomplishment. Clearly, bike couriers could fall into this category, which is why so many messengers companies list their riders as such, or have done so in the past. However, independent contractors, by the IRS definition, have absolute impunity in turning down work they do not want, something most companies are unlikely to grant. As such, many riders, at least by auditors' assessments, fall into the category of employees.

Messengers uninterested in legality sometimes view independent-contractor status or the nonstatus of working under the table as a method of tax-free income. For those not wanting or willing to dodge taxation, however, filing as an independent contractor represents a sizable economic burden. This is because employers are responsible for covering a portion of their workers' taxes. Independent contractors, however, are considered self-employed and must cover their entire tax liability. For this reason companies are eager to consider their riders contractors. Other reasons include insurance and workers' compensation issues.

Payments and Benefits

In New York, nearly all messengers are paid on commission. These messengers make between 40 and 60 percent of the price paid for a job. Most messengers average between three to five dollars per delivery, but on occasion a single package can be worth several times more than that (a late-night, oversize, or double rush delivery, for instance). New York messengers average sixteen to twenty-five deliveries a day, but it is not uncommon for some messengers to complete fewer than twenty runs while others do more than forty. In 2002, one hundred dollars a day was considered a respectable day's wage in New York, but it is worth noting that, in the early 1980s, some messengers were also making this wage. Today, while some messengers (some of the time) can make more than this, many riders are making far less (most of the time). Since the golden age of the 1980s, a rider's real wages have been cut in half—if not more.[18] Riders today are making about the same dollar amount as they were twenty years ago. In Seattle, many of the messenger companies pay hourly. The pay is between $9.50 an hour and $15 an hour. Commission riders in Seattle make a comparable rate to that of riders in New York, and make a similar number of deliveries. In San Diego, all messengers (aside from Kenton, who runs his own company) are paid between $7.50 and $15 hourly.

In my year of work in New York, on some days I made less than $30, and on others I made over $150. In the course of ten months in Seattle, I started at $10.50 an hour and finished making $10.90 an hour (in a quarterly raise system based on relative performance across employees). In San Diego, I was paid $10 an hour.

In all places, messengers shoulder payments for bicycles, bike repair, courier bags, and traffic violations. Some companies offer funds or discounts for bike parts and maintenance, but most do not. For workers not counted as employees because they are independent contractors or working off the books, injuries incurred on the job are not covered by workers' compensation. For individuals performing such dangerous labor and making very little in return, this represents a *serious* financial risk. Even for messengers who are considered employees, health insurance for injuries sustained off the job, as well as for general sickness, is uncommon. For example, both CLS and Sprint offer health insurance to employees who have been with the company for a year or more. At those companies, however, a year of employment is a rarity. Further, many qualifying riders opt out of coverage because they cannot afford to pay their portion of the plan.

Companies may also fire employees who have gotten hurt. At commission companies the process is even simpler, as dispatchers can simply refuse to allocate work to disliked riders, forcing them to quit. Upon getting a job at a larger New York company, Becka, a recent college graduate with a BA in literature from The New School, was given a list of accidents that responsible couriers *never* have. The list consisted of the most common injuries an urban cyclist *does* have (e.g., getting doored by a car, colliding with a pedestrian, being hit by a car, sliding out on wet pavement, etc.). Becka was then informed that since responsible couriers do not have these accidents, if they did happen to her, she would be fired. While the company might claim that such a policy helps weed out reckless riders, their list was far too broad and their policy far too stringent. What the company was really doing was trying to avoid its responsibilities as an employer operating in a hazardous industry. Also, the warning Becka received was a threat. If she wanted to keep her job, accidents (some of which are simply inevitable) should be kept secret—lest she get labeled as reckless and lose her job.

Job Allocation

Regardless of how she is paid and her status as an employee or independent contractor, a messenger spends her day roaming the city. The company's other riders are also dispersed throughout the city. Messengers keep in contact with their company through various means. In the 1980s, messengers used pay phones to call their companies to receive new jobs. Today, most messengers use two-way radios or, more commonly, Nextel cellular phones with direct connect, which allows the phone also to be used as a walkie-talkie. Some use regular cell phones or pagers with text messaging. Jobs are allocated among the company's riders based on where they are located (at a given moment) and what other deliveries they are holding. This process is known as dispatching. Depending on the number of riders working for a company, there may be only one person answering calls from clients and dispatching jobs to riders. At Aloha, Kenton, the owner, does all his own administrative work while also making deliveries himself. Alternatively, companies like Sprint have separate order takers and several dispatchers, each assigned a set number of riders to manage.

Dispatchers are almost always former messengers themselves. This is because an intimate knowledge of the city and a messenger's ability to travel through it is essential to handling the workflow of the company. Most companies, including all those I worked for, practice direct dispatch. This means that it is the dispatcher who monitors all incoming work and decides unilaterally which riders will do what jobs. Efficient dispatching in this manner requires a rather astounding set of mental operations. Good dispatchers are able to calculate where each of their riders is (or should be) at *any* moment. As Cindy, a part-time rider and part-time dispatcher for CLS observed, "[Dispatching] is like playing an adult video game. You have to clear everything off the board [i.e., the computer screen listing incomplete jobs]. It is multitasking, but in a fun way." Beyond the sheer chance of who happens to be near jobs when they come in, dispatchers also make decisions based on rider seniority and their general disposition to individual riders. At commission companies, therefore, a good relationship with the dispatcher is essential to making decent money. A less common method of dispatching is the free call system. In free call, jobs are announced to all the company's riders over an open radio channel, and the messengers decide among themselves who should take the various jobs.

Once a job is allocated, the messenger must first pick up the item and then make the delivery. A messenger does not want to be holding only one job at a time. Instead, a messenger wants to always have his bag filled with multiple jobs. Dispatchers attempt to assign new pick-ups near drop-offs for the work riders are already holding. On an ideal day, a messenger's route is a series of circles around the city—picking up, dropping off, and repeating without pause. An absolutely essential part of the delivery process is getting proof of delivery. This is usually a signature or a company stamp on a delivery manifest. Because messenger work is so

Figure 5. Seattle dispatcher at work

time-sensitive, riders and their companies must be able to verify that the recipient, who is usually not the company's client, received the package on time. In fact, *proof* of delivery is more important than the delivery itself. If a receiving firm loses a package (a rather common occurrence in large offices) and the messenger company cannot verify that the item was delivered, it might as well not have been delivered.

On the other hand, if a rider can make a late package appear to have been delivered on time, most messenger companies are quite satisfied with the outcome. A retired messenger, for example, described some of his past exploits as a "problem solver" for his company. Mainly, this involved surreptitiously rolling back date stamps at law offices and court-houses to make deliveries performed days late appear on time. An office worker for another messenger company also extolled the value of a former problem solver who worked for them. Among other things, this individual had supposedly procured an electronic time stamp from the local courthouse, allowing the company unencumbered manipulations of delivery verification.

Selling Speed

Those not familiar with bike messengers often think the job sounds quaint. Delivering packages by bicycle might even sound idyllic. The reality is quite different. Bike messengering is intense, and the occupation exists because of the speed it can offer. Clearly, these couriers are not selling velocity. Even the fastest professionally competitive cyclists in the world max out around forty miles per hour, and these top athletes can sustain such an effort for only a very brief period. Instead, a bike messenger's speed comes by traveling through the city *on average* far more quickly than a motorized vehicle. Bicycles are smaller and lighter than cars. This makes them more maneuverable, allowing riders to weave in and out of gridlocked traffic. Also, bicycles can be parked anywhere there is a stationary object that the rider can lock the bike to. In cities like San Diego and Seattle, messengers sometimes do not even bother locking their bikes to anything but merely place the lock around a wheel and the frame (rendering the bike unusable were someone to try to steal it).[19] Further, unlike mopeds and motorcycles, bicycles have an ambiguous legal status. This allows bike riders to travel on sidewalks and go the wrong way down one-way streets. For these same reasons, cyclists can also run red lights by skillfully maneuvering between the relatively small spaces separating moving vehicles.

As I will explain in detail in chapters 4 and 6, a talented messenger has an absolute understanding of her speed, the speed of surrounding objects, and the time it will take her bike to travel between two points. The best messengers can slip through seemingly solid walls of moving traffic seamlessly. Andy, a longtime Seattle messenger, called this "skills with spatial capacity." An example from my November 14, 2002, field notes is telling: "I saw Squid [Kevin] in traffic today. I was stopped on 23rd Street at Broadway. The traffic coming down Broadway looked impenetrable, but then Squid just appears between two moving buses, weaving out of pedestrian traffic. He wasn't going fast or anything. He just slipped through it." Bicycles really are the fastest known way through the morass of downtown traffic.

As the example of Kevin crossing Broadway illustrates, much of what messengers do to make their deliveries is technically prohibited and clearly dangerous. Courier work, therefore, exists on the margins of the law. One messenger, nervous about having his picture taken for this project, sarcastically expressed his reservation: "I don't know, something about having to break laws every minute of the day." In describing his job, Matt, a young and enthusiastic rider for CLS, explained: "We're pretty much just paid outlaws." As Rebecca Reilly, a longtime bike messenger and folk historian of the occupation, notes, "By merely dispatching jobs of that nature [i.e., fifteen-minute deliveries], there is the implied order to the courier to break the law."[20] At the same time, legal enforcement is inconsistent and minimal at best. Aside from police officers specifically assigned to write traffic citations (and places like New York have officers designated for such tasks), most cops do not consider cyclists a priority. For instance, Becka calculated that she ran more than ten thousand red lights before receiving her first (and only) ticket. Alternatively, strong enforcement tends to come after a serious accident involving a messenger (or a cyclist assumed to be a messenger) and a pedestrian. These events, especially if given media attention, can quickly raise public outrage and prompt at least temporary police interest in biking scofflaws.

The need and desire for messengers to break traffic laws are compounded by the method of job allocation. First, some jobs require fast delivery. Working as a messenger, I was often given jobs that could not possibly be completed within the confines of the law, or even common sense. Consider, for example, an excerpt from my field notes from June 5, 2003: "Ian radioed me and said he had a 'super rush.' He told me I had less than 15 minutes to go to Broadway Video [at 54th Street and Broadway], and make it down to Deutsche [at 15th Street and Eighth Avenue]. I did it in 12. I did the actual distance in seven (the other five minutes was lost inside Broadway Video)." This is only a distance of two miles, but in the congestion of midtown traffic, an average speed of seventeen miles per hour can be maintained only by running red lights and traveling the wrong way down one-way streets. More cavalier messengers could cover this distance even more quickly.

Second, for commission riders, the faster they make a delivery the more deliveries they can make. Third, courier companies, even those that pay hourly, give preferential treatment, when dispatching jobs, to their fastest riders. This helps to keep them from looking for employment with other companies. One of the first things new messengers are told by the manager at Sprint is, "Don't tell me you are a 'pro messenger' and you deserve the sweet runs. Don't tell anyone that." His admonition was clear. The only way for new couriers to get the "sweet runs" is to demonstrate that they deserve them. Rookie messengers, therefore, must constantly prove their mettle in order to someday receive preferential treatment.

A dispatcher asked a group of us at CLS: "Who is feeling fast today?" Matt answered: "I'm always fast"; and such eager bravado was not lost on the management. As Kenneth Peyser, the vice president of another courier company, remarked, "Speed is the name of the game.... [Messengers] make as much money as they dare....We don't want kamikazes, but we do hire risk takers. There is a macho element involved."[21] We will see in chapter 4, however, that neither money nor client demands are entirely adequate explanations for this risk taking.

It is worth mentioning that, while both messengers and the public at large focus on the speed at which bike couriers travel through the city's streets, much of messenger work (at least half of it) is spent inside of buildings. Beyond careening through traffic, messengering is about riding in elevators, standing in lobbies, waiting at front desks, and traipsing up stairs. As many messenger company managers are quick to point out, and as many young messengers are apt to ignore, a rider's paycheck has more to do with her speed in buildings than outside them. Primarily this sort of speed is about the messenger knowing building layouts and policies. It is about being ready for security guards who check bags, and knowing if there are stairs in addition to elevators. It is also about being able to solve problems, from circumventing security measures to deducing a mislabeled package's true destination. The pragmatic, cognitive skills of building knowledge and problem solving, however, are given only cursory attention in the images put forth in the messenger subculture. As one messenger remarked, "I could care less about who's the best courier. I just want to know who's the fastest."[22] That is, the issue is not actually making deliveries—being the best courier. For those in the subculture, the issue is often simply who is the fastest on the streets.

The Price of Speed

One of the most notable aspects of messenger work is its danger. Environmental-health researchers Jack Dennerlein and John Meeker report that bike couriers have an injury rate three times higher than workers in the infamously dangerous occupation of meatpacking. The national average for injuries in the workplace is three lost days of work per year per hundred workers. Meatpackers lose over five times this amount. Messengers, however, were found to lose a staggering forty-seven days of work per year per hundred workers.[23] Dennerlein and Meeker looked only at Boston, and they used a convenience sample with no method

for cross-checking the accuracy of their respondents. Regardless, their findings, even if inflated, are sobering. As a longtime messenger and dispatcher in New York City commented, "A messenger from the moment he hits Manhattan, and he's on his bike, he's in danger. I don't recommend messenger work to anybody.... I've seen a lot of people, a lot of my friends, die doing this work."[24]

Because there are no industry-wide statistics on bike messenger injuries, deaths and mishaps must be pieced together from newspaper articles and personal stories. Thankfully, it does not appear that any messengers died during my time in the field, but less than a month after I left New York, two messengers were killed in quick succession. Just over a year later, another messenger was killed when he collided with a delivery truck's opening front door.[25] No San Diego messengers have died on their bikes. The last Seattle messenger death during work was in 2000. Of course, more messengers are injured than killed on the job. During my fieldwork, all of my key informants in every city had at least one minor collision with automobiles or pedestrians, and some were not so minor.

"You ride your bike enough, you're gonna wreck. Hopefully you're not going to get run over by a car, but you're going to have an accident. It's a fact. The more you ride your bike, *you will have an accident.*" This is Dan's outlook on urban cycling. A big guy, and a veteran of the first Gulf War, Dan had cut his chops messengering in Texas. By the time he moved to Seattle he already knew several couriers from traveling for various alleycats and championship races. Dan made his rather fatalistic pronouncement through a mouth missing several teeth. His orbital was broken, and his face was still swollen, discolored, and adorned with fifty-seven fresh stitches. During our interview he proudly informed me that this was not a record number of facial stitches for him. Years earlier he had been in a mountain biking accident resulting in eighty-six sutures in his face. That accident, however, while breaking his nose and orbital, did not claim teeth. Dan acquired his ghastly new wounds in a cycling accident after work, but his point holds true for the workday as well.

As an example, take Matt. He's the messenger who claimed he was always fast. More than anything, Matt was a messenger with true spirit. In his early 20s, he was eager to work and willing to put his life on the line. When CLS started ranking its riders, Matt jumped at the opportunity to assert himself as the company's fastest, and he was truly gushing when he finally achieved the number one ranking. Matt had two major collisions with automobiles in the ten months I worked with him. In one incident he slammed into a door while speeding down a hill in excess of twenty-five miles per hour. His front wheel and fork were crushed, but he acquired only minimal injuries to his person. In the other, he made a left turn from the right side of a lane assuming, incorrectly, that the car behind him was also turning. His front wheel was again demolished, but he survived with only minor scraps and bruises once more. Both accidents, though not requiring hospitalization, left him physically sore and psychologically rattled for days—just not enough to appreciably alter his future behavior. While he did not miss work, in both incidents, Matt came incredibly close to extreme bodily harm, and his survival was largely a matter of luck. Further, Matt's accidents not resulting in inoperable machinery go unrecorded in my field notes, but many more near catastrophes were cataloged in the flesh of his legs, arms, and face.

The injury of one rider can be a financial opportunity for another. When Buck severely sprained his ankle, his company quickly moved to replace him. Being a small company, it could not operate otherwise. Travis, working for Sprint Courier, was offered the job. The switch represented a substantial pay raise for Travis. Buck's company was small and paid a high commission (60 percent), under the table. Travis's good fortune, of course, was nothing but bad news for Buck. Not only was he injured and not covered by either health insurance or workers' compensation; he was out of a job altogether. This story illustrates just how cutthroat the piece-rate system can be. According to Buck, upon hearing about the injury the owner simply replied: "If you don't want to ride for me I'll just find another rider." Moreover, the owner's behavior failed to raise the eyebrows of the New York messengers who heard the story. This indifference was true even among those generally quite critical of their companies.

For both riders and owners, there is an agreement that company loyalty begins and ends with a messenger's ability to perform. And, conversely, employee loyalty ends the minute a better offer comes along. It should be stressed here that the letter of the law is totally irrelevant in these situations. There is no legal record of Buck's relationship with his company. The company in question consists of one man answering phone calls from his tiny apartment. Whatever recourse Buck may possibly have in the technical sense, if he could prove his relationship to the company, is (for all practical purposes) irrelevant. So much so I never overheard messengers discuss the possibility of legal recourse for these situations. Both Buck and his employer agree that he is just a guy that got hurt riding his bike, not an employee with legal entitlements for being injured on the job.

The dangers of the occupation are apparent when one considers the realities of urban cycling. For starters, a bicycle usually weighs less than twenty-five pounds. It offers no protection to the rider. This fact is compounded by the messengers' ambivalence about helmets. Drivers turn unexpectedly, make lane changes without looking, and speed up or slow down erratically. In New York, taxis are especially dangerous. They regularly make sudden stops and turns without signaling or checking their mirrors for cyclists. The biggest threat, however, is parked cars. The sides of the street are lined with vehicles whose doors might fling open with no warning. In fact, being "doored" is one of the most common causes of injury. People are another latent danger for the cyclist. Pedestrians look for cars, but often their attention passes over bicyclists as they step into the road. At speeds that can exceed thirty miles per hour, a cyclist (and also the pedestrian) can easily be injured or killed in such a collision. Back in the 1980s, for example, Calvin spent a week in a coma after colliding with a pedestrian. Weather conditions can increase these risks. Rain, snow, and ice reduce braking power, turn metal fixtures into slippery glass, and conceal potholes and other hazards. This is a danger greatly intensified by Seattle's hilly topography.

Discomfort, Dirt, and Disdain

Beyond the mortal dangers, the work environment itself can be exceedingly uncomfortable for messengers. Winters can be painfully cold, summers can be insufferably hot, and the addition of rain can transform even mildly cool days into shivering nightmares. Snow on the ground means slush on the roads, and when it snows, there is nothing (and I mean *nothing*) that can keep a rider's feet dry. Messengers spend these days walking into buildings on nubs of painful nerves throbbing beneath their ankles from feet that are just not quite numb enough to totally disappear from consciousness. Regardless of the weather, riding in traffic all day exposes the cyclist to noxious fumes, roaring engines, honking horns, and black exhaust. My first few weeks as a New York messenger, I was shocked at how much dirt accumulated on my body throughout the day. After work, my legs and face were covered in dark soot.

Worse than the environment itself are the other people in it. Inconsiderate and irresponsible drivers are a constant source of stress. Beyond the physical threat cars and trucks pose to cyclists, there is a pervasive indifference exhibited by many drivers that infuriates and demeans bike riders. For example, on more than one occasion drivers in New York attempted to intimidate me by passing so close as to brush me with their vehicles. One passenger in a van actually leaned out of his vehicle and tried to push me over. This man was angry because as a cyclist using the road, I was in his vehicle's way. But he seemed less concerned with causing injury to all the automobile drivers also in his way. Another driver chased me for blocks screaming out threats at me (and my mother—who was not present, but her responsibility for my existence was enough to warrant her indictment). My transgression in this incident had been knocking on the window of his car to alert him of the fact that he was merging into the bike lane, and inches from squishing me between his vehicle and the cars parked on the side of the road.

The most serious road tensions arise between cabdrivers and messengers. When tempers flare, cabbies are known to speed around messengers, swerve in front of them, and then slam on their brakes in an attempt to cause a collision. Their thinking, I suppose, is to conceal (for legal purposes) who is at fault by having the cyclist rear-end the cab. The resulting accident would be more ambiguous than if the cabdriver simply collided with the cyclist from behind. Everyone, of course, experiences road rage. Cyclists, though, because of their exposure, are extremely vulnerable to such behavior. No one, for example, wants to be part of a rear-end collision, but a car aggressively swerving and braking in front of a cyclist turns what might just be a matter of property damage when done to another motor vehicle into the frightening possibility of serious bodily harm. Further, because of the nature of messenger work, bike couriers experience more road rage than other types of cyclists. Couriers are probably the bicyclists also the most likely to dish out their own road rage.

After I expressed my disbelief at many of the driving practices I experienced firsthand, Jason replied: "Can't believe it? Why not? This shit happens every day!" Months later, a delivery truck passed so close to Jason that his bag snagged on the side of the vehicle, pulling him from his bike and dragging him a block up Sixth Avenue before stopping. Jason survived with only minor injuries, but neither the truck's occupants nor the police arriving at the scene believed that the driver had committed any violation of traffic law. Cyclists in general, and messengers in particular, therefore, see themselves as under siege and legal enforcement as biased against them. Efren, a feisty Latino messenger, commenting on this tension, explained: "That is one of the reasons I stopped being a messenger. I was getting stressed out all the time. Fighting everyone." There are, of course, many laws on the books meant to protect cyclists. As Jason's story reveals, though, their enforcement is often nonexistent. At the same time, increased efforts to improve safety for cyclists are always tied to efforts to increase the cyclist's compliance with traffic laws.[26] Thus, in many ways, messengering is wedded to these dangers and tensions.

Even the messengers' own clients can be a source of frustration. Couriers riding for small companies usually have positive relationships with their clients. Firms that use larger companies like Sprint and CLS, however, generally treat messengers as nuisances, despite the fact that they endure numerous hardships in order to make deliveries for minimal compensation. Worse, they are often treated as dumb nuisances. Recounting his experiences, Jack Kugelmass, an anthropologist who conducted the first ethnography of bike messengers, notes: "My own sense of resentment at being treated as a messenger by clients made me all too ready to use my title, Dr., as a weapon, to shock the people I was serving."[27] This resentment is a common facet of both Travis Culley's and Rebecca Reilly's personal writings about messenger work. The *New York Times* editorialist and former messenger Tom Leander writes of this treatment: "I discovered that the messenger is second to the bottom of the Manhattan pecking order....As my work clothes got grubbier, people stood clear of me in elevators. I grew accustomed to rudeness....I gave up making hopeful eyes at receptionists at agencies uptown because I looked as if I had just come through a war zone."[28]

The Labor Market

It is not surprising that the messenger industry has an extremely high turnover rate. This is especially true in New York. According to Sprint Courier, over 50 percent of their rookie messengers quit work within two months. A good portion of riders do not make it past the first week. Cities like Seattle and San Diego have tighter messenger markets and tend to have more stable workforces. Regardless, five years is a long time to be a messenger, and ten is a rarity. Because of the high turnover, more seasoned couriers view rookie messengers negatively. "Real messengers" are measured against the assumed characteristics of rookies. Rookie messengers are perceived to lack knowledge of the city, not know how to handle themselves in traffic, lose packages, and stay home on cold and rainy days. Generally speaking, a messenger is no longer a rookie after a full year of work. Still, many longtime messengers socially snub new couriers for much longer. The messengers who have spent several years on the road are considered veterans. Veteran status garners a high degree of respect among other messengers. In New York, a handful of couriers have ridden for several decades, and these "original messengers" are treated reverently by their peers.

In New York, a vast majority of messengers are minorities and immigrants. This is not true in Seattle, where approximately 80 percent of riders are native-born whites. In San Diego this number is usually around 90 percent. Most messengers are men in their early 20s to early 30s. In New York, women make up less than 5 percent of the population. In Seattle, females constitute around 20 percent of messengers, and in San Diego it is usually about 15 percent. In all places, though, for people with no formal education, criminal records, drug addictions, or undocumented work status, messengering is often the best job option. This is especially true in the loose labor market of New York. There, a courier who messes up at one company or gets in a dispute with his employer can easily move to another company. As one New York messenger told me about his company, "Every morning at eight, they'll hire anybody who wants to work." Such a structure allows people who cannot (or do not want to) keep regular work routines to use messengering as one method of many forms of income.

In part, because of this flexibility, the occupation attracts not only the disenfranchised, but also those disillusioned with more routinized forms of labor. It is the disillusioned, more than the disenfranchised, who make up the messenger subculture. Which is to say, messengering in places like Chicago, New York, and Washington, D.C., can be a semiformal occupation for a marginally employable workforce willing to face extreme risks for small rewards. In all places, however, it is also a job that attracts middle-class bohemians lured by a promise of freedom. Specifically, the job offers freedom from the watchful eyes of one's employer and the potential thrills of dodging cars.

Couriers, even those paid hourly, are on their own for the most part and left to their own devices. They are assigned work through a communication device and are expected to complete the job by the deadline. As long as that is accomplished, nothing else is expected. In doing their work, therefore, messengers have a high degree of independence. This independence is extremely high in comparison to other low-wage service jobs. In between deliveries ("on standby"), messengers have even more freedom. They can run errands, read books, people watch, get intoxicated, or any combination of these things. Of course, getting intoxicated often requires some degree of concealment from employers and clients. But at many smaller companies such behavior may actually be encouraged. For example, Dragonfly was a reference to both the owner's Welsh nationality (Wales has a dragon on its flag) and the fact that he and his riders (with the exception of myself) were stoned for significant portions of the day ("flying around high all the time"). As one Seattle messenger summed up courier work, "You're either hanging out getting drunk or you're delivering a package." In either case, the implication is that being a bike courier is always an ideal job.

THE LIFESTYLE

Fannin and I started working in Seattle on the same day. Fannin got the job because his friend already worked at the company (and Fannin's friend had gotten the job from another friend already working there). Fannin applied for the job because he needed work, and it turned out to be a perfect fit. Over the many months we worked together his enthusiasm never seemed to wane. In fact, more than once he seemed dumbfounded as to why he had not started working as a bike courier sooner. Remarkably, he felt this way even after the sun and warmth of summer had long since been washed away by the incessant drizzle of winter.

Just into his 20s, Fannin had a thick beard, dressed like a punk rocker, and listened to hip-hop. He was a graffiti writer, and he was always working on various artistic projects. For days I watched him making sketches for a children's book during his lunch break. He also had a large multimedia showing at a Seattle coffeehouse, and his various pieces sold quite well. The sales were no doubt spurred by Fannin's refusal to charge much beyond the cost of the materials used in his artwork. More than anything, Fannin was attracted to the anarchy of messengering—not just the freedom, but a freedom tinged with danger and social disorganization (think Johnny Rotten, not Mikhail Bakunin). As Fannin happily described it, "Pretty much, we're totally above the law. That's the way I honesty feel about my job....I can do whatever all day: run lights, do graffiti during the whole day, whatever, get drunk if I want to. I'm just a paid criminal, I guess, at this job."

When Fannin started messengering he did not have a particularly strong interest in bicycles, but his appreciation and knowledge of the machines would grow. Unlike Fannin, Hultman, a fit and slender man in his early 30s, did have a deep appreciation and knowledge of bicycles before becoming a messenger. He even had a professional-quality bicycle workshop in his garage. Hultman knew how to build wheels (one of the most complex aspects of bicycle mechanics) and enjoyed debating the finer points of which parts do or do not get greased on a bicycle (believe it or not, among cyclists with an interest in mechanics, this is a very provocative topic). Like Fannin, on the other hand, Hultman was attracted to the edgy side of the occupation, particularly the excitement and the danger. Surprisingly, though, messengering was not Hultman's riskiest occupation. In the summer he was a firefighter for the forestry department, but in the winter there are no forest fires. So Hultman worked as a Seattle courier.

Hugo was a New York messenger who really liked the action of the job. Only in his early 20s when I met him, Hugo had already been a messenger for three years. Born in Texas, raised in Guatemala, and coming of age in Tennessee, Hugo saw messengering as a way out of the poverty he grew up in. As I got to know him, he was starting to make a name for himself in the scene. He would go on to become one of New York's fastest racers. Hugo, along with many of the younger New York couriers in this study, actually stopped formally messengering about two years after I left New York. Instead, he started working as a food delivery rider in Brooklyn. Hugo made the shift because he could make more money doing food delivery. However, Hugo still considered himself a messenger and continued to participate in races and parties. When I last saw him in 2007, he was spearheading a cooperatively run food delivery service, Snap Delivery. His company had arrangements with numerous restaurants, and he managed a handful of full-time riders. He was also expanding the co-op's activities to include traditional on-demand delivery services for Brooklyn. This novel idea garnered Snap media attention and a surprisingly successful niche in the local economy.[1]

Kenton was similar in some ways, but different in many others from Fannin, Hultman, and Hugo. When I first met Kenton, at my first messenger

Figure 6. Kenton, owner of Aloha Bicycle Courier

race in San Diego, he was in his early 30s. He came from a working-class family in the Midwest. He was a former collegiate swimmer and had a degree in technical illustration. For his first few years out of college, Kenton worked primarily in graphic design but was also a waiter and even a swim coach. Eventually, Kenton decided he would rather ride his bike for a living. He knew nothing about bike messengers, but he did know he wanted to be active and his own boss. An entrepreneurial drive more than the seduction of excitement brought Kenton to the courier business. In 2001, after a good deal of research, Kenton moved to San Diego and started Aloha Bicycle Courier.

The first years were rough. Kenton had no office space and only a few clients. He spent most of his days reading in parks downtown and his nights working in restaurants to cover his rent. He even spent some of this time living on a docked boat. Eventually, Aloha started to thrive; there was enough work to support another full-time rider, and Kenton often enlisted other messengers for help throughout the day. For a brief period Kenton and his wife, Mimi, rode for the company together, but the impending birth of their daughter changed that. Kenton started looking into retiring from the business, or at least moving into the office full-time. Ideally, he wanted to become a documentary filmmaker. His first major undertaking, in fact, is a feature-length documentary on bike messengers—*Career Courier.*[2]

Jacky started messengering at CLS soon after I moved to Seattle. She was an outgoing (if not hyper) college student in her mid-20s. She had a quick, sarcastic humor that could light up any situation. She was messengering, in addition to holding several other part-time service jobs, to pay for her education. Jacky was one of CLS's best riders and was soon promoted to working part-time as a dispatcher. After graduating college she briefly left the road and worked with a local sexual assault center and the ACLU. However, she eventually returned to messengering. As she explained, "I couldn't resist, as you can probably understand. My legs were losing definition, my mood was getting grouchier, and I missed the edge of messenger living....It's been great. You know that movie where the main character is a secretary by day, hooker by night? The transition from office work to messengering feels very similar."

Worlds apart from the other messengers I have just described, but an icon to any courier that ever saw him ride through traffic, was Calvin. A messenger since the 1970s, Calvin exercised a Zenlike control of his machine—as if cycling was a martial art, and he was a master practitioner. To watch him ride in New York traffic was to watch perfection in motion. When I knew him, Calvin's bike was almost completely covered in stickers (and he had more than one decorated this way). Many of the stickers were self-made, cut from magazines and newspapers and stuck to the frames with packaging tape. The images and slogans ranged from bicycle advocacy to pornography to simple absurdity. As a rookie rider, I was surprised and encouraged by Calvin's friendly wave (usually a peace sign) when we would cross paths in traffic. In many ways, Calvin stands as the supreme representation of both the highs and the lows of the occupation. Even into his 50s, Calvin still attended alleycats and parties. He kept up with the "old cats" and the "young bloods" alike. Conversely, as a poor black man, Calvin was never provided the material compensation worthy of the physical sacrifices he made as a messenger. Presumably, failing health prompted Calvin's departure from New York and his retirement (if you can call it that) from the occupation.

Being a Bike Messenger

When asked directly most messengers cite money as their motivation for working. As one messenger sarcastically answered, "Did I mention rent? It could be that they like to eat."[3] Or, as one boisterous New York messenger often yelled to other couriers as he wove his way through traffic, "Gotta make that dollar!" Certainly, for some individuals, bicycle delivery may be their most lucrative job option. The actions and attitudes of many messengers, especially those in the subculture, however, cannot be reduced to simple economic necessity. As a case in point, no one was paid for the Warriors Fun Ride (not even the organizers who spent months planning it). Summing up the incongruence between her financial compensation and her psychological satisfaction, a Milwaukee messenger informed me: "I make shit, but I love my life." Or, as a popular sticker made by Mark, a longtime Seattle messenger and self-directed graphic designer, screen printer, and blogger, reads, "It's a quality of life issue."

Some of this "quality of life" arises from the occupation's flexibility and independence, but, in itself, it does not explain much. Nighttime security guards, for example, have a high level of independence, but they do not have a subculture surrounding their job. Likewise, white-collar workers may appreciate the implementation of flextime by many companies, but it has not resulted in the widespread fusion of work and leisure as we see it in the messenger world. But we are getting ahead of ourselves. I will start to unravel the subcultural puzzle in the next chapter. For now, we need not be concerned with *why* the subculture exists, only *what* the lifestyle consists of.

Bikes and Beer

At its most basic level, the messenger lifestyle is about bikes and beer. Or, more accurately (but losing the alliteration), the lifestyle revolves around urban cycling and various forms of intoxication.[4] First and foremost, messengering is a bicycle subculture. Messengers love bikes and love biking. "Urban cycling," as messengers use the term, can be characterized as a combination of an ecologically minded view on alternative transportation and an aggressive assertion of one's self within traffic. At the same time, the courier's devotion to bicycles should not be mistaken as a devotion to athletic asceticism. Nothing could be further from the truth. Alcohol, cigarettes, marijuana, and harder drugs are mainstays of any messenger gathering. Clearly, it takes a special sort of person to regularly intoxicate himself while riding in traffic. While the majority of messengers may remain sober during the workday, it is a rarity for a messenger not to drink after work.

One messenger I was about to interview began by asking: "Do you mind waiting for like five minutes? I just want to drink another beer and smoke some weed before we get started." Another messenger proudly informed me, without the slightest hint of irony, that he had "stopped drinking." He said this while nursing a pint of Guinness. For this messenger, not drinking did not mean not ingesting alcohol; it just meant not ingesting alcohol until he blacked out. To really drive this point home, one of my first interactions with members of the messenger subculture involved one messenger asking another courier what happened to him after he left a bar the previous night. The messenger replied: "I don't remember. All I know is I woke up with bloody sheets and a wobbly front wheel." For his part, the first messenger followed with his own tales of blacking out—the most bizarre of which involved him awaking on the roof of his apartment complex, in his underwear, holding his bicycle.

Alleycats

For messengers subsumed in the subculture, there are two main forms of socializing: drinking after work and racing bicycles. Social drinking is far more common, but races are *the* main social event. Most messenger races are far less complex and far less cosmopolitan than the Warriors Fun Ride, and most do not attempt to conceal that they are, in fact, races. That is, they are called "races" not "fun rides." These smaller events are known as alleycats, and like the Warriors, they take place in open traffic with no approval from city officials. Alleycats mimic the basic structure of the job. Race organizers, who are messengers themselves (or former messengers), give racers a manifest with a list of checkpoints. Some races require a specific sequence, but other races allow the courier to determine the best order. This is just like the workday, where some runs are given priority by dispatchers, and other times messengers determine how to arrange their pick-ups and drop-offs. At each checkpoint, the racer must have his manifest signed (just as in work). In some alleycats, messengers must perform certain tasks. For example, I've been to races where riders were required to puncture their own tire and replace the tube or do push-ups before their manifests would be signed. These tasks mimic the myriad ways things may go wrong during the workday, from mechanical difficulties and mislabeled packages to clients who are unavailable or trouble with security guards. In this regard, unlike traditional bike races, alleycats test not only one's speed on the bike but also one's efficiency at solving problems, although the problem solving is altered and simplified.

Competitive cycling events like the Tour de France are generally about physical strength and endurance. They involve teamwork and strategy, but mainly they test human power as transferred into the forward momentum of a machine. The routes are known, and the conditions (more or less) standardized. In alleycats, by contrast, cardiovascular fitness is of small consequence. This is because messenger races are extremely short by cycling standards. Messenger competitions are rarely over fifteen miles. More importantly, there are very few rules in alleycats. Or, as several people have pointed out, "There are no rules." These races are not intended to be athletic events in any usual sense of the term, and accomplished competitive cyclists are by no means particularly accomplished at messenger races. Alleycats are events of loosely controlled chaos, and standardization runs counter to the very nature of the competition.

Joan, a short, cute girl whose smile and enthusiasm contrasted with her dreadlocked hair and grungy clothing, captured the unique nature of the alleycat quite well. She was still a teenager when she started messengering in 2002. Originally from an affluent neighborhood in Boston, Joan was not only a courier but also an undergraduate at New York University. Like Hugo, she quickly made a name for herself racing. In one of her first notable victories, Joan, well under the legal drinking age, actually won a "year's supply of beer" (365 bottles delivered to her apartment) at an alleycat sponsored by a local brewery. Despite her racing prowess, I was surprised to learn she had absolutely no interest in traditional cycling competitions. She derided those competitions, in which, she observed, "it's just you." Instead, she relished the buzz of the traffic and the uncertainty it brought to the competition. In alleycats, riders swarm the street, scream at pedestrians, and bully their way through intersections in a way that defies the expectations of the typical workday. That is, in a real workday, there are lots of slow deliveries and maybe one or two rushes punctuated by pauses and lulls. An alleycat, though, is one long double rush with no elevator rides to slow the rider down.

The difference between an alleycat and other forms of bicycle racing is apparent at first sight. Hardly any racers will be wearing spandex, and few will be wearing helmets. Baggy shorts or pants cut off above the ankle are much more common, and almost everyone will be wearing a huge messenger bag slung across their shoulder. The bicycles are not carbon fiber or titanium racing bikes with sixteen-spoke wheels. They are solid bikes with frames often made of steel. They are machines that must handle abuse every day at work. For this reason, couriers draw a strong distinction between a messenger's bike and a yuppie's bicycle. The latter are for "weekend warriors" on training rides. The former are for men and women doing practical work—day in and day out. Many messengers ride expensive machines, but these meet important stylistic and functional criteria. The end result of the messengers' style is a scene that looks like "a collision between the Tour de France field and the cast of Mad Max."[5] Some racers will be drunk or high long before the competition even starts. Some of the intoxicated riders seriously embrace the competition, while others ride with no interest in winning at all. As Arnold, a massive man with tattoos adorning his neck and decorating his bulging, muscular arms, exclaimed at the 2002 New York City Halloween race, "I don't want to win. I just want to get drunk and hopefully cause some damage to this city." The competition itself was ancillary.

Races always conclude (and often start) with a party. Like all aspects of courier life, drinking and other intoxicants are a major component of the race environment. Organizers of one New York race, for example, debated whether drug dealers should be formally invited to the event. In the end it was decided "real drug dealers will know to be there anyway." As a case in point, a group of Canadian messengers had smuggled a rather large quantity of psychedelic mushrooms across the border in jars of salsa.

Many messengers come to races and do not even bother racing, choosing to enjoy the partylike atmosphere surrounding the event instead. A group of Philadelphia messengers told me after an alleycat in Boston: "We didn't race, but we came for the party." Almost all the New York entrants at a Montreal alleycat dropped out after the first checkpoint and rode to a strip club instead. In alleycats, like all races, prizes are awarded for the fastest riders, but some messenger races also have a prize for the messenger who finishes "DFL" (Dead Fucking Last). Two of the races I participated in even had alternative rides for messengers with no interest in competing but only in social drinking.

A Note on the Prominent Races

Messengers within a city organize any number of alleycats throughout the year. These may or may not draw riders from surrounding scenes. Other races are nationally and internationally recognized. First and foremost is the Cycle Messenger World Championships (CMWC). The CMWC has been held annually since 1993. Hundreds of messengers, along with former messengers and those interested in the messenger lifestyle, attend. Several of my informants cited the CMWC as a life-changing event. For them it marked a realization that messengering was of profound importance to not only themselves but countless others as well. This was definitely the case with MAC, a woman who had made a name for herself in the Seattle scene several years before I met her. She reflected on her first CMWC: "I was pretty much a rookie. I'd been working for like three months. I was like, 'Everyone here is wearing Sidis [a brand of cycling shoe] and looks weird. This is my community. I'm home." There are also annual continental championships: the European Cycle Messenger Championships (ECMC), the North American Cycle Courier Championships (NAC3), and the Australian Cycle Messenger Championships (ACMC).

These world and continental championships are huge, formally organized alleycats. Messengers in various cities bid among themselves at various gatherings for the rights to hold the event. Cities are usually selected one to two years in advance. Because of the size of these events, organizers must get permits and hold the races on closed courses. In fact, a large part of the selection process is based on messengers from the would-be host cities convincing others that they will successfully conduct all the necessary planning. During the championships, there are helmet policies due to legal issues and qualifying heats due to the sheer number of participants. The winners of these races are given bragging rights for a year: the world's and continent's fastest couriers. They are prestigious titles. At the same time, many messengers are cynical of the format of these races, and there is a certain disdain for their rules and formalities. As one New York messenger quipped about the 2003 NAC3, "It has nothing to do with the skills of being a messenger." However, despite their sanitation, the races do attempt to replicate the occupation. Riders make "deliveries" to various checkpoints, and "bike thieves" prowl the course to penalize racers who leave their machines unlocked at checkpoints.

Beyond the championships, several cities hold large annual races that attract riders nationally and internationally. The most notable of these are New York's Fourth of July Race, Halloween Race, and Monster Track; Minneapolis's Stupor Bowl; Portland's Westside Invite; and Seattle's Dead Baby Downhill. There are also one-time events like the Warriors that can draw international participation. It is worth mentioning that cities like San Diego hold alleycats, but they attract no outside riders. However, messengers from these cities will often travel to the larger championships.

A Fixed Bike Won't Brake

Couriers can ride any number of bikes. The three most common machines are mountain, road, and track bikes. Mountain and road bikes need no introduction. A track bike, on the other hand, is a more exotic piece of equipment (though it is quickly becoming less exotic). A track bike (also known as a fixed gear, fixed, or fixie) is a bicycle specifically designed for racing on an oval racetrack with banked corners called a velodrome. Track racing gets most of its mainstream exposure during the Summer Olympics.

Track bikes have a fixed gear, no brakes, and a rigid geometry. Rigid geometries are good for speed and quick handling but are harder on the rider's body (especially when riding on a surface other than a velodrome). A fixed gear means the bicycle does not have a freewheel. So if the rear wheel is spinning so are the pedals. With fixes, therefore, there can be no coasting. The rider controls the bike's speed with the pedals, and (with a certain degree of skill) the bike can be made to skid to a stop. This is why track bikes do not require a brake. If the rider leans forward, removing some of her body weight from the rear wheel, and locks her legs, she can force the rear wheel to stop moving and produce a skid (sometimes called a skip). Track bikes should not be confused with children's bikes with coaster brakes or with beach cruisers. In addition, forcing a bike to skid or skip to a stop is only necessary when using the machine on city streets; when raced on a velodrome there is simply no need to come to an abrupt halt, because no one else has brakes either.

Although it is a somewhat esoteric point, all track bikes are fixed gears, but not all fixed gears are track bikes. The term "track bike" technically refers to frames and components that have been purposely engineered for velodrome racing. Road bikes and mountain bikes can be converted into fixed gears by altering the retching mechanism connected to the rear hub or by replacing the hub, but they cannot be made into real track bikes. Some manufacturers also produce fixed-gear frames that are not true road bikes because they lack fittings for derailleurs, but these do not have track geometry.[6] Fixed gears can also be fitted with brakes, but most real track bikes do not have holes in the frame in which to mount brakes. Among messengers who ride fixed, having a "real track bike" (and not just a fixed gear) is often an issue of major social importance.

While only a minority of messengers actually ride track bikes, most, nonetheless, consider fixes *the* bike of choice among messengers. There are many reasons for the track bike's popularity among messengers. First, there is very little to steal from the bike. Second, being able to control the speed of the bike through the pedals (as opposed to combining hand brakes with coasting) offers a huge degree of control in traffic and on wet or snowy roads. In hilly conditions, however, a fixed without hand brakes provides less control—and even less on wet or icy hills. Third, unencumbered by additional components, track bikes are often lighter than similarly priced machines. Fourth, there is very little that can break or needs to be tuned up, but among the remaining components that can break (such as the drive chain or various parts of the wheel system) not having a brake greatly increases the risk of physical injury should the malfunction occur while riding. Fifth, many cyclists believe that riding fixed is more enjoyable than riding a freewheel bicycle. As Joan, the NYU rider with a year's supply of beer, explained, "[A track bike] is like an extension of your body." Sixth, tying in with the fifth reason, there is a mystique about riding a track bike, since it has no brakes and does not allow you to coast. A track bike helps separate the initiated from the uninitiated. It is considered something that only a true "pro" can ride. As Rick, a fast and aggressive New York messenger (on and off the bike), remarked, "People on track bikes know what they are doing. On a mountain bike, you can get away with a lot more." Conversely, as track bikes gain mainstream popularity, Rick's distinctions hold less truth.

Occupational Messengers and Lifestyle Messengers

It must be noted that not all couriers attend races and messenger parties. For some messengers, the occupation is not a lifestyle; it is only work. As Craig, a prominent member of the Seattle courier subculture, noted, "So many messengers are just job-only kind of people." These people

Figure 7. New York messenger working in regular street clothes

may or may not find work enjoyable, but it does not overtly define who they are. The difference between job-only kind of people and those who are integrated into the bike-courier subculture is illustrated nicely in the contrast between the comments of Craig and Lester. Craig was in his mid-20s and had been a messenger for several years. He was considered one of Seattle's fastest couriers (at work and in alleycats). In fact, he won the 2010 CMWC, and he was quickly making a name for himself in traditional cycling races as well. Lester was also in his 20s with several years of experience and a solid reputation as a top rider at Sprint. However, unlike Craig, Lester did not ride his bike at all when not working. He would actually leave his machine at Sprint's office and take the subway home.

Craig explained why he participated in alleycats: "I think that it's mostly because I like what I do enough to want to do it again. And, if I'm not [racing] on Friday night, it is funny how much you find yourself talking about it. It's ridiculous." Conversely, Lester, when asked if he went to a messenger party the previous weekend, replied: "I see these kids every day. Why would I want to party with them too?" Chapter 5 will explore

Figure 8. San Diego bike messenger riding in the Gaslamp Quarter

the reasons for these variations in social integration; for now I want simply to give a basic description of the variation.

In New York, only a small minority of couriers(fewer than two hundred) fully participates in the messenger lifestyle. Among this group, whites and females are overrepresented. Nearly every female messenger in New York, and most of the whites, are participants in the subculture. In larger messenger cities, an unspoken tension can exist between messengers involved in the subculture and those who are not. During the same conversation, Lester expressed his frustration with the lifestyle messengers' integration of work and leisure, explaining that at these events attendees "all had their messenger clothes on, and their bags." As it happened, Lester's friend Malcolm lived next door to the party. Malcolm, unfamiliar with the subculture, walked in because he recognized people from work. However, he found the whole situation rather perplexing. Agreeing with Lester, he exclaimed: "Can't [they] be normal for just one day?" In contrast to the occupational messengers' derision of the lifestyle, within the subculture the formal rhetoric states that there is no difference between messengers. One New York messenger, irritated with my question on the issue, summed it up as follows: "It doesn't fucking matter."

Regardless of the subcultural rhetoric of occupational unity, in large messenger cities, there is a practical divide that all messengers recognize. A Chicago messenger explained it simply: "They don't come to alleycats. Of course, because they don't love riding their bikes." Representing the other side of the issue, a veteran New York messenger offered this criticism: "Some elements within the messenger scene only want to portray one part of it. I went to these people and said, 'You're not representing New York. You have to go all over.'" This courier, one of New York's "original messengers," felt excluded by the specific image many within the lifestyle portray to the outside world—the hip, bohemian side of the job over its working-class realism. At the same time, the Chicago messenger was adamant that if Chicago hosted the NAC3, the event needed to include not only lifestyle messengers, but occupational messengers as well. By contrast, in smaller cities like Seattle and San Diego, there is no clear divide between full participants in the lifestyle and occupational messengers. Which is to say, in smaller cities, all messengers are at least partially integrated into the subculture.

To summarize, bike messengers, as members of a particular occupation, are part of a social world. Within this world, however, is a subculture. This book is primarily about those within the subculture. They are what I call lifestyle messengers, and they can be contrasted with occupational messengers. By emphasizing certain aspects of the occupation, lifestyle messengers give the act of delivering packages avocational value and imbue urban cycling with grand meaning. That is, they see delivering packages as an authentic form of action connected to their real self. The point of this book, therefore, is to explain how and why this happens.

The Local Scenes at My Research Sites

During my time in Seattle, very few messengers regularly raced. Talking with older messengers, I learned the frequency of alleycats in the city has fluctuated over time. I was there in a lull, but, even during this dip in racing enthusiasm, at least five local alleycats were held in the course of ten months. Many Seattle messengers traveled to Portland for the Westside Invite, to Philadelphia for the 2006 NAC3, and to San Francisco for the 2007 NAC3. A few even traveled to Australia for the 2006 CMWC. The Dead Baby Downhill and an annual backyard-boxing event at which messengers box each other were, as always, attended by virtually every messenger in the city (as well as by many former messengers). Moreover, up to 40 percent of the city's riders might have socialized together on any given Friday evening. During the workday, the Monorail, an outdoor coffee stand, functioned as the primary spot where messengers would socialize.

The vibrancy of the Seattle scene was epitomized by the various efforts of Mark. In his late 30s (although he looked much younger), Mark was a very quiet man. His words, soft-spoken as they may have been, proved him to be a keen observer and a folk historian of both the messenger subculture and cycling more generally. During my interview with Mark it was obvious that he was worried about wasting his potential. For example, he asked me what my parents thought about me working as a messenger. A graduate of a top liberal arts college, he was clearly a man who could be doing a lot of other things, and during our talk it was obvious that his parents had never really come to terms with the choices he had made. I knew Mark for only a tiny fraction of his numerous years on the road, but he was a great example of someone who helped make messengering more than just a job, and whose efforts enhanced the lives of Seattle couriers. Most notable among his efforts were his zine (*Kickstand*) and his website (pilderwasser.com).

Through these outlets he was a bicycle advocate, messenger pundit, and T-shirt and sticker designer. One of his shirts, for example, depicted the evolution of humanity from our beginning as apelike creatures to our zenith as messengers on bicycles. In a rather obscure way, another of Mark's shirts asserted the messengers riding for a particular company were alcoholics (a comment that was taken as a point of pride, not an insult). The shirt read: "Fleetfoot messengers cannot give alcoholics advice." The Fleetfoot shirt was a play on an earlier shirt that read: "Messengers cannot give legal advice." This first shirt was a spoof of a common sign in filing rooms at courthouses: "Clerks cannot give legal advice."[7]

When I moved to San Diego, alleycats were new to the area. James, a messenger originally from Seattle, introduced them. Prior to James's arrival, there were messengers in San Diego, but no messenger subculture. Remembering the days before James's influence, Kenton commented: "It never crossed my mind to hang out with other messengers. I thought all we had in common was low pay." James introduced not only alleycats

Figure 9. San Diego messengers drinking coffee at Tony's Coffee Cart

but other aspects of the messenger subculture too: Messenger Appreciation Day and self-published magazines detailing the local courier scene. Messenger Appreciation Day is October 9 ("10–9" is radio code for "repeat last message"). The zine James started was called *Chillowmode*. San Diego's first alleycat was in the fall of 2003. James left San Diego very shortly after my arrival there, to continue working as a messenger in Portland. His zine only survived an issue or two after his departure, but San Diego messengers still toasted to October 9, and, more importantly, races were still going strong.

Aside from Kenton, most of San Diego's veteran couriers did not race, but younger riders, along with couriers transplanted from other scenes, vigorously participated in local alleycats. As in Seattle, a coffee stand, in this case Tony's Coffee Cart, functioned as a workday hangout. Tony's, though, was only a morning spot, closing in the early afternoon. Further, this budding messenger subculture had not established formal after-hours socializing, nor did its members hold alleycats that attracted

Figure 10. Kevin (aka Squid) in Washington Square Park

messengers from other cities—not even from Los Angeles, which is just
a short train ride away.

In New York, messengers involved in the subculture raced a lot, and
there were lots of racing options. Not only did New Yorkers regularly
hold local races, but the city's couriers traveled up and down the Eastern
seaboard for alleycats. New York's messenger scene was large enough
to have several notable figures, but none were as well known as Kevin
(often called by his nickname, Squid). He represented everything positive about New York messengering. Working since the early 1990s, Kevin
had tirelessly supported both the occupation and the lifestyle. He was
a tall, lanky guy with a punk-rock haircut, even though he was well into
his 30s. He had organized benefits, gathered corporate sponsorships
for various events, and functioned as a media spokesperson. Known by
messengers across the globe, Kevin still made a point to talk to rookie
riders—to ask how they were doing and to make sure they knew about

upcoming races and parties. During my time in New York, Kevin won several prominent races and organized several memorable ones himself (like the Warriors). While Kevin loved the competition of alleycats, he always stressed fun as the only purpose of the events. Also, like Calvin, Kevin's experience on the bike gave him a seemingly supernatural control of his machine.

When I lived in New York, there was no functional messenger zine, but there were several messenger websites providing both editorial comments and information about upcoming and past events. After I left, even more websites sprang up. Many even included pages for the sale of shirts and other bric-a-brac for insiders and outsiders alike. As for socializing, Tompkins Square Park and Sophie's, a bar in the East Village, were the two primary places for messengers to meet after work. Various cliques had their own haunts, but Tompkins and Sophie's were the primary places of congregation, especially on Fridays. Perhaps because of New York's size, there was no main place for socializing during the day in the city. In San Diego or Seattle, on the other hand, regardless of where a messenger just made a drop-off, it was usually just a short ride to Tony's or the Monorail. In Manhattan (divided between downtown, midtown, and uptown) there was no one central place to congregate. Unlike messengering in San Diego and Seattle, therefore, courier work in New York was very atomized. Riders might constantly cross paths with other messengers, but they rarely stopped to talk, and even when they did, the exchange lacked the relaxed character of the socialization that occurred at my other sites' designated meeting places.

The Subculture and Outsiders

As is the case for many subcultures, outsiders have appropriated various aspects of messenger style. For example, correctly or not, messengers have been credited with starting the 1990s hip-hop fad of rolling up a single leg of one's pants.[8] Most noticeably, numerous backpack and bag makers from Eddie Bauer to the Gap now produce "messenger bags." These are single-shoulder-strap bags whose main opening is closed by a large fabric flap over the top, but they are only vaguely similar to the bag a working messenger would actually use. Cashing in on the urban mystique of the messenger image, however, these bags have become quite popular. A middle-aged businesswoman in an elevator, for instance, proudly displayed her "messenger bag" to me but then for clarity's sake (which certainly was not necessary) informed me: "I only have the bag. I'm not an actual messenger."

Interestingly, bike messengers actually fit into the bohemian revival of the Pabst Blue Ribbon beer brand. In what *New York Times Magazine* columnist Rob Walker calls "murketing"—that is, nontraditional and sparsely funded marketing campaigns relying on word-of-mouth buzz and the potential for things to go viral on the Internet[9]—Pabst has provided free beer (along with some other minor forms of support) for alleycats. It has done the same with bike polo, which is an offshoot of the messenger subculture.[10]

Particularly notable in all of this is the fact that Pabst's new ownership and new nonunion production have greatly damaged the brand's original blue-collar support. But messengers are largely ambivalent about unionization—as we will see in the conclusion. Of course, it is unlikely the marketing executives at the company knew about bike couriers' indifference to unions. All the same, in supporting messenger events and providing various promotions at the dive bars messengers patronize, Pabst successfully tapped into a subculture that has helped renew the beer's credentials as a gritty, salt-of-the-earth beer—and helped market the brand to other postindustrial urban trendsetters.

While unionization is not a going concern for most couriers, numerous other matters of authenticity are, as chapter 5 will show. At this juncture, though, I want to address two highly related issues: the boundary between rookie and veteran riders and the boundary between messengers and nonmessengers. When I started messengering in New York, the most salient boundary was that between rookie and veteran messengers. I began the job working on a track bike. This resulted in messengers either incorrectly assuming that I was not a rookie or, if they knew me to be a rookie, their subtle (and sometimes not so subtle) admonishments on the danger riding fixed posed for novices. It was assumed that only "pros" could handle themselves on such a machine. At the same time, while alleycats were open to anyone, it was almost exclusively current and former messengers who competed. The small attendance of outsiders was not considered a threat to the subculture's sovereignty. In other words, messengers focused on the boundary between rookie and veteran riders, not on that between messengers and nonmessengers (for the latter was considered inconsequential).

The popularity of track bikes beyond the messenger's world has been increasing since the late 1990s, and starting in the mid-2000s, the trend exploded. Bicycle retailers across the country now sell fixed-gear products, even in places that do not have velodromes and where messengers have no cultural resonance. Concurrent with the mainstreaming of fixies is the expansion of alleycats outside the subculture. While more obscure than track bikes, alleycats now occur in cities with no messengers. For example, places like Raleigh, North Carolina, and St. Petersburg, Florida, have held such races, and San Diego and Seattle alleycats (while still considered messenger events) are attended by more nonmessengers than messengers. These developments reflect the emergence of a new and different cultural phenomenon—the bicycle hipster. Although the term "hipster" is rather vague and clearly could apply to more than just those interested in bikes, nonmessengers who ride track bikes and race in alleycats are commonly referred to as such.

Having been initiated in New York before the influx of hipsters, I was originally blind to the threat many messengers increasingly believe outsiders pose. A dispute at a Boston race in 2003 illustrates how the matter of outsiders has changed. In that instance, several veteran Boston messengers disputed the legitimacy of an alleycat being organized, in their estimation, by a rookie messenger. The organizer worked only parttime and was thus not a real messenger by Boston standards. In speaking about this conflict to other New Yorkers, Joan stood up for the organizer: "He's fast as shit! What does it matter if he's a messenger? He's a fast urban cyclist." For the New Yorkers at the race, the organizer's credentials were based on his skills in urban cycling. Indeed, he had previously placed quite well in a New York race. His time working as an actual messenger was seen as secondary, or even irrelevant, to the matter.

In fact, at the time New York flyers for upcoming alleycats were likely to specify that all urban cyclists were welcome to attend. Even among the Boston couriers, the issue was not about insiders and complete outsiders. No one would have complained if the organizer attended a Boston race. He had certainly done so on numerous occasions. His offense was stepping too quickly into the role of a veteran. That is, he set out to assert his right not only to compete, but to organize. As such, the individual in question was not so much an impostor as an upstart.

Increasingly, though, the appropriation of track bikes by nonmessengers and the mere presence of outsiders at alleycats are viewed as problematic in the messenger subculture. Seattle messengers, in particular, started policing their borders against outsiders. In interviews, I heard time and again variations of how hipsters made messengers look bad in the public eye. The validity of this claim is certainly debatable, but it was accepted as gospel. Seattle lore was also filled with stories about hipsters who try to pass themselves off as messengers to other outsiders. Again, the accuracy of these claims is questionable, but their acceptance by messengers was universal. In 2007, even the New York messengers, previously so indifferent to the presence of outsiders, have sought to place barriers between themselves and hipsters. For example, Hugo, one of the New York messengers present at the disputed Boston race, told me about his plans to organize a "messenger-only" alleycat. His hope was to help return the event to its true roots as a competition between messengers.

Messengers and the Public Sphere

I started this book by claiming that outsiders, or at least those living in older metropolitan hubs, have a fascination with bike messengers. Outsiders' characterization of messengers may be positive ("daredevils") or negative ("maniacal and dangerous"). In familiarizing oneself with messengers, it is instructive to look at how they have been portrayed in the media. The *New York Times,* in particular, offers a valuable window into public opinion on messengers and some additional historical context for the occupation.

In the *New York Times'* first article on couriers, William Geist portrays messengers as lovable outlaws (i.e., folk heroes).[11] While acknowledging that couriers break laws, Geist, to a large extent, valorizes their behavior. Jack Kugelmass's ethnography of messengers also paints an image of folk heroes. Regardless of racial, class, age, or gender differences, Kugelmass writes, "all share a kinship with the heroes of the Wild West. They are romantic adventurers who prefer the exhilaration of danger to civilization's deadening routine."[12] The portrayal of the messenger as the ultimate urban man reached its zenith in 1986 with the release of *Quicksilver,* a Hollywood movie starring Kevin Bacon as a stockbroker turned free-spirited bike courier. In 1995, couriers would again be given the limelight in a briefly aired sitcom on CBS called *Double Rush.*[13] Not surprisingly, neither of these fiction vehicles even remotely captures what messenger life is like. For dialogue purposes (as well as filming costs), messengers in these stories are almost always stationary. They don't make deliveries so much as hang out at the company office or sit and chat in a diner—in the middle of the day no less.

While the idea of the "romantic adventurer" has intrigued the public, it also demonizes the messenger. In response to Geist's article, one

New Yorker angrily wrote: "[The article] dealt with the problem of wild and dangerous bike-riding messengers as if it were some interesting and benign cultural phenomenon, glossing over the extreme hazards these self-styled entrepreneurs pose to the public at large." The *New York Times* ran its own editorial piece slamming messengers one week after the publication of Geist's article: "What motivates those cyclists who whiz along the blind side of traffic lanes, plunge through intersections against the light and otherwise terrorize New York City drivers and pedestrians? For the worst offenders, the answer is money." Then: "Are bike messengers capable of such contempt? You bet."[14]

While occasionally depicted positively, from the mid-1980s on, messengers were quickly turned from folk heroes to villains, at least in New York. They became "the speeding bane of New York's pedestrians and motorists." For example, the *New York Times* review of *Quicksilver* suggested: "You may need a soft spot for the bicycle messengers who bring such thrills, chills and spills to New York's streets and sidewalks to get a bang out of [the movie]." Admittedly, the movie is so awful that the required soft spot would probably need to be in one's skull, but the larger point remains: messengers were increasingly seen as a menace. The New York City police commissioner went as far as to claim: "What [messengers are] doing is scaring the public to death, and we've got to do something about it."[15] Beyond New York, Bob Levy, a columnist for the *Washington Post,* probably worked harder than anyone to demonize messengers. Levy went so far as to accuse messengers of not only engaging in reckless riding, but also causing an epidemic of bicycle theft throughout the city and, with no humor intended, killing innocent squirrels.[16]

In response to public outrage over messengers fanned by the media, Mayor Ed Koch gradually started increasing police pressure on bicycle scofflaws throughout the 1980s. Police more than quadrupled their citations to cyclists between 1982 and 1983. In 1984, a bill was passed requiring messengers to wear identifying vests, and companies to keep logs of where messengers had been dispatched. The original version of this bill, which Koch refused to sign, actually included criminal penalties and possible jail time for offenders. The bill that went into law, however, was civil, not criminal. Commenting on the original bill, a *New York Times* editorial stated: "Given the dangers posed by speeding bikes that defy the traffic law, jail is wholly appropriate in some cases." Three years later, in an effort to tame "the dangerous habits which threaten the safety of any New Yorker who is not blessed with eyes in the back of his or her head," the mayor attempted to ban all bicycles on three midtown avenues (between the hours of 10 a.m. and 4 p.m.). The proposed bike ban was blocked by a court order on the eve of its implementation.[17]

Ten years after the failed bike ban, a pedestrian was killed in a collision with a food-delivery biker, and New Yorkers reignited their moral condemnations of *all* bicycle delivery riders. Of course, motor vehicles represent a far greater threat to pedestrian safety. In 1996, 256 pedestrians died from accidents with automobiles in New York. Only 1 died from a collision with a cyclist.[18] Regardless, the bicyclist drew the greatest amount of public attention. In 1997, a Boston bike courier put a pedestrian into a weeklong coma. The pedestrian happened to be rather well connected—he was a vice president of the Federal Reserve Bank. In the aftermath of this accident a similar moral panic broke out in Boston too. It is worth noting that in this incident the pedestrian was crossing *against* the light, but it was the courier who was both legally fined and publicly blamed for the event.[19] Speaking of the New York death, Mayor Rudy Giuliani stated: "Bicycles are a very big quality-of-life problem.... It may be the thing that was most mentioned to me when I was campaigning, particularly in Manhattan." As a writer for the *New York Times* notes, "While the number of deaths is small, many pedestrians said...that the statistics did not take into account the daily close calls they had encountered on the city's crowded streets."[20] While certainly true, this observation fails to account for why the daily close calls with automobiles are so easily ignored.

Bad press is part of the reason messengers view themselves as outlaws. The good press is part of the reason messengers view their subculture as special. It is probably already apparent to the reader that I believe both are true. Messengers are outlaws, and their subculture is special. At the same time, while journalists have produced compelling stories, many filled with rich pieces of data, as products of the mass media they do not provide an adequate theoretical analysis of bike messengers. I see my task in the chapters that follow to connect the pieces—the good and the bad—and construct an explanation for why couriers do what they do and how they do it. Not simply why they run red lights, but why those in the subculture spend so much time and effort in their nonwork lives reproducing the very acts that vilify them in the press. In doing so, we will learn about how emotions and space are integral to meaningful identity construction—through a process I call the affective appropriation of space. Before focusing on the nitty-gritty, however, it is worth looking at two competing sociological explanations for the messenger subculture: masculinity and dirty work.

MEN'S WORK AND DIRTY WORK

Without a doubt, bike messengering is a masculine occupation. Not only is it a job overwhelmingly performed by men, but many of the skills it requires exemplify a certain type of machismo. It is a job that involves an athletic negotiation of danger and the management of interpersonal hostility. Moreover, the courier subculture exaggerates the stereotypically male aspects of the job by turning workday practices into even more dangerous competitions.

A Macho Element Involved?

Many researchers have shown that men use the difficulties of manual labor as a prop for greater self-esteem over and against women.[1] It is, perhaps, tempting to explain messengering the same way. However, the job of bike messenger and its surrounding subculture does not easily fit into such a conception. Women, while numerically underrepresented, are prominent in both the occupation and the subculture. In fact, as already pointed out, the percentage of females is disproportionately higher in the subculture. Thus neither the work nor the subculture of messengering can be seen as a site of homosocial bonding. Men regularly interact with women performing the same tasks. Often the women are more successful than the men. At CLS, for example, several women were readily acknowledged, by men and women alike, as the company's top riders and dispatchers. And these women received promotions accordingly. Male messengers, therefore, cannot use their labor (paid or otherwise) to valorize themselves in opposition to women.

Regardless, to write about messengers is to write about men—even when one is including women in the discussion. What may be plain to the sociologist, however, goes largely unmentioned among messengers. In fact, any attempt to emphasize the gendered aspects of messengering is likely to make many couriers, both male and female, balk. This is because men have an invisible gender.[2] In other words, manifestations of masculinity abound in our culture (and certainly within the messenger subculture), but its ubiquitous nature leads to its elusiveness. Which is to say, masculinity and the male perspective are often considered the default positions in our society, and we can see this clearly with bike couriers. However, messengers did not set out to create a fraternal association, nor have they *intentionally* erected barriers to female participation.[3] While the same could not be said of many all-male workplaces or social groups, among bike couriers, women willing to do the work and endure the tribulations of a male-dominated workplace are welcome members of the messenger's world.[4] In fact, this is often a point of pride among the subculture. Everyone, it is maintained, is treated equally—or, if not equally, at least on the merits of their performance.

The female messengers I encountered in my research, by definition, are women with the ability to successfully perform messenger labor and deal with male-centric environments. However, even for this select group, being a women in the occupation and the subculture is not without its struggles—largely because messengering is so stereotypically masculine. Mary, a former cook, covered in tattoos, provided a telling explanation:

> It takes a certain kind of girl to be a messenger. You've got to suck it up....
> I hear really gross stuff all day long [over the radio]. It's nothing new. Interacting with guys [is different]. Sometimes I'm like Todd, "Today [Larry] was so mean to [Cedric]." He's like, "That's how boys get along." ... I've learned that's just how boys interact.... They've been short with me over the radio, and I've had to be like, "[Cedric], what's going on? Is everything okay?" And he's like, "What are you talking about?" ... He won't even

remember what I'm referring to. I take things really personally, and I think they just fucking forget about it right after it happens.

For Mary, "to suck it up" involves two things. First, working at a company that uses an open radio channel, she hears her male coworkers discuss—in what she considers to be rather gross detail—the positive and negative attributes of various women they encounter throughout the day. Second, Mary must accept her coworkers' gruff and callous methods of conflict resolution—a form of interaction that she clearly finds distressing and perplexing. In order to continue being a messenger, Mary has made a conscious effort to adapt. And, for better or for worse, adapting to male forms of interaction and accepting their topics of discussion are an inevitable part of the messenger lifestyle for women.

Beyond the crass and the hostile, female messengers are often the target of sexual advances (directly and indirectly). A former Portland messenger, for example, characterized the beginning of her career as being "fresh meat" for male couriers. Likewise, a dispatcher at Sprint was renowned (at least among female messengers) for eagerly, if not aggressively, inviting female rookies to hang out at Sophie's Bar on Friday nights. Oddly, there is a positive flip side to male messengers pursuing female rookies as potential mates: these women are quickly inducted into the messenger subculture. And, as long as these women succeed in the occupation and accept the norms of male interaction, their acceptance within the subculture is not predicated on making themselves sexually available to male couriers. When I asked MAC if she was treated differently being a female messenger she replied:

> Yeah, definitely. I know the guys I worked with liked working with a girl, at least at my first company. They liked having a female voice on the radio. . . . If there is a cute messenger girl, all the guys are on them. I was always friends with people, and they were always rooting for me. I don't know how much sexism was going on in the industry. . . . I don't think [male messengers] really realize what they're doing, and that is even more condescending in a way. . . . I've definitely gotten more perceptive about that sort of thing and maybe more sensitive to it now that I am an older woman. Maybe a lot of it I just didn't notice at the time, but I definitely didn't feel like it was an issue. I definitely felt different because I was a female, and I was definitely singled out in a certain way, but it was almost like a romanticizing of the messenger industry, "Oh, this is a lot of respect."

In other words, looking back, MAC believes that there was sexism going on, but, at the time, she took the extra attention she received as respect.

One of the common issues brought up in my interviews with female messengers was the matter of having to prove oneself. Whether purely self-imposed or indirectly cajoled by others, the women I met (more than the men) felt compelled to assert their competence as messengers. Of course, male messengers are also eager to prove their mettle, but in interviews they never couched their behavior in this way. None of the men I interviewed talked directly about wanting to prove to their dispatcher, their company, or their coworkers that they were good messengers. Instead, men simply talk about wanting to be good messengers (or maybe even the best messenger). Clearly, they wanted to impress others, but this desire is distinct from the female messenger's direct fear of negative appraisal.

According to sociologist Cynthia Epstein, such self-consciousness is common for women in male-dominated settings.[5] Mary, for example, felt a pressure to perform at her new company but could not exactly pinpoint its source: "I think they have the same expectations of you. If I say I'm going to do something I'm going to do it and I'll do it on time. I think I've shown the people I work for that I'm willing to bust ass and that I work hard. . . . I don't know if they saw it that way, but I felt it. I didn't want them to regret hiring a girl. Maybe I was worried about it, but I don't think that they were." In a similar vein, Cat, a Seattle messenger with a master's degree in education, explained:

> I don't know. Maybe it is in my head, but I feel that I had to prove myself. . . . Every so often I will get a comment, "Oh wow, you did that!" or "You made it. You made that deadline!" I want to be like, "Fuck off." If I was a guy doing that job there would be no question of whether that job was going to get done. Whereas me being a female, I think that he's saying it because I'm a female. Maybe it is in my head, but I do think that.

Karli put it bluntly: "There were people out there that made it very apparent to me that I needed to prove myself." Karli said this in response to a question about women being treated differently from men in the messenger subculture. However, Karli quickly switched the discussion away from gender to the topic of rookies. She made it clear that all rookies (men and women) need to prove themselves to seasoned riders: "When new people start here, I'm off-stand-ish. 'Prove yourself, kid.' I've seen people come and go, and come and go. I feel like, if you're serious about it, you're serious about it, and if not, go." Working with Karli, I experienced this pressure directly; it took close to a year for Karli to do more than scowl whenever we crossed paths.

Particularly notable is the gendered division some women made between messengers. Only two of my respondents made this point, but it captures a powerful discrepancy between the motivations of male and female messengers. MAC stated:

> I think generally you're going to find a high percentage of strong-work-ethic, high-achiever females gravitating toward this job, and with men it is a lot more of a crapshoot, a lot more antisocial guys, and guys that maybe don't have anything else to do.... There's definitely a range of guys, but 90 percent of the time the female is going to be...hardworking. They don't necessarily have all the same interests or anything, but they just have this general personality style that gravitates toward the job.

Almost identically, Cat noted:

> I don't want to make blanket statements or blanket generalizations, but just in terms of the people that I see, right now, on the road, I think there is a tendency towards [messengering]: it draws a certain type of female, and it draws a certain type of male, but it is definitely not the same type of person. I don't know that I can elaborate entirely on that, but I think there is a lot of common traits to a lot of females on the road, and there is a lot of common traits to the males on the road. But it is not necessarily that both males and females are the same....I think generally...there is a lot of hard workers among the females. Not that there's not a lot of hard workers among the males too. But, I think being a female on the road there is a [different] element.

These observations indicate that men and women may have different underlying motivations for becoming messengers. For men, being a messenger is often a refusal to meet social expectations (i.e., dropping out or refusing to enter the rat race). For women, being a messenger is a way of defying social expectations (i.e., wanting to do a dangerous physical job, on the same terms as men). As Cat stated, "For me, as a woman, I like [being a messenger]. It is a physical active thing that I can do. I don't know what other job is possible for that. I don't want to work construction."

More than anything else, we should see messengering as offering an escape from the feminization of postindustrial labor,[6] and this holds true for men as well as women (even if their underlying motivations are somewhat divergent). Like other low-end jobs proliferating in the new economy, messengering is service oriented. Such service jobs are characterized by typically feminine qualities. They are not about rough-and-tumble production, but about catering to the needs of others. However, the services provided by messengers *do* exemplify stereotypically male traits. It is dangerous, bodily labor. Messengers please their clients with feats of skill and strength—like a last-minute filing, sprinted into the courthouse just in the nick of time. Social pleasantries may exist, but they are not part of the job description. These masculine aspects are why some journalists have constructed a romantic, cowboy-esque image of the occupation.

The various points about gender, gender relations, and gender differences are certainly interesting—interesting enough that I hope another researcher takes them up as a focus of study. However, they are largely ancillary to the argument developed in this book. Men may dominate the messenger's world enough to set the rules of the game, but the game itself is available to women as well. Most importantly, job tasks that contain male stereotypes do not, by default, lead to lifestyles built around occupations. Despite its masculine characteristics, therefore, it would be a mistake to take messengering's macho element as an explanation for *why* couriers identify with their occupation and find such meaning in its lifestyle. Gender is part of the puzzle, but it is not an answer to it. The affective appropriation of space is applicable to both genders.

The Bottom of the Pecking Order

Related to the masculine nature of courier work is the stigma associated with it. Messengering is, literally and figuratively, dirty. Dangerous, grimy, servile in nature, at times highly unpleasant, and often the focus of moral reprimand, bike messengering certainly qualifies as what occupational sociologists refer to as dirty work. Researchers have long studied how individuals working in stigmatized occupations maintain positive identities, and it is well known that workers in socially degraded jobs attempt to

Figure 11. Cat, *second from left,* and Rachel, *far right,* socializing with other Seattle messengers at the Monorail coffee stand

recast their situation in a way that destigmatizes their occupation. Dirty workers, it is claimed, overcome the physical, social, and moral taint of their occupations by reframing, recalibrating, and refocusing the stigma of outsiders.[7]

Bike messengers are no exception. Take the case of track bikes and riding styles from the previous chapters. Bike messengers often agree that riding brakeless bikes is dangerous and careening through traffic reckless—*just not when a messenger does it.* In other words, one solution to their occupation's stigma is to reframe the matter away from couriers. The real issue, many messengers contend, is not working bike couriers, who through their on-the-job training are said to possess enough skill to safely do what others cannot. Syd, one of CLS's top riders (as well as part-time dispatcher), for example, explained: "You develop a sense of the way certain people drive and know how to cut a line around them because of that." She went on to explain that while there are reckless messengers (most likely rookies), "for most messengers it is safer because they've spent a long time studying the way traffic moves and the way people walk around streets and stuff. Whereas if you're just a commuter and you just bike every once and a while you don't really pay attention to the streets."

Alternatively, when condemned for their riding, bike couriers also refocus the matter to stress the valuable service they provide to the local economy. As Matt explained about the job, "You're helping the system run." Or, as Syd said about CLS, "We do some serious stuff. If you mess up a court filing a kid might not get their child support." In doing so, messengers take behavior that is being labeled dangerous or selfish and position it as a necessary unpleasantness. Sometimes they even paint the messenger as a bit of an altruist for taking on such danger to keep the wheels of commerce rolling. Cory, for example, asserted that he rode the way he did because he was paid to do it, but it is dangerous work: "I was a messenger doing my job. . . . I almost get myself killed every day."

Beyond reframing and refocusing, messengers are also eager to recalibrate the threat their riding poses to the general public. In fact, I did this very thing in the previous chapter when I contrasted the deaths caused by bicycles and those caused by cars in New York City. The point being, even if the courier's urban cycling is morally wrong, it must be kept in perspective with other nonstigmatized dangers. In Andy's words, "I expect motorists to understand that I am working and that they'll just have to deal with it."

Ultimately, what needs to be stressed is that the "dirty work" approach sociologists take toward occupations ignores emotional involvement. From such a perspective, identity is treated as an entirely cognitive phenomenon. But, going back to the discussion of Durkheim in the introduction, we know that meaning has an *affective* component. As researchers, though, we often neglect to take into consideration the difference between the words a person is able to say and the emotional weight of what someone actually feels. Again, my point is not to deny that stigmatized individuals frame, calibrate, and focus condemnation in a way that does not threaten their positive assessments of themselves. Throughout the book such processes will be apparent. At the same time, such explanations fall short of adequately explaining the messenger subculture. In fact, in the sociological literature dirty workers are generally shown to *separate* their real selves from their work selves. Morticians wear bright, cheery clothing when not on the job, and topless dancers construct fictional personas to act out on stage.[8] Further, even in occupations with strong work identities and dense social networks such as those of typographical workers and underground miners we do not see the replication of labor in leisure activities the way couriers merge the two in alleycats.[9]

In setting up the theoretical background for my argument, therefore, I am proposing that the existing sociological literature does not provide an adequately clear guide for understanding the courier world. Certainly, masculinity is one of the materials from which much of the messenger puzzle is cut, and the reframing, recalibrating, and refocusing of stigma represents one piece of the more complex solution. Neither paradigm, however, resolves the question posed by the Seattle businessman and discussed in the introduction: what is the lure of delivering packages? As it stands, sociologists are constrained by a theoretical tool kit stocked with instruments ill suited for analyzing the lived emotions of bike messengers as they manipulate the physical environment of the city. It is these points—emotions and space—that we will now address.

PLAYING IN TRAFFIC

As we saw in the introduction, people (at least in the Western world) increasingly draw boundaries between their work selves and their real selves. Even before Marx, social critics and theorists emphasized the monotony of paid labor. Today, perhaps more than any other company, McDonald's epitomizes such de-skilling, and in many ways McDonald's has become a model for other facets of Western society.[1] Through semiautomated food preparation and computerized cash registers, nonscripted encounters with customers are not possible.[2] Which is to say, workers at McDonald's are shielded from nearly every possible contingency. There are no problems left for employees to solve. No creative thought is required, or even allowed, because everything happening during the workday has been preplanned. Even the pickles at McDonald's have a standardized width. In sum, the more a workplace is standardized and the more workplace behavior can be scripted, the more contingency is replaced by predictability. Under such conditions it is difficult for labor to be engrossing.

Parts of the messenger's job, like numerous aspects of all daily life, are semiscripted. For example, messengers and clients normally behave in rather formalized ways during the pick-up and drop-off of packages.

Typically, there is a polite but brief exchange of simple pleasantries followed by a quick conveyance of any necessary information. For instance, the client may tell the messenger exactly where a package needs to be taken and who needs to sign for it. Both parties follow a script meant to facilitate the courier's quick departure from the building. In traffic, the true workplace of the bike courier, however, nothing is pre-scripted, nor can it be. Instead, messengers must write their story anew each moment. The point of the story, of course, is entirely predictable; messengers want to get where they are going as fast as possible. But, their plot, by necessity, is in continual revision. There are unexpected twists and turns as new problems arise and are continually compounded. For example, to go from the Empire State Building to Washington Square Park involves more than riding a straight line down Fifth Avenue. It requires an infinite series of adjustments, and these adjustments get trickier and trickier as the rider's speed increases. It is these skillful moment-to-moment adjustments that distinguish messenger work from so much of contemporary labor (particularly low-end service jobs).

Flow as Optimal Experience

In Michael Burawoy's famous ethnography of factory production, the machinists he studied eagerly worked harder than necessary because they were able to turn their labor process into a game.[3] Like many messengers, the machinists in Burawoy's study were paid a piece rate, and the game was to beat the company's daily quota. In their factory labor, however, the game the machinists played was little more than a sugar-coating to an otherwise miserable job. Bike messenger labor, by contrast, cannot exist without the spontaneous, creative actions of the rider. As we will see, even couriers paid an hourly wage become enraptured in workday games. They participate in these games even though they earn no extra money for their harder work and added risks. Indeed, the messengers' game is less about money and far more about what psychologist Mihaly Csikszentmihalyi calls flow.[4]

In flow, individuals are engrossed by their activities. They are subsumed in the moment. In seeking out flow, individuals put themselves in situations where the tasks at hand are perfectly matched by their skills. In a game of tennis, for instance, playing against an opponent far below one's skill level is boring. Alternatively, playing against an opponent of far superior skill is stressful. In either case, the players are consciously aware of themselves and the game. When a player is matched against someone of equal talent, however, the game takes on an entirely different character. It is at this threshold of boredom and anxiety that the player can truly focus his attention in the moment, and *only* in the moment.

The state of flow is distinct from normal life. In most day-to-day activities we are not engrossed but are reflexively aware of ourselves. Instead of being *in* the moment, we think about the past (how we got ourselves into the present activity) or the future (when will we stop doing it). Csikszentmihalyi refers to flow as an optimal experience. What makes flow such an important type of experience is that by dampening (and often completely halting) reflexive thought, actions appear utterly authentic. The individual in flow feels as if her mind and body are perfectly in tune—as if operating on instinct alone.[5]

While it is doubtful that any of the messengers I met were familiar with the work of Csikszentmihalyi, it is remarkable how many used the word "flow" in describing their work. In fact, Csikszentmihalyi calls flow a native category. That is, he uses the term because his informants—chess players, rock climbers, dancers, and surgeons—repeatedly used the word to describe their activities. Likewise, messengers extol their ability to flow with, through, and around other traffic. And it is this negotiation of the urban morass that makes bicycle delivery a valuable part of postindustrial production. The physical flow that bike couriers have in traffic relates directly to the emotional flow of optimally lived experience described by Csikszentmihalyi. In other words, messengering involves an engagement of both mind and body. Unlike routinized forms of labor, urban cycling requires constant adaptations to new challenges. Instead of following scripts, bike couriers, by necessity, must creatively construct new scripts from moment to moment.

As the occupational literature indicates, individuals fail to identify with their labor precisely because it lacks flow. It is this lack of flow that makes the workplace a site of boredom and indifference. It estranges us, and so our paid labor feels alienating—it fails to engross us. Of course, there are varying degrees of alienation in the workplace, and even seemingly monotonous factory work can be made enjoyable.[6] Regardless, outside the workplace is where we tend to find flow. Leisure time is when individuals can play, and play is the antithesis of alienated labor.[7] Flow is the very essence of play, and this is why, as many observe, young children will modify games to keep the tasks and skills of players balanced. Play can take many forms, but what distinguishes it from other activities is its creative, spontaneous character.

Routing through the Urban Maze

For the bike messenger, traffic is an ever-shifting puzzle. To borrow the title of the New York Bike Messenger Association's former publication, the city's streets are an "urban death maze." The first step in unraveling the puzzle of the messenger subculture, therefore, is to understand that the job itself is an endless series of puzzles that messengers solve. Talented messengers do so with an air of inevitability. That is, they appear to make their way through seemingly impervious traffic flawlessly, as if they choreographed their movements with the other users of the road. Less talented messengers also work their way through the maze, but in a less fluid manner. The rookie's movements appear less choreographed and reveal a process of trial and error.

In thinking about traffic as a puzzle and the flow it can generate, my field notes for May 29, 2003, are illustrative: "I rode behind Eddie this morning. He is such a smooth rider. It was like the seas were parting for him. As I followed in his wake everything just cleared out of our way. As soon as he turned off, the tide of cars poured back in, and I was once again drowning within them." As I rode behind him, it honestly appeared that cars were moving out of Eddie's way. I remarked in my field notes that it was "eerie." Eddie, an experienced New York messenger, had intimate knowledge of how pedestrians and vehicles moved.[8] In comparison, I had nowhere near the same skill set. When our paths diverged, I was left to make my own choices, and those choices were far less efficient.

The eeriness of Eddie's riding deserves greater explanation. To quote one messenger, "Let me tell you something about being the best in New York. It's not about being this fast....It's about having a sense of direction and [knowing] where you're going. If you know where you're going, and you know how to get there, that's the most important thing. You ain't got to be fast."[9] In other words, as discussed in chapter 1, it is not a rider's velocity that matters; it is how she *routes* herself. But routing has two components. There is the typical use of the word, what I will call a macro-component. These are the roads and shortcuts a courier uses. Then there is a micro-component—the small choices a rider makes within his larger course of travel. These are moment-to-moment adjustments. This micro-routing is about whether cyclists go left or right around a slowing car, or whether they take the left, middle, or right of a lane going into a turn. Urban cycling involves a countless number of such tacit decisions. Taken together, these choices can shave minutes (not just seconds) off a rider's traveling time. Knowing where you're going and knowing how to get there involve far more than having a cognitive map of the city. In other words, knowing Washington Square Park is due south from the Empire State Building is only a tiny part of being able to get there successfully in the same time as a skilled rider like Eddie.

Cat, in describing the tacit knowledge of urban cycling, remarked: "I think people look at us when we're riding, and they think we're being reckless. But, actually, our eyes and our ears, and everything, are in touch with what is going on around [us]. You know that door is going to open before it opens. . . . Doing it every day, you learn things that other people don't." In fact, almost all experienced couriers highlight their ability to foresee the future of traffic. Jordan claimed: "You totally see two seconds into the future at all times." To this Craig added that riding in the city is "less reacting and more predicting." As Rachel expanded, "You know those situations where you're riding behind a car, and you just go to the left, and you don't know why, and all of the sudden they swerve off to the right. Had you been there you would have been killed, but something in you said, 'Don't go there.' It's just a sense that you build up from being on your bike ten hours a day."

None of this, however, is to assert that couriers believe they are invincible. These riders are equally quick to point out that there is not always something in them warning them of danger. As Craig added, "You can't predict everything." But the more time they spend on their bikes, the more riders hone their senses and build up a reserve of knowledge that allows the experienced messenger to really flow (in both senses of the term) in traffic.

Conversely, when I asked Jacky, a rookie, if she liked her job she replied: "Overall it's fun, but some days it's frustrating." When I asked why, she answered: "Pedestrians and cars get in my way and I can't flow." At the same time, Jacky realized that with more training she could flow: "I realize that you can always have flow. When a car pulls out in front of me, I don't have to hit my brakes." Months later, Jacky proudly (and somewhat sarcastically) referred to herself as an "artist" after Justin, a veteran messenger, complimented her increasing skills at urban cycling (i.e., in keeping her flow). In describing the riding knowledge he had obtained since working as a messenger, Erik explained that now he could "flow through traffic." "Before," he observed, "I probably would have either given the pedestrian the right of way or let the car go the right of way. But, finding those ways to absolutely get myself out of anybody's way and still keep moving, it's something I never really did before."

Beyond moving around and between pedestrians and other vehicles going in the same direction, messengers also use their micro-routing talents to get through cross-traffic. Which is to say, couriers run red lights. Often, they run *a lot* of red lights. The best bike messengers have an exceptional understanding of time and space. In thinking about this the reader should recall the description in chapter 1 of Kevin traversing what I believed to be impenetrable traffic on Broadway. Andreas, in describing riding styles, said of Kevin: "Have you ever seen Squid ride? It is not that he rides that fast, but he can get through traffic.... He can use every little space between cars."

Of all their behaviors, running red lights and stop signs is what makes messengers seem the most reckless to outsiders. Of course, many, if not most, commuters and recreational cyclists will do little more than a "rolling stop" through intersections when no clear danger is present. For messengers, though, what constitutes a clear danger can be vastly different from what other cyclists perceive, and the speeds at which messengers assess situations are often far quicker, which is why Cat notes that outsiders view messengers as reckless. Cory, venting against what he considers the foolhardy practices of other cyclists, observed:

> [Bicycle commuters] will pass you from here to that pole, which is not more than twelve or fourteen feet away, and they'll pass you at a high rate of speed going to a red light, and they'll stop at that red light right in front of you. I've already been looking at that red light for like ten seconds. I already know what I'm going to do when I get to that red light. And those people are like jamming past you just to hit on their fucking brakes and have no idea what's coming at them. Okay, you want to do that? I'm already looking at three different directions coming at me, and I'm just going to keep riding my bike at the same speed. You just blew past me to get to that red light and stop. I'm going to keep riding my bike right through that thing and not disrupt the flow of traffic or anything like that.

At the most basic level, messengers tend to have a confidence that they can fit between cars in situations that other riders might balk at. As

Andy explained, "When you've been on the road a long time with cars, you know how it goes, when you see that opening, and you know if you can make it or not. And anybody else who looked at it would be like, 'You're fucking insane,' but you're not. You just know exactly how fast you're going and how fast they're going, and you can do the math." At the more advanced levels, running red lights is more than a progressively greater faith that one can dart straight across an intersection. No matter how well one can do the math, there is a point where it will no longer add up—especially on roads with more than two lanes of cars. Instead, messengers learn to keep their speed coming into an intersection, turn to go with the cross-traffic and then swerve—lane by lane—to the other side. While done in a relatively short span of time and space (an intersection is only so wide), this technique allows the rider to make various adjustments to his speed to allow cars to pass or to pass cars, as he sees fit.

Messengering as a Game

Under any circumstances, bicycling in city traffic requires a dedication of one's senses; there are too many variables for the rider to be inattentive to his surroundings. The micro-routing decisions couriers make mean that their minds are even more focused. Urban cycling, therefore, often requires messengers to be fully engrossed in their action. As Erik noted, "It's not necessarily a logical thing. You're not sitting there analyzing. You don't know why you're doing these things, but your mind is occupied and kind of taking in the fact that there is a car with its left-turn signal on over here, there is a pedestrian right there." Or as Hultman indicated, "I don't know how the mind works. I'm not consciously saying, 'Should I go?' or 'Should I stop?' I'm making decisions really fast." It is precisely this instinctual quality that makes creative, spontaneous action appear authentic. As Rachel observed, "[It is] a natural thing that your body just does, without even really thinking about it."

At the same time, this "natural" action occurs within the framework of an occupation. In other words, it is in making deliveries that bike couriers feel authentic. To begin, if messengers play in traffic, their games must have boundaries to give their actions purpose. For messengers, the constraints of their play (e.g., having fixed pick-up and drop-off points) relate directly to their paychecks. This makes for an interesting combination of the skillful leisure pursuits paramount to identity formation in a

Figure 12. Seattle messenger on a track bike

job that might otherwise just be considered dangerous, demeaning, and strenuous.

The Labor Process as a Game

The game messengers play is delivering packages. The macro- and micro-routing decisions couriers make are only relevant to the degree that they facilitate more deliveries, and, of course, that they do not get the rider injured or killed in the process. In explaining their work (to insiders, not to outsiders), messengers will occasionally liken their labor to other forms of delivery. They do this to emphasize that what they do is, in fact, very mundane. Fannin referred to himself as an "errand boy." Likewise, Kelsey, a Seattle messenger with training as an audio engineer and a passion for exotic travel (which he copiously documents with photography), commented: "By far, I am a glorified mailman." At an abstract level, Fannin and Kelsey are certainly correct. Bike couriers are just moving packages from one place to another. This is a task that hardly seems entertaining. But, the glory, so to speak, comes from the game. Instead of drudgery, every delivery is an opportunity. The workday is the game day, and the tally of one's deliveries is the score. It is a game played largely against one's self, but one's employer and one's peers do take note of both over- and underachievers. As we will see in the next chapter, the game of delivery (specifically, the danger of playing the game at high speeds) is sanctified in alleycats.

For Burawoy, factory production can become a game when workers are paid a piece rate and thus are unsure of the day's outcome. Conducting participant observation, Burawoy became as immersed in the game of factory production as the workers he studied. Like Burawoy, working as a messenger in New York, I quickly found myself engrossed by the game. As a commission rider, the better I played the game, the more money I could make. However, I was more concerned with the symbolic importance of the game. The more deliveries I completed in a day, the more I demonstrated to myself and to others that I was less a rookie and more a "real messenger."

For Jason the piece-rate system provides not only enjoyment, but a chance to realize one's full earning potential. In talking about why he would not want to be a dispatcher, Jason explained: "The money is not as good. . . . You're on a salary. . . . Being a messenger you can earn as much money as you want to make, or as much money as you *can* make." Here, Jason emphasizes the importance of uncertainty. Working as a dispatcher, an individual knows what he will make. Working as a commission messenger, there is always the chance to make out better, and the threat of making out worse. The issue here goes deeper than pay. Many people can and do make more money as dispatchers. They are also less likely to incur job-related injuries and receive traffic citations. The issue for Jason is self-determination. He frames the discussion in terms of making as much money as one's individual talents permit.

Jason's comments about dispatching are echoed in Travis Culley's frustrations regarding a daily guarantee: "Sure I was riding my bike, sure I was free to navigate my own way through the city without any boss or manager telling me how to do my job, but I didn't feel that I had a chance to succeed. No matter how hard I worked, I could never significantly compete with their guaranteed pay. Every check would be a statement of what I couldn't accomplish."[10]

Common sense, of course, concurs with Culley's and Jason's assessments of commission riders. Messengers risk their lives and terrorize other users of the road to make *more* money. To quote again from the *New York Times* editorial, "What motivates those cyclists who whiz along the blind side of traffic lanes, plunge through intersections against the light and otherwise terrorize New York City drivers and pedestrians? For the worst offenders, the answer is money." However, the prestige and pride of the game hold true even when money is removed from the equation. The authenticity of messenger work—its flow—is separate from purely monetary concerns. That is to say, for the worst offenders it is not money at all. It is flow played for its own sake. As noted earlier, only a small number of the Warriors' participants left the event with more money. Most returned home with far less.

Negating the importance of his commission, Bob asserted: "No matter how bad my day is, if I get a direct rush then I just go [makes the motions of riding fast].... This job isn't about money. It is about having fun anyway." Fannin, paid by the hour, explained: "There are actually real times when there are [extremely hard-to-meet deadlines], where, if you wait at red lights, you are not going to make the job. But almost 90 percent of the time it's not like that. I want to get it done as fast as possible. Even if I have like an hour or something to get eight blocks, it is like I want to be there in one second. So I'll just run every red light. It's funner to go way faster."

To understand why messengers work harder and, consequently, make a dangerous job more dangerous for nonfinancial rewards is to rethink much of how sociologists (and other social commentators) conceptualize work. It also goes a long way toward describing the lure of delivering packages. As Cat, in explaining why she does not like slow days, remarked, "For me, at least, it's not even because of commission, but because I don't want to sit here anymore, and I don't want to ride in circles for no reason."

So far the discussion of messengers in traffic has covered only what I call the micro-components of routing. This is the tacit dimension of negotiating the city. At the discursive level, however, there are the macro-components of routing: that is, the streets a rider chooses to take and the order in which she does her deliveries. These cognitive issues of routing are a major part of the messenger game and constitute a popular subject of discussion. This is especially true in Seattle, where, because of the massive and steep hills downtown, a change of one block can have a noticeable effect on one's ride.

Routing at this level requires basic map knowledge. First, the rider must know his current location, the various locations he needs to get to, and what streets provide the most direct route. Second, routing can incorporate shortcuts—alleyways, parking lots, or sidewalks that provide even more direct connections between places. Third, it involves knowing the buildings one will be entering, from elevators, staircases, and entrance locations to floor numbers and security measures. Finally, previous experience with clients can influence the order in which packages should be picked up. For example, if a client regularly calls in jobs before they are ready, the rider may want to make another pick-up or drop-off before going to that office.

I have focused on micro-routing because it is the less obvious component of urban cycling and a more difficult concept to grasp (for insiders and outsiders alike). The macro- component of routing, however, is a major part of the game. When riders are busy, they are not just holding one or two packages; they may be juggling well over ten jobs. Deciding the order in which they will make their pick-ups and drop-offs and the streets they will take to do them is a substantial cognitive challenge. Further, it is a skill enjoyable in its own right. As we saw with the Warriors Fun Ride, both macro- and micro-routing are part of alleycats. That is, riders must figure out how (at both levels) to get from one checkpoint to the next.

From Flow to Edgework

The creative, spontaneous actions required in urban cycling allow messengers to achieve optimal experience in their labor. Which is to say, in messengering, the rider is engrossed in the spontaneity of her actions. Of course, messengers are not always flowing. There are times that the job is slow and boring. But, as Fannin noted, there are also times when, unless riders push their skills to the very limit, the deadline will not be met. It is at these times that messengers not only act without conscious reflection, as Erik and Hultman explained, but willfully risk their bodily safety to make a delivery. In these situations, the flow of the game becomes what sociologist Stephen Lyng calls edgework.[11] Lyng uses edgework to describe intense mental and physical engagement brought about by individuals intentionally placing themselves in extremely dangerous situations, such as drug binging, motorcycle racing, or skydiving. Edgeworkers take the optimal experience of flow and raise the stakes by inserting their own corporeal safety into the equation. Matt described the experience: "You get that kind of adrenaline rush, and you kind of look back and say, 'Whoa, man, I could have been killed by this car and this and that.' It's shit you don't realize when you're riding because you kind of zone everything out except for the cars within a couple of inches from you." The "experiential anarchy" described by Lyng is a more extreme version of flow.[12] In edgework the engrossing action of the experience becomes more than optimal; it becomes essential. Most people, after all, find it hard to be ambivalent about their own survival.

There is, perhaps, a seeming contradiction here. Fannin's claim that even when he is not technically rushed, he still feels compelled to take risks seems to imply that messengers are, in fact, ambivalent about the goal of survival. The same, of course, can be said for all edgeworkers. If they were so serious about survival, they would not pop pills, speed around on motorcycles, or jump out of airplanes. However, the risks (regardless of how outsiders assess them) are calculated with insider knowledge. Edgeworkers weigh their talents with the tasks ahead and plan accordingly. Cat observed: "I don't think I'm reckless, I guess. And, I mean, sometimes the nature of it is, you have to pull moves. Because, your life depends on cutting that turn the right way. Maybe it was a reckless turn, but maybe the alternative would have been worse." Messengers put their skills to the test because it is what they are paid to do (whether it is piece rate or hourly), and, more importantly, because it is more fun to go fast. When I asked Justin, for example, what his favorite part of being a messenger was, he replied that it was the same as his favorite part of riding bicycles: "dipping into corners at about thirty miles an hour." He went on to claim: "If there is one thing that gets me high, gets my rocks [off], everything, my adrenaline, [it is] flying through traffic....I do it because I love working. *I love to ride my bike.*"

Creative Work

Work, generally speaking, is alienating because it lacks flow, and, therefore, it does not engross. We can think about this in terms of clock-watching—"a characteristic disease of those burdened with alienated labor." Alternatively, "those engrossed creatively are oblivious of the passage of social time or the dimensions of physical space."[13] This is why the machinists in Burawoy's study voluntarily work harder and faster (i.e., consent to higher levels of exploitation). As he explains, "Playing the game eliminated much of the drudgery and boredom associated with industrial work."[14] Of course, the game of messengering requires attentiveness to time—the packages must be delivered by their deadlines. The messenger's attention to time, though—like a basketball player attending to the shot clock—is tacit. It is not clock-*watching*. It is an embodied sense of time, distinct from the very disembodied cognition of impatiently waiting for time to pass. It is, instead, time flooded with one's subjective being. Further, this nonreflexivity state is intensified by the extreme flow found at the edge of survival. As Jordan stated,

> The job is sort of like a game anyway. You claim like six jobs in like six different parts of town. You're exercising and you're breathing heavy, and you're next to dead because you haven't had time to get lunch or whatever, but then you have to exercise your head as well, to keep you upright, to keep you from getting doored or getting sideswiped or getting hit or whatever, and you also have to totally be able to route yourself and plan where you're going. It is like totally a game. It is the most fun job I will *ever have in my life,* without a doubt.

In my own field notes, I often described the joys I found during the workday. For example, on July 3, 2002, I wrote: "Despite the heat...it was a fun day. I got three sweet little runs at the end of the day....It was fun because I was just rushing to get the jobs dropped off as close to 5:00 as I could. It was like 4:40, 4:55, and 5:20 (I feel like that could have been faster, but I was flying as best I could)." Or, as I wrote almost a year later, on June 5, 2003, "I had one crazy...rush at the start of the day. It was sort of stressful, but it was also fun." At CLS, when I would ask fellow riders how their days were going, their answers were almost always expressed in terms of how many rush jobs they were assigned. Erik, in particular, would explain his day in these terms: "I got some good jobs, some ten-minute double rushes." This sort of answer is especially remarkable from CLS (and other hourly) riders because they make no extra money for doing rushes. Still, they are the most coveted jobs. Matt, at a loss for words, described it as a "runner's high."

For most people, the mental and physical engagements required in their workplace are, at best, marginally, and only rarely, flowlike. In contrast, the ways in which messengers describe their busy and slow times denote just how significant, in an almost spiritual sense, the flow of messengering can be. Conversations I had with Stan are telling in this regard. A messenger of several years in the Midwest, Stan moved to New York and got an hourly job requiring very little riding. I saw Stan waiting around one day for another delivery, and he commented: "I hate this. You do a job and then just sit around. You don't really do the job." The point being, "the job" is speeding through traffic, not standing still. Not only did Stan assume his work should not be dull, but he felt cheated that he was not given more work. Stan only did around eight jobs a day, and had the rest of the time free. Although he had a guaranteed wage and could travel anywhere in the city when not on a delivery, Stan constantly complained of boredom. He clearly missed the excitement of making rushed deliveries.

As explained in chapter 1, there are major differences between messenger work and other forms of employment. Most workers, if they are to get paid, must stay at their workplace. Stan, however, could go anywhere he desired in Manhattan while on standby. As a case in point, Jason and Rob, who were both paid a commission, reminisced about a summer where they made no money because they stopped working around noon every day to get drinks and eat chicken wings in Times Square. Rob, an experienced messenger from Boston who had moved to New York a few years prior, recalled: "It would be like noon, and I'd be like, 'I want to stick around and make some money,' and [Jason would] be like, 'There isn't going to be any more work, let's go drink." Beyond chicken wings and drinks, when on standby, messengers can run personal errands, make phone calls, and read. As a case in point, I was able to do a bulk of the readings, and even some of the writing, for my graduate field exams during the slow spells at CLS. As the Seattle courier observed, "You're either hanging out getting drunk or you're delivering a package"—his point being, slow or not, there is nothing to complain about. However, while messengers cherish the freedom to do what they want when not making a delivery, most cherish the thrill of the game far more.

To fully understand why the thrill is so desirable, we must again turn to Lyng. In pushing the edge, individuals experience a sort of "hyper-reality." That is, by focusing attention only on the factors necessary for survival, one feels "a sense of cognitive control over the essential 'objects' in the environment or a feeling of identity with these objects."[15] At the extreme reaches of flow, therefore, individuals are not only engrossed; they actually feel omnipotent. An article in *Urban Death Maze* wonderfully captured these sensations by describing "the line."

"The line" is a common cycling term used to denote one's micro-route of travel. A rider must find her line through a turn or his line through an intersection. In my earlier description of Eddie's riding, I was following his line (and not making my own). In the *Urban Death Maze* article, however, the author is using the term to indicate something more unique. He is describing what might be thought of as a super-line—moments when the rider perfectly pilots a course through seemingly unpredictable traffic:

> The line is not an easy thing to describe.... The line demands one hundred percent of my attention. I'm in complete harmony with my bicycle. The red lights are not an issue; the line [goes] right through the crosstown traffic.... A feeling of omnipotence washes over me and all fear and hesitation is gone.... The line knows nothing of traffic regulations, it just burns before me commanding I follow. Everything except me and my bicycle moves in slow motion, spinning out of our way whether they see us or not. It's musical the way everything flows together, as if orchestrated by some unseen conductor.... I've achieved perpetual motion, and I'm not stopping for shit.... All extraneous thoughts have left me. My mind is in a state of such absolute clarity that I don't even have to think of my next move. My bike moves by itself perfectly in tune with my instincts.... The moment ends rather abruptly.... So I go back to the grind, turning around to grab the packages I missed, but I don't lose sight of the fact that for a few brief moments I was the center of the universe. And none of you motherfuckers could touch me.[16]

Likewise, Fannin, reacting to another messenger's comment that when in the right zone you are invincible, said: "I don't know how true it actually is that when you're in a zone you're invincible, but for the most part you feel invincible downtown." Or as Kelsey explained, "I love...riding in traffic and the feeling of knowing that pretty much nothing is going to get in my way anymore, and I can just flow. It's skilled riding, too. It uses every skill I have on the bike and uses them all. It takes everything I can do to make it all happen, and make it happen quickly and smoothly."

Thus the messenger game not only eliminates drudgery, as Burawoy describes it, but also draws the courier into a world in which her "instincts" appear perfectly attuned to the environment. This is an immensely enjoyable state. Whereas many people struggle to find this sensation even in leisure, messengers are able to actualize this optimal experience in their paid labor. For this reason, Fannin described messengering as "the biggest non-job I've ever had." Or, to use Hultman's analogy, "the urban equivalent of mountain biking is bike messengering." Which is to say, the joys of mountain biking, which is a popular leisure-time activity, can be had for pay by working as a bike courier.

Identification with the Occupation

When one thinks about messengering in terms of flow, the lure of delivering packages is less mysterious. While by no means always enjoyable, messengering, far more than most occupations, involves elements of play and at times can become edgework. As we have seen, Fannin barely considered it work. Similarly, Rick claimed: "I'm going to work, but I love it!" And Mary, thinking back to her first week as a messenger, recounted: "[The dispatcher] sent me out to 1100 Dexter North [an address just outside Seattle's downtown core], and it was sunny out. I'm like, 'I cannot believe I get paid for this shit.'" Cat, in her typically articulate and thoughtful manner, explained:

> Some days I think, 'Where would I be without this job?' And some days, I'm like, 'You know what, it's a nine to five, I'm working for the Man just as much as anyone else is working for the Man.' ... I'm still working for the Man, but I think that there is also ... I'm also doing it for me. I think if I was still working at Specialty's [Cafe and Bakery], what about that is doing it for me? I can't imagine. Or, if I had a job as a receptionist or somewhere else downtown, I don't know how that would be giving me as much as I feel this job gives me.... There is a satisfaction and a joy that I get out of this job, even if my face may not be showing it most of the time. There is a joy that I get out of this that I don't get out of any other job. When I was working with kids, it was satisfying because education is an amazing thing. But it's not like that joy. Most days I actually enjoy coming to work, you know. To me that's huge. I don't like getting up in the morning *ever*, but I don't dread coming into work.... Most [nonmessengers] can see that I get something out of this, but they don't get it. People tell me I should quit messengering, and, to me, you know, I can't. I just can't. One day I will. I'm not going to do this until I'm, whatever, I don't know how old. One day I will quit. And that's the kind of weird thing about this job. Everybody who does it knows they can't do it for the rest of their lives. Most jobs, if you

want to keep doing [them] for the rest of your life, you probably could. But this job you physically can't, you know. There is going to come a time when you can't do this job anymore.

Unlike typical workers, who make a compromise between the satisfaction they find in leisure activities and the pay offered in nongratifying paid labor, messengers emphasize that they are paid to play—although, admittedly, they are not paid much.

The story of Jordan is illustrative here. When I met Jordan he was no longer working as a messenger. After a serious work-related bicycle crash, he got a job at a successful independent record label. Originally from the Midwest, it was actually the job he had moved to Seattle hoping to get. By most people's standards (or even by his own earlier standards), Jordan had moved on to a far better occupation. He now had a career, in the typical sense of the term. He had financial security, benefits, and a fair amount of social prestige, at least among those who follow Seattle's revered independent music scene. In fact, Jordan was featured in a Seattle weekly newspaper column about people with dream jobs. Despite this, Jordan, now healed from his injuries, wanted back on the road: "I always think about coming back. I just went and talked to [Ultra Fast Courier] the other day in hopes that 'When a spot opens up, I want it.' That is what I told them. It is weird because I have a good job now, but I wasn't ready to quit when [my injury] happened."

Jordan has stayed connected to his friends in the occupation. In fact, I met Jordan because he had come to the Monorail to socialize with other messengers after work. The surprising part is that Jordan still kept up with the social minutiae of Seattle courier life: "Most of the people I'm really good friends with now are messengers or ex-messengers, but even after a year of being out of being a bike messenger, I still kind of keep tabs on who's new. It is really, really weird. 'Who do they work for?' 'How much are [Ultra Fast Courier] riders making these days?'...For whatever reason, I totally care about it still. It is completely insane." Jordan conceded that these questions should have no bearing on his current life, but, regardless, he felt compelled, even when employed elsewhere, to stay connected to the most fun job he will ever have in his life.

Even when physical injuries are removed from the equation, leaving the occupation does not necessarily mean leaving the subculture. Few people actually schlep packages for more than five years, but lifestyle messengers continue to race and party long after they have "retired."

One dispatcher remarked pejoratively: "They don't want to leave this life. It's all they want to do." Just as in Jordan's case, these messengers reminisce about their days on the road. Tony, for example, worked as a messenger for two years. When his girlfriend became pregnant he decided he needed a safer job that paid more money. Working in the mailroom of an advertising agency, Tony was miserable. I ran into him one day after he had gotten off work. He was elated to be out of the office and wanted to ride. He simply shouted, "Lets go play!" and darted off into traffic. While his new job provided security on many levels, he now found himself in a job that lacked the joy described by Cat. In talking about messengering, Tony commented: "It's tearing me up not doing it." Likewise, the owner of a New York courier company lamented: "When I started the messenger service I thought, 'Okay, great. I'm finally going to be making the boss's end.' And I tell you, after all this time, I wish I was a messenger, still. Out of everything I've done in my life, that's what I wish I was still doing. So enjoy it while you've got it."[17]

Despite the fact that quitting the job does not mean abandoning the subculture, many messengers feel guilt and apprehension over the prospect of moving on. With six years under his belt, Adam proclaimed: "I can't take another winter." But he sounded dejected telling me about looking for a job in graphic design. One New York messenger explained: "It's a subculture. It's more than just a career. It's like you feel that if you leave you will be dissing your subculture by leaving."[18] But, as Cat noted, whether mental or physical, there is a point past which few can remain. The reality of this fact, though, can be a source of tension.

In contrast, when I returned to New York in 2007, Jason had nothing positive to say about messengers. Once a regular attendant at CMWCs around the globe and a staple supporter of local alleycats, Jason now claimed: "I'm over that scene." However, he said this at a barbecue being held at his house where nearly everyone present was a current or former messenger. Moreover, he even invited a traveling messenger, in town on his way back to the West Coast after attending the CMWC in Dublin, to the barbecue. Jason did not know him but felt compelled to treat this messenger with hospitality.[19] As noted earlier, in the description of the Warriors Fun Ride, the messenger subculture dictates accommodating traveling couriers.

There are two types of occupational identifications at stake here. First, as Cat and Tony show, messengers identify with the flow found in the job—they do not want to leave it, and they lament leaving if they do.

Figure 13. Jason, co-owner and bartender at the Second Chance Saloon

For Jason, the attachment appears to be largely social—he is enmeshed in the subculture. But, as Jordan shows, loving to play the game and caring about its players are two sides of the same coin. Sidelined by injury, Jordan's attachment to flow is manifested in his attempts to keep up with the social aspects of the scene—who's working where, and who's earning what. How the flow of the job relates to a social attachment to the subculture will be discussed more explicitly in chapter 5. For now, we will turn to the flow-producing alternatives couriers turn to when and if they retire from messengering.

Alternatives to Messengering

Because of my position in the field—at first a rookie New York messenger and later a semiexperienced but new-to-the-area San Diego and Seattle messenger—I do not have systematic data on what occupations people enter when they exit messengering. I only got a chance to briefly know the vast majority of messengers with whom I came into contact, and I often had little time to ask questions before we parted ways. Moreover, in New York, I spoke directly with only a small portion of the city's large, diverse courier population. Thus I've only been able to track the lives of my key informants, and many of those have disappeared over the years. I cannot speak for messengers as a whole, but only for the more dedicated subcultural participants truly wedded to the thrills of the game. For them, leaving is often decided for them by injury (like Jordan) or circumstance (like Tony).

Some riders are incorporated into the messenger company's administrative structure. Like riding, dispatching, as noted in chapter 1, is a satisfying game. In this case, though, it is more of a cognitive game, involving macro-routing a series of riders and lacking the physical tribulations of urban cycling. Many messengers view dispatching as a respectable job to which to "retire." However, only a small number of messengers can actually become dispatchers, as there are far more riders than dispatchers at any given time, and the turnover rate among the former is far higher than that among the latter.

If they do not make a move to dispatch, riders who willingly leave messengering seem to quit it for an occupation that (in theory at least) promises some sort of flow. For example, I have met several former messengers now involved in the commercial arts. Numerous bike messengers are aspiring graphic artists, and many come off the road when they have a chance to pursue this career. Similarly, Kelsey worked part-time as an audio engineer and claimed he would happily make it full-time once he built up a large-enough client base.

While by no means representative, some messengers choose to move into jobs that not only offer mental flow, but keep them physically engaged as well. Construction, for example, is a common occupation for ex-messengers, although, for those I have discussed it with, the physicality construction offers lacks the satisfaction of flow or the excitement of edgework. In chapter 2 we discussed Hultman's dual career as a forest firefighter and messenger. Similarly, Rob actually left messengering to work as an EMT. When I asked him why he chose the job, he cited "being outside and moving around." Helping people was not mentioned. Rob was drawn to the job for its promise of action. Jason applied to become a firefighter but in the end did not make the selection. Like Rob, he wanted a job with more financial security than being a bike messenger, but he still wanted a job that would be exciting. Arnold attempted to become a Navy SEAL. He did not make the selection but did enlist in the military. Like Rob and Jason, he craved excitement and adventure; he cited neither duty nor chivalry in his motivations. For Arnold the military offered the potential of a steady paycheck for thrilling, dangerous work. In particular he said he wanted work that would give him stories to tell his children.

Russ's life history is worthy of a novel. Russ was born and raised in Nairobi, Kenya, to an American missionary family. He did not move permanently to the United States until he was 18, and soon after joined the navy. After his time in the military his primary source of income was from his job as an Alaskan fisherman, but he only worked sporadically, spending the rest of the time traveling in the Lower 48—sometimes by very unconventional means, such as hopping freight trains or bicycling across the country. Russ lived that way for nearly seven years. He explained: "It's a wild lifestyle. You work eighteen-hour shifts, sleep for six. Then you go into port and party." He said of the actual fishing: "I like the adventure, being out in the wilderness, hunting the prey." But it was also a hard lifestyle; and after taking a fishhook to the eye (which permanently impaired his vision) and a year later being cast into the frigid sea during a storm, Russ decided to head south to find a (somewhat) more stable occupation. Messengering, to some extent, therefore, was a compromise for Russ. It was a tamer adventure, but it did offer parallels to his former lifestyle.

In contrast to the novelty of Russ's life, most of the messengers I met worked in other service industry jobs before becoming bike couriers. These riders used to be bank tellers, department store clerks, kitchen workers, or waiters. Some came to the job as a stopgap after college or as part-time work to make ends meet in college. Andreas, for example, was an articulate and bright individual with a degree from a prestigious liberal arts college. When I asked him why he continued to work as a messenger he first gave me a platitude: "I wanted to be a messenger. What else was I going to do? Go to grad school?" When I probed more, he quickly grew frustrated and exclaimed: "I don't want a career!" Andreas had options and, like Rob, became an EMT. At the time, however, messengering was a quality-of-life issue for him. Mark, the Seattle bike pundit, is another well-educated messenger. In Mark's case, a summer job before graduate school has lasted over a decade. In his words, "Every time I think about working in an office, or doing so many other jobs that pay way more money, I don't regret it. I don't feel sad. I don't feel like I'm wasting my life away. I'd much rather be outside riding than working

Figure 14. Longtime Seattle bike messenger Russ

in a law firm, doing research, or whatever. I don't do this job because I'm not qualified to do other jobs."

Some people came to the job because they already knew about couriers and felt that the job offered the life they only dreamed of. Justin, for example, grew up in a small town in the Pacific Northwest and as a teenager saw a bike messenger working in Portland. From that moment, he knew what he wanted to be. He connected his current occupation with his childhood job as a paper boy: "Right off the bat, it was almost destiny to deliver shit. It is what I know." Rachel, who grew up in Seattle, talked of having her mom drive circles around downtown so Rachel could watch the messengers work.

On the other hand, Nick worked as a car messenger and became a bike courier only after his car broke down and he could not afford to fix it. However, that was six years before I met him, and Nick has been an active member of the Seattle bike messenger scene for many years. In New York, I met a messenger who used to live in a housing project. As a

teenager he got the best job that he could, which was working as a runner for a local drug dealer. The dealer had his workers use bicycles. This
is a practice supposedly common in New York. This individual enjoyed
the biking far more than the dealing and soon found employment at a
legitimate courier company.

Of course, messengering is not for everyone. As we saw in chapter 1,
even among those foolish enough to try it, most do not stay long, especially in New York. For example, a reporter attempting to spend a week
working as a messenger stopped on his fourth day. He wrote: "I'm scared.
I want to do [five] days, but I've made it through [four] without a mis-
hap. The odds are against me."[20] However, for those who can handle the
danger, the discomfort, and the disdain, messengering offers a chance to
turn the workday into an engaging game. When I asked Mary to compare
her positive experiences working as a cook (she had previously attended
culinary school) and her positive experiences working as a messenger,
she stated that while both cooking and messengering gave her satisfaction, she enjoyed cooking to "a lot lesser extent." She went on to explain
how working in a restaurant compared to messengering: "Working at a
restaurant and being super busy and you get through the rush and you
do a good job and you didn't fuck up anything, it is just like that, but not
as pronounced."

Thinking back to her time as a messenger, Lady Jake, now working
in the messenger company's office (but not as a dispatcher), remarked:
"I felt very alive." Comparatively, she described her current job as being
"trapped in this box." For this reason Dan, the messenger with the broken orbital, missing teeth, and fifty-seven facial stitches, refused to turn
his part-time job as a waiter into a full-time one. By his own admis-
sion, he was a great waiter and could make more money in restaurants,
but he did not want to come off the bike. Instead, he waited tables
solely as a means to supplement his courier income. As a point of fact,
Dan's previous messenger company mandated that he work part-time
as a driving courier. While that job paid more, Dan wanted none of it.
"I worked at [Ultra Fast Courier] for about two months. They wanted
me to drive. I was driving half the time, and they kept me on my bike
about half the time—just enough to keep me there. Finally one day, I
was like, 'Fuck this. *Fuck this.*' . . . Fuck driving. . . . I really wanted to be a
bike messenger." So he left and found employment at a company that
let him stay on his bike. However, his new company initially hired him

only part-time. So he took a severe pay cut just to stay as a bike-only messenger.

It is easy to be critical of messengering. It is an extremely dangerous job that pays little and rarely provides its workers with other tangible benefits like health insurance or pension plans. Messenger companies, as the saying goes, get rich off the backs of workers. Messenger bodies are used, abused, and discarded with only minimal compensation for their labor. As Burawoy observes, the piece rate—regardless whether workers find the game enjoyable—benefits the owning class at the expense of labor. At the same time, it would be a mistake to ignore the positive benefits of flow, and the positives exist even if the flow is generated at the edge of disaster. The playful quality of messenger labor is the first major piece in the puzzle of the messenger subculture. As we have seen, many messengers sincerely love their jobs, and many who leave look for ways to keep some aspects of its flow in their lives, and stay connected to its subculture.

Despite its low status and low pay, therefore, messengering is a form of what Stanley Aronowitz calls creative work.[21] It is the playful quality of messenger work that separates it from alienated labor. Hidden between the recesses of work and sleep, play provides another side to the one-dimensionality of capitalist logic. At the same time, Aronowitz insists that estrangement from the self cannot be resolved solely in leisure-time activities. The alienation of production must be addressed: "The soul cannot be healed unless divided labor is reintegrated, unless the lost 'instinct of workmanship' is found within the sphere of ordinary labor rather than becoming an 'avocation.'"[22] In this sense the game messengers play represents a subterranean challenge to the alienating rationality of Weber's iron cage.

The flow of courier labor is only the first part of the messenger puzzle. Engrossment generates emotions, but emotion in isolation does not explain the subculture. To understand the subculture we must look at rituals. As we will see in the following chapter, flow and rituals work together to help sustain the highly integrated lives led by many bike messengers. Ultimately, it is the sanctification of flow in rituals that really explains why Cat cannot just leave her job and why the ever-cynical Jason is still inviting unknown messengers over to his house.

THE DEEP PLAY OF ALLEYCATS

We have seen how the flow of urban cycling reduces reflexivity and results in "instinctual" actions that are enjoyable, at times even giving riders feelings of omnipotence. Compounding this individual experience are the social interactions in which they are produced. In alleycats, flow does not occur in isolation. It takes place within a group of one's peers. And, even for those not racing, alleycats are still part of a collective gathering focused on racing. As Émile Durkheim notes, "It is by shouting the same cry, saying the same words, and performing the same action in regard to the same object that [individuals] arrive at and experience agreement."[1] It must be asked, then: What agreement are messengers experiencing? How are messengers imagining their subculture?

The Power of the Collective

Before arriving at answers to these questions, consider some scenes from Monster Track IV, an annual track-bike-only race held in New York. It was a cold Saturday afternoon in February. Remnants of snow still clung to the shady pockets around the trees of Tompkins Square Park. Even by messenger standards, the event organizers arrived late. When not working, bike couriers are rarely punctual. These organizers actually showed up to their own event a full two hours after the scheduled start time. An hour later, everyone was finally registered. Strewn across the park were over 120 track bikes, and the racers were lined up about fifty feet from the collection of bicycles. Separating them and their machines was a three-foot iron fence that divided the park. The race would start LeMans-style, with the competitors running to their bikes. Moments before the final countdown, some competitors were joking and talking; others stared straight ahead (their minds apparently lost in deep concentration). At this point, I had participated in several alleycats, but it was the first time I really planned to race, and my stomach was thoroughly planted in my throat.

As usual, the countdown began at three and ended just before two. People sprinted toward the fence, jumping or vaulting over it. People were shouting, and people were tripping. On their bikes, they pedaled off in different directions. There were only four checkpoints for the race: Upper East Side and Upper West Side stops and Lower East Side and Lower West Side stops. The riders could do them in any order, but there were only two logical choices. Whoever made it back to the park first would win. I headed north up Avenue A. There were about thirty riders in my immediate sight. Swarming through the East Village, we turned left onto Fourteenth Street and then right onto First Avenue as bystanders stopped dead in their tracks. We were not even slowing down for the coming red lights. Weaving in and out of cars, we screamed at pedestrians, demanding they get out of our way. By the time I hit Eightieth Street, I was starting to get fatigued. By cycling standards this was an extremely short distance, but, like most messengers, I was not rationing my energy; I had been riding all out from the start. At this point, the pack was starting to thin. Stronger riders were well ahead of me, and weaker riders just behind me. However, I could still see some racers in front of me, and I could hear the churning of chains beside me.

When I got to the first checkpoint, bikes were strewn across the ground. People crowded around an organizer signing the manifests. As it goes, there was no orderly queue for the manifest signing, and there was very little courtesy. It was not about who arrived at the checkpoint first, but who could *leave* the checkpoint first. Manifest signed, I hopped back on my bike. Three checkpoints later, racing from the Financial District back to Tompkins, I felt downright delirious. I stopped thinking about anything, save for finishing. A messenger from Washington, D.C., lost in Manhattan, was riding behind me. Not from the area, he followed my route to find his way through Chinatown and the Lower East Side. Unfortunately for him, I was not the best racer to follow. Still, I tried my best. Only a few blocks from the finish, I saw a Boston courier just ahead of me. I strained that much more, wanting to overtake him. I flew up Avenue B and tried to slow as little as possible crossing (almost blindly) through intersections against the light.

I never caught up with the Boston courier, and long before reaching the park, I knew that there were many riders far ahead of me. I had no promise of prizes, and I never considered myself a contender for them anyway. Still, for over an hour, I willingly embraced far more risks than I would have on any given workday. At the finish line there were no cheers, and I rolled in unceremoniously. People were already relaxing and drinking beers.

The D.C. messenger who finished just behind me would later tell me that it was the most fun he ever had at an alleycat, and I have heard numerous messengers make this claim at many different events. I have either had the good fortune of going to some of the world's best races (which are only getting progressively better), or (more likely) in the festive mood of many alleycats, participants are so caught up in their immediate experience that the past is swallowed by the reality of the present.

Putting Meaning to Flow

Action produced in the state of flow (or edgework) appears unquestioningly natural, even instinctual, and as such is innately enjoyable. The flow of messengering, however, should not be studied in isolation. Its significance extends beyond the individualized emotions of each rider. While it is true that the authenticity of flow is, in and of itself, a motivation for action, the lure of delivering packages derives from more than the individualistic thrills of solving the urban maze.

Bike messengers are part of a subculture, and in a subculture the feelings of the individual must be connected to the group. Alleycats are crucial in this regard. As collective gatherings these races turn the individual emotions of urban cycling into a group experience. Alternatively, not all messengers are part of the subculture; many have varying degrees of commitment to it. It is in alleycats, therefore, that we see how couriers become more thoroughly or less thoroughly bonded to the messenger lifestyle. In looking at alleycats as rituals, I want to highlight the creation of affect-meaning (i.e., the *felt* reality of culture). I also want to connect the reduction of reflexivity created by the flow experience to the designation of objects and ideas as sacred symbols. These symbols, in turn, allow the power of the alleycat to be transported beyond the ritual event, and thus reinforce messenger identity in everyday life.

In Durkheim's theory, rituals are both collective *and* effervescent. In modern times calling something a ritual is often pejorative. The term can be used to imply that an event lacked excitement or genuine interest for a participant; for Durkheim, however, a ritual is an emotionally intensive event. Successful rituals, therefore, are not times of reflexive contemplation (much less boredom). They are events of spontaneous actions. Thus, just as with play, flow is the essence of rituals. This point may sound counterintuitive. Play is creative and spontaneous; rituals are structured and predetermined. However, when individuals play together (no matter how creatively or spontaneously) there are always some rules and boundaries or else the game would devolve into atomized nonsense. Of course, rituals are not the same thing as play precisely because they have a preordained quality. The rules of a game can be understood as arbitrary; the rules of a ritual cannot. But the remarkable characteristic of a successful ritual is its ability to take the formulaic and make it appear as the product of spontaneous performance.[2]

Just as flow is an experience separate from normal day-to-day activities, ecstatic rituals also stand in stark contrast to mundane life. This is true regardless of whether they are religious or secular events. In rituals, individuals congregate together and are focused on the performance of a rite. It is through this collective action that individuals become subsumed by the perspective of the group (shouting the same cry). Crucial to this claim is that such experienced agreement is not perceived as coercion but is felt as part of a person's individual disposition.[3] The source of such a disposition, Durkheim argues, is entirely social but is obscured by the ritual process to feel as if it were inherently natural. Really, it feels more than natural—supranatural. Ultimately, it is in ritual participation that Durkheim locates the distinction between the sacred and the profane.

From the Durkheimian perspective, the most significant consequence of rituals is the transmutation of emotions. Collectively generated emotions are moved from inside the body of the individual onto the objects used in the ritual. This is to say, rituals do more than just differentiate the sacred from the profane. By collectivizing lived experience, they denote certain materials (what Durkheim calls totems) as sacred symbols. These become physical embodiments of the emotions generated during rituals. In a tangible form, the exaltation of the ritual can be transported into mundane daily life through the use of ritual totems. That is, sacred symbols serve as markers, continuously reminding the individual of the power of the collective.

Take, for example, the various rock band T-shirts and stickers (e.g., for Metallica, Phish, or the Grateful Dead) so ubiquitous within youth groups. These items not only mark individuals as fans of a particular musical group, but they also invest nonconcert life with memories of more remarkable times. That is, such paraphernalia serve as reminders of the experience of the concert. Further, this symbolic power is located not only in physical objects, but also in ideas. The First and Second Amendments to the U.S. Constitution, for example, have taken on an affective charge that far exceeds the words they contain (and overpowers the political significance of the other twenty-five amendments).

Ideas form the myths on which religious doctrines are based. However, for Durkheim, rituals precede belief.[4] That is to say, religion generates its power, not from its ideological content, but from the communal emotions of ritual activity. Activities feel sacred (i.e., supernatural and unquestioningly righteous) because they at once feel instinctual to the individual *and* are engaged in by others (presumably equally enraptured by the event). This collective effervescence, not the words spoken at the time or the discursive justifications given after the fact, is the real source of meaning.

Of course, in modern times many rituals fail to generate effervescence (think about most high-school graduation ceremonies or even many weddings). In these instances, the "ritual" is nothing but its discursive explanation. Thus the participants feel that the event is utterly empty.[5] In successful rituals, however, flow provides affect-*meaning* by connecting otherwise individual self-feeling to the larger collective. In this process the individual feels energized. This energy starts in rituals but continues in mundane life through its fortification with sacred symbols.[6] Most importantly, it is only by connecting with the collective—that which is greater than the individual—that the individual can feel purpose in action and belief. Clifford Geertz calls this the "really real."[7] It is meaning generated in collective action and rooted in the lived experience of emotion.

Anatomy of the Race

Rituals, if they are to generate collective effervescence, require bodily co-presence, a barrier to outsiders, a mutual focus of attention, and shared mood.[8] Lifestyle messengers associate largely among themselves. After-hour relaxation, parties, and weekends are often spent with other messengers. When I asked Karli, the initially standoffish messenger from chapter 3, how often she socializes with bike couriers outside the workday she replied: "A lot. A lot. My boyfriend's a messenger. A lot of my best friends are messengers. We're taking a camping trip for three days next weekend: Chuck, me, my boyfriend, [David], [Brett], all bike messengers." Similarly, Kelsey explained:

> During the day, I hang out with other messengers *a lot*. Whether it is popping in [wherever other messengers might be] saying something for five or ten minutes, or if there is nothing going on so I'm sitting at the [Mono]rail for an hour, hour and a half.... Quite often, you're hanging out with other messengers who also aren't working at that time. And, then, after work, now, two or three days a week I go [rock] climbing with other messengers. I [traditional bicycle] race with a lot of other messengers as well [on a team comprised specifically of current and former messengers].

What makes someone a lifestyle messenger, of course, is that one's job and the rest of one's life blur together. This is perhaps best exemplified by Jason's inability to extricate himself from the subculture even though he claimed that he was finished with it (described in chapter 4).

When messengers hang out they spend a great deal of time discussing urban cycling. Specifically, they talk about the edgework of riding. Accidents, amazing feats, and wild behavior are common topics. This talk generates foreknowledge of what to expect and excitement over what is to come at an alleycat. For example, the numerous head injuries one messenger sustained while racing over the years were a popular source of good-natured ribbing among his friends. And, as a rookie, I was introduced not only to the dangers of alleycats, but also to how injuries were framed by the subculture. Basically, as long as the rider can walk away from it, it is all just fun and games.

Likewise, messengers who performed in some special or exceedingly dangerous way were often brought up in discussion. For example, during the final sprint of a 1998 New York race, the second position rider reached forward, grabbed the seatpost of the leader, and pulled him back as he propelled himself to the lead. The rider was disqualified. Even in a race with "no rules," this rider's behavior transcended acceptable norms. In fact, because of the general chaos surrounding alleycats, being disqualified ("DQed") is common. It generally results from competitors skipping checkpoints and attempting to hand in their manifests as if they were complete. In this particular story, five years after the fact when I heard it, the tale was told to valorize the rider for displaying a sort of unbridled fortitude.

Similarly, Cory, who has pedaled, full speed, down one of Seattle's steepest hills on a track bike (multiple times), has earned his place in the oral history of the local scene. The hill, Queen Anne Hill, is punctuated by numerous traffic lights. Because it has no brake, inertia and gravity make a track bike nearly impossible to stop (or even appreciably slow down) on a steep decline. Thus Cory took an enormous gamble on what sort of contingencies he might meet at the multiple intersections on his way down. But during a race it was no doubt much faster than taking a less steep route to the bottom.

During an alleycat, racers, without a doubt, are focused on the event. Messengers push the edge during work, but they push it further and sustain it longer in a race. At the same time, riders are engrossed not only because of the competition. The biggest issue is simply their own corporeal safety. Everyone knows the stakes are high. Conversely, other competitors are almost always in sight. In other words, there is bodily co-presence. Thus racers are not riding against a clock as in work. They are riding against each other. An alleycat, therefore, is a series of double rushes, but those double rushes are not measured against an abstraction of time. They are measured against other racers. To this end, the rider's focus is not only on her own speed, but also on the practices of others trying to outpace her. Thus there is a mutual focus of attention. Alternatively, those outside the race are ignored or treated simply as obstacles to be overcome. Thus there is a barrier to outsiders. Even extremely polite couriers can take on fierce personas during a race. Cars are cut off, and pedestrians are yelled at—whatever it takes to keep one's speed.

Overall, the mood of an alleycat is festive competition. Many racers have no intentions of winning. Remember that Arnold only desired a chance to ride wild in the streets. In Rob's words, "Winning doesn't matter. It is about having fun. No one remembers or cares who wins." This statement is not entirely true, but it captures a dominant sentiment of the subculture. An alleycat is more about having fun with fellow messengers and demonstrating your skills in urban cycling. This is why the organizers of the Warriors ride called it a "fun ride." During my time in New York, Kevin set up several alleycats that he labeled fun rides. After one "ride" (i.e., race), there was a dispute about whether a competitor should be disqualified. As one courier screamed at another, Kevin calmly asked: "Did you have fun? Then what are you worried about? The point was to have fun." Similarly, at the 2003 NAC3, one messenger raised his voice over what he felt was unfair treatment by the organizers. He believed his time had been incorrectly marked. Others in attendance voiced their own disapproval at this racer's overt focus on the technicalities of competition instead of the festive atmosphere.

Messengers treat prizes somewhat ambivalently. On one hand, like a rider's wage, prizes serve as a discursive motivation to race. That is, racers often mention the potential of winning something as the reason to race. For example, during the 2003 NAC3, the several Washington, D.C., messengers organized a separate alleycat to be held in conjunction with the national championship. The purse was $500. The possibility of winning this large payout provided lively discussion throughout the day. Similarly, a group of New Yorkers spent several weeks training for a team race in Boston because they wanted the first prize of a $400 wheel set for each rider on the team. There were hard feelings when they did not take first place.

Yet prizes are mentioned far less than antics when messengers recount past races. Moreover, unlike the examples listed above, most races offer far smaller material rewards. Often, riders are competing for little more than bicycle bric-a-brac donated to the organizer by a sympathetic shop owner. By and large, few racers who enter alleycats believe they have a chance of winning, but this does not necessarily alter their dedication to the event. As Kenton explained, "Just riding around as fast as I can. That's what I get out of it. I don't care if I finish first, second, or last, as long as I get to go all out. I get mad at myself for mistakes I make, but that lasts all of like five minutes. I have fun."

The start and finish of an alleycat is crowded with messengers, bikes, and bags. People mill around, drinking and socializing. Even for people not racing (and many messengers, it should be remembered, come to party and not to race), alleycats offer an environment with ritual components. For these people, however, the flow of the ritual is, obviously, less intense than for those engaged in the edgework of the race itself. For messengers, whether racing or merely socializing, pre-race and after-race events offer bookends to the race itself. There is anticipation of the race about to start, and a recounting of the race that just finished.

Rituals and Meaning

Geertz proposes that cultural practices should be analyzed as texts. That is, events, whether they are religious rituals, sporting contests, or theatrical plays, say something about the culture in which they are produced. In his famous example, Geertz argues that Balinese cockfights represent a "sentimental education" for those who witness them. Cockfights are only marginally about avian combat; the fights are ultimately physical metaphors for the life of Balinese men: "Like any art form…the cockfight renders ordinary, everyday experience comprehensible by presenting it in terms of acts and objects which have had their practical consequences removed and been reduced (or, if you prefer, raised) to the level of sheer appearance, where their meaning can be more powerfully articulated and more exactly perceived." Geertz goes on to state that what a Balinese man learns at a cockfight "is what his culture's ethos and his private sensibilities (or, anyway, certain aspects of them) look like when spelled out externally in the symbolics of a single text."[9]

Alleycats as Deep Play

The cockfight, however, is not just any single text. All practices are open to semiotic analysis, but some activities say more about a culture than others. Geertz refers to cockfighting as deep play. Deep play extends beyond instrumental rationalization. That is, the potential consequences of the act appear to outweigh its material rewards. Specifically, cockfighting is a sport of gambling. Betting on most matches is relatively trivial, but in deep matches significant sums of money are at stake. The money, however, is a surrogate for status. Men are not betting for financial reward. Instead they bet for their own pride and the honor of their relatives and village.

Alleycats, like cockfights, are a form of sentimental education. Races, for competitors and onlookers alike, enact and display what messengering means. As Edward, in justifying the actions of couriers to outsiders exclaimed, "You don't know about our life and how we live.... This is our life." As I have stated, alleycats are an extended double rush. These messenger races represent the perfection of flow. Alleycats provide all the excitement of urban cycling with none of the boredom or frustration. There is no being put on standby; there is no waiting on clients or haggling with security guards. There is only the urban maze for the messenger to solve (using both macro- and micro-routing). Jordan explained: "An alleycat boils down your job, like the game aspect of your job, and it is fun to be good at a game."

Clearly, the generally small material rewards offered to the top placers in alleycats do not exceed the risks. Arguably, neither do the larger ones. Further, traveling messengers take time off from their paid labor to compete in events that cannot possibly reimburse them for lost wages. In this sense, alleycats are deep play. More importantly, the value placed on racing, whether the focus is on winning or merely having fun, is deep because the race, like the cockfight, is a stand-in for something else. The organizer of the first Monster Track event explained: "This is what we do for a living, you know. We make deliveries out riding our bikes everyday doing deliveries. So, in the scene, in the messenger scene, we always talk about who is the fastest guy, you know. So, now, here we determine who is the fastest guy, who is the best on the track bike."[10] Somewhat more cynically, Andy described alleycats as "a king of the shit pile kind of competition."

However, placing well in a race is *not* an objective measure of one's ability to be a good earner on the road. Alleycats test the routing skills of urban cycling far more than they test the problem-solving skills discussed in chapter 1. Further, being deemed the fastest guy (i.e., the king of the shit pile) does not move one up the ranks of one's company. Only workday performances can do that. These points aside, to place well in an alleycat is taken by those in the subculture, and only by those in the subculture, as indicative of a messenger's overall ability.

Alleycats as Objective Reality

As we have seen, alleycats emphasize the excitement of urban cycling where flow is pushed to the edge. Performed collectively, the otherwise individual self-feelings of flow move beyond the realm of the subjective. Which is to say, behaving in unison with a group, an individual feels her actions and thoughts as transcendental. The seemingly instinctual quality of flow, therefore, is not felt merely as the property of the actor.

Instead, the actor experiences it as part of something greater—as part of the collective. In other words, actions are reduced to instinct, and those instincts are mobilized by a set of conditions that, because of their social context, seem *objectively* real. Building from the collective effervescence of the group, the individual feels the power of the subculture. While this power is the product of individual minds, the actor feels as if it was a force located outside of the self: "It is then no longer a mere individual who speaks [or acts] but a group incarnated and personified."[11]

The objective power of the alleycat is most clearly illustrated in how messengers describe their attendance at large races, especially the CMWC. As we saw in chapter 2, MAC described the experience of her first championship as coming home. It was a home she had never been to before, but immediately felt connected to. At the time of my interview with her, MAC had been working in CLS's office for several years. Sometimes she was a dispatcher, but mostly she did other administrative work. She described a rather protracted process of removing herself from the messenger lifestyle. It was a lifestyle that, after years of involvement, she felt was too concentrated on intoxication. However, when I asked her to elaborate on her experiences at her first CMWC, MAC responded: "It was really exciting." In simply saying these words, her tone changed. Almost gushing, she further recollected the event:

> It was so exciting. I didn't know how big of a thing it was. I wasn't very urban at the time. I grew up in the suburbs and didn't go into the city very much, and I started to know a lot of people who did it in Seattle, but I didn't realize that it was all over the world. Seeing people from Japan was like really cool. The guys from New York...It was just really exciting. There was just so much energy, bright colors, awesome bicycles, and crazy skills of these guys. It was like nothing I'd ever seen before, and it was awesome....I'm sure I stayed in this job for years longer than I should have because of that. For sure, I was very impressionable at the time.

MAC is not alone in these feelings of awe. Cory had similar feelings about his first CMWC: "That was like my big messenger experience, right there. Going out there and fucking seeing like seven hundred people lining up to race bikes and do messenger work. That was cool....That was fun shit, man." More than characterizing the race simply as cool or fun, Cory located the relevance of the race in its connection to the work and the universal qualities of those that do it: "It's just the community. It doesn't matter. Works the same, everywhere you go. It doesn't

Figure 15. Award ceremony at the 2005 CMWC in New York

matter who you work for, what company you work for. Whatever you do, it's work. Everybody's riding their bike, and it is just as dangerous [for everyone]. Everybody has a job that they have to do, and it's fucking dangerous. But...there's a community." Or, as Karli put it, "It totally changed my perspective. I just thought it was this small group of people, you know, but then there were thousands of people that were messengers from everywhere. I was completely overwhelmed. You want to meet everyone.... It's like a family."

To a greater or lesser extent, these feelings are present at all alleycats, for they all gather messengers together and emphasize (certain aspects of) the job. Further, while a messenger may be disconnected from the edgework of the race, his mere presence at an alleycat still connects him to the deep play of the ritual. Cory went on to explain:

It was eye opening. It was a good scale, just the amount of people that were there.... Aside from [the] racers, there were another four hundred

Figure 16. Bikes laid out for the start of the 2005 CMWC

spectators watching that shit, cheering them on, giving them water, ... some of those people have been messengers from way back when, some have been boyfriend or girlfriend to a bike messenger, or just knew somebody that was a bike messenger. That's the great thing about it, you go to those events and you cover every aspect of what could possibly be bike messengering.

Cory's final comment, that championships are about more than the actual competitors, underscores the subcultural depth of the ritual. The event is an outward expression of the thrills of urban cycling, and that is the ritual's focus.[12] But the ritual itself encompasses not only those who race, but those who simply party. It is a mistake to consider nonracers "spectators" because there is very little of the race to see at an alleycat, aside from the start and finish. Instead, those who come only to socialize are an integral aspect of the ritual itself. They are not only onlookers, but participants in a festival celebrating the messenger lifestyle. And this lifestyle, through its collective enactments, is not understood as a set of loosely collected eccentrics. Instead, it becomes a worldwide community—an objective reality above and beyond any one individual. This is Karli's point about realizing that messengers comprised more than just a small group.

On a personal level, I was at once enveloped by the emotions of the group and disconnected from them. Spending my days working as a messenger and my weekends riding, partying, and racing, I found myself utterly inspired at events like the Warriors and Monster Track. Like the title of Travis Culley's book about his life as a messenger, I felt like I was part of an "immortal class." It seemed as though we understood a secret about the city. We could travel faster than anyone around us. We flew through red lights while others cowered before them. We did not fear traffic; we played in it. Clearly, I was in the throes of what Durkheim considers social solidarity.

Conversely, as a sociologist, I was forced to step outside the reality of the bike messenger subculture. So much of what seemed unquestionably valid within the collective was uniformly rejected by others. This is why Cat's nonmessenger friends do not understand what she gets out of her job. At the finish of Monster Track, for example, I listened to outsiders as they strolled past us in the park. It was clear that they did not see us as immortals. Instead, we were strangely dressed men and women playing with children's toys. Our skills were useless to them, and what messengers called bravery was understood as simple foolhardiness. These nonmessengers were disconnected from the collective effervescence of the ritual, and, consequently, they did not share in the reality messengers create. Which is to say, the subculture's meanings, rooted in affect, appeared meaningless to those removed from the flow of the alleycat.

Designating the Sacred

The discrepancy between outsiders' views and the image messengers hold of themselves comes from more than the emotions generated in the sheer moments of collective action. More importantly, the objective reality created by the ritual is taken as something separate and special from normal, mundane activities.[13] This is Durkheim's differentiation of the sacred from the profane. As we have already seen, the sacred force of the ritual is not confined to the collection of individuals who unwittingly

Figure 17. Various patches on a San Diego messenger's bag

produce it. Instead, the effervescence of the collectivity is transferred to the objects and ideas surrounding the ritual. Further, actors can comprehend this religious force only through these objects. Ultimately, it is sacred symbols—totems—that carry the emotions of the ritual into everyday life. By recalling the lived experience of the individual engrossed in the actions of the collective, symbols keep the objectivations of the group alive. In mundane life, therefore, the individual is given small, and sometimes not so small, reminders of the sacred.

From Objectivation to Objects

Bicycles, messenger bags, clothing, radios, and more have symbolic value for messengers. At the most basic level, they designate insiders from outsiders. In this sense they are membership symbols.[14] Not surprisingly, bicycles (especially track bikes) serve as the most important of these totems. As mentioned in chapter 2, I started working in New York on a track bike, and this confused many messengers who would have otherwise, and rightly, labeled me a rookie. On several occasions, couriers did a double take when they discovered I was on a track bike. One messenger I'd been talking to remarked: "You're a rookie? But that's your fixed outside, isn't it?" This messenger, a mountain bike rider, had trouble believing a neophyte could handle himself on a fixed.

While track bikes have recently grown in popularity among nonmessengers, for over twenty years couriers could claim near exclusivity in this object's use on city streets. Adam snidely commented one day: "Track bikes are trendy now." For Adam, track bikes were a distinguishing feature of messengers, and their use among outsiders was mildly irritating. Or, as Audrey told me, "Every time I see someone on a track bike I feel like I should know them." Today, it is inconceivable that Audrey could still feel this way. In 2003, however, messengers still felt they had ownership rights to the machine. One evening after work, for example, I was with a group of messengers at Columbus Circle. A man on a sparkling new track bike rode by. He looked uncomfortable on the bike and not at all confident. Several people in the group laughed as he passed. Alex, a rookie from Portland with a crusty punk-rock background, smirked: "Maybe we should ask him if he wants to ride with some *real* messengers."

Because of its growing popularity, messengers have had to, at least partially, relinquish the symbol of the track bike. Far more nonmessengers are riding fixies today than there are messengers and ex-messengers combined. However, couriers have not fully given up their claims to to the track bike. Now, however, the focus is on how one rides the bike. It is not in simply displaying the symbol, but in the nuances of how they use it that messengers make claims to it. Specifically, messengers tend to believe that they are the only people capable of safely riding fixed and thus are the only legitimate users of the symbol.

One evening in Seattle, a large group of messengers was hanging out after work. A hipster on a track bike rode by, moving fast. Approaching an intersection with a red light, he appeared as if he was intending to run it, but then at the last moment put the bike into a skid and stopped. Upon seeing this, most messengers in the group burst into laughter. One yelled to the cyclist: "Way to almost get popped by a car!" This was followed by more laughter from the group. There was nothing good-natured about the laughs or the comment. They were meant to ridicule the rider, who was outnumbered and had no choice but to wait at the light while being openly mocked. By my own estimate, the cyclist demonstrated perfect control of his machine and had not almost gotten "popped" by a car. However, by riding a fixed around messengers, he opened himself to severe criticism.

In trying to justify his disapproval of hipsters Jordan observed:

> It's a fashionable thing, and it's rad that it's on bikes, but at the same time, it's kind of patronizing. It's like, "What's up? What's going on? You know, you're kind of dressing like 'em. You're doing a little fronting here [i.e., pretending to be something you're not]. What's going on? You've been biking for like eight months and you're bombing [i.e., speeding down] Madison [a street on a very steep hill] on your brakeless track bike, and it's like, 'What's going on upstairs there, buddy?'"...I don't want to have negative thoughts, but at the same time, it's a co-opting of our counterculture, of our subculture....It's like a co-opting that is just unsettling....I'm trying to articulate it better....It's difficult to articulate....People I know [that are not messengers] will be like, "So, what's your deal with these 'possengers' [i.e., a person "posing" as a messenger]? Why do you have such a problem [with them]?" It's like, I don't have a *problem* with it. It's just a matter of like...Their argument is that, "So anyone with a messenger bag and a fixed gear bike is kind of trying to be like you?" It's like, "No, but yeah."

Jordan has difficulty expressing his point. He wants to be supportive of people riding bicycles. Like most lifestyle messengers, he believes that bikes improve people's lives. This, of course, is an integral part of the subculture's sacred ideal. At the same time, he feels that by wearing certain items and riding a fixed, nonmessengers are transgressing into a symbolic territory in which they do not belong. That is to say, beyond the ideal of having more people on bikes, messengers feel the need to protect the sacredness of their objects from the pollution of outsiders. Thinking rationally, Jordan had a hard time sustaining his stance, but it is clear that emotionally, he had a stake in these objects, and he wanted them protected. In fact, everyone of my respondents who addressed the subject of hipsters prefaced their complaints with the disclaimer that it is great people are on bikes. However, they immediately followed this with a firm and unconditional "but" statement, just as Jordan had.

Of course, it is not only track bikes that are sacred. While track bikes serve (or, at least, once served) as membership symbols, bikes, more generally, are profoundly important to messengers. For example, eight messengers and I met in Central Park for a day of riding. On our way up to the Bronx, we rode to a large statue of Buddha for a picture. We all hung our bikes across a fence surrounding the statue. The sight of our nine bikes clinging to the iron fence and dangling over our heads led us all to a moment of contemplation. We crossed the street and gazed upon the impromptu art. Hugo simply remarked: "Beautiful." We were not looking at profane things: welded steel, spokes, and wheels. We were staring at something that seemed far bigger. An issue of *Urban Death Maze* sums this up perfectly with an adaptation of the Marine Corps Rifleman's Creed: "My bicycle is my best friend. It is my life....Me and my bicycle are defenders of our freedom. We are the saviors of my life."[15]

Bicycles, particularly track bikes, therefore, are objects set apart from more mundane things. Messengers would not, for example, ride to a statue to hang their T-shirts over it, and if they did, it would certainly not prompt the same reverence as the sight of the hanging bicycles. Likewise, the offense and humor that experienced messengers express toward neophytes (and even highly skilled hipsters) on track bikes are efforts to protect the object from the desecration of outsiders. Jason, for example, upon hearing that several rookies would be traveling to a swap meet at the Trexlertown velodrome, huffed: "All these new jacks doing all this shit."

As with track bikes, veteran messengers speak negatively about rookies who too quickly adapt other messenger symbols. For instance, at a party Jason jokingly commented to several other veteran messengers that two rookies had arrived with their bags and radios on. Jason himself was wearing his bag and his radio, and so was nearly everyone in attendance. In other words, the joke was not about radios and bags, but about unworthy messengers wearing two hallmarks of messenger style. In another instance, Jason trained his ire on another rookie: "He's the guy that wants to *look* like a messenger: wearing the little hat [i.e., a cycling cap], but can't remember to roll up his pant leg [to keep it from getting caught in the bike's gears]. And he can't ride a fixed." Neophytes in all subcultures yearn to distinguish themselves as members but in doing so often only highlight their naïveté.[16] More importantly for the present discussion, such symbolic overstatements tarnish the sacredness of the totem. That is, the objects that messengers hold dear lose their charms if rookies or outsiders can easily appropriate the style.

Sacred Ideas

It is not only certain objects that are sacred to messengers. The effervescence of alleycats spills over onto ideas as well. For example, there is the idea that bicycles improve one's life. As another, speed and a disregard for traffic laws can be thought of as a purely economic matter during the workday. As we saw above, alleycats were ostensibly created to settle arguments over bragging rights. They determine the fastest guy. But races do not really determine who's the best at the job. Chuck, a Seattle courier and avid traveler for messenger events, broke down the basic differences between work and racing: "One, you rarely ever actually pick up anything. Two, you rarely ever lock and go into a building. You do sometimes, but it's very rare." Further, "If you pick up something you just smash the shit out of it." That is, racing is about finishing the urban maze, not the finesse of actual delivery work. But, as we have seen repeatedly, the thrills of urban cycling are of value in themselves, and it is the ritual that sanctifies this value. This is optimized in chapter 2 by the messenger who stated: "I could care less about who's the best courier. I just want to know who's the fastest."

More importantly, alleycats sanctify the very notion of messenger work. We can see this in the quotes about the CMWC. Respondents repeatedly mention that messengers across the globe are all doing the same job. The validity of these statements is apparent. Their significance is somewhat more obscure. Janitors and waitresses the world over are also doing the same jobs, and so are dentists and heart surgeons. The difference is that lifestyle messengers see themselves as part of a family—citywide, nationally, and internationally. Alleycats bring couriers together, and, as Durkheim insists, the collective effervescence generated in the ritual allows messengers to identify themselves as a family. That is, it is the ritual, *not* the job, that allows messengers to conceptualize themselves as part of a global subculture.

It must be remembered that at races no one is actually working. There is, in fact, no verification offered at alleycats or at the larger championships that everyone (or anyone) does the same job. Instead, what is verified is that everyone present has an interest in pushing the flow of urban cycling to the edge, or, at least, in socializing while others do so. While messengers couch their explanations of their participation in alleycats in terms of their work, what is really eye-opening about the races is not their paid labor, but the values attributed to flow. In other words, it is the flow of the race that becomes proof positive for messengers that they are part of a family.

Rituals and the Permeation of Boundaries

Alleycats represent what could be called the institutionalization of flow. Actions are institutionalized to the extent that they have occurred before (and will presumably occur again) and the individuals performing them fall into specified roles. Moreover, institutionalization is a process in which habitual activities take on an objective character.[17] What would otherwise be subjective and, therefore, ethereal ideals about messengering are dramatized collectively as an objective, undeniable reality in alleycats. It is this courier reality that gives birth to the messenger subculture and a lifestyle that spirals beyond the workday.[18] By performing in the ritual, the individual is brought into contact with the divine conceptions of her culture.

Alleycats are a perfect example of this duality. They are modeled after work, but they become models for work. For example, Rick described the informal races he would have against a fellow messenger he did not like: "I never say anything to him. I hate people that talk like that, but whenever I see him, I race him. I'm sure he used to be fast, but he's not willing to take the risks I'll take. His time has passed." For Rick, taking additional risks during an already dangerous workday is logical. Clearly this is deep play; Rick receives no material compensation. Further, these races have no audience or scorekeeper and thus offer no increase in social prestige. Instead, it is simply the value of the race (who's the fastest) superseding the value of the occupation (who's the best courier).

The essential point here is that the value of the alleycat, which, by extension, is the value of the subculture, is not produced simply through cognition. In fact, discursive explanations provide rather inadequate answers. To claim that the work is internationally undifferentiated, for example, or that older riders are more cautious does not explain anything. These replies say nothing about why couriers re-create (at least partially) their labor in their free time, or why couriers re-create the risks of racing in their labor. Looking at the workday as a flow-generating game, and alleycats as the ritualized perfections of this flow, explains this behavior. Thus alleycats are models *of* reality, but more importantly they are also models *for* reality.

Further, rituals transmute the flow of urban cycling into sacred objects and ideas that reaffirm the emotions of the group even after the group has dispersed. Riding like one is racing when not actually racing, for example, brings the effervescence of the alleycat into mundane life. Speeding through streets, the messenger reaffirms to himself that he is part of the group. Just as Christians reading the Bible in isolation recall the power of the congregation, the messenger swerving between cars inserts these actions into the schema of her social world. With actions produced collectively, and reaffirmed individually, the messenger can feel confident that her actions have meanings that are in no need of conscious introspection. As Durkheim points out, "When a belief is shared unanimously by a people, to touch it—that is, to deny or question it—is forbidden."[19]

The Authenticity of the Lifestyle

No intrinsic boundary exists between the sphere of labor and the sphere of leisure.[20] Instead, individuals construct mental categories of how home and work should be separated. Some people lead highly integrated lives, while others have highly segmented ones. To some degree, class determines this. White-collar professionals tend to blend the different spheres of their lives, and manual laborers tend to keep the spheres separate. Lifestyle messengers, as the name implies, are extreme integrators. The existence of alleycats alone is a testament to this.

The fusion of leisure and work, however, goes much further than races. It goes to the core of the self. As Tanya, a Seattle messenger bemused by my use of the term "occupation" in an interview, explained, "Yeah, when you say 'occupation' that makes me laugh. Like 'bike messengers'? When I did my tax returns this year it said 'occupation.' I was like, 'Do I put bike messenger?'" To this Kelsey added: "It doesn't seem like a job, I know"; and Tanya expanded: "I think it is more like a lifestyle. I know that sounds really cheesy, but it is *your lifestyle*. It's not what you do. Well, I guess it is what you do." Tanya is using "do" here to mean "do for work," and it is a description of messengering that seems to strip the word of its larger significance as an all-encompassing lifestyle. Kelsey elaborated:

> It's what you do for a living, but it's not *just* what you do for a living. It becomes way more than that. It comes to the point where you see us outside work and we still have our workbag on, . . . we're riding our work bike.

You're transferring from work into social life, and there's not really much of a change. You're still riding your bike around the same. You're still carrying the same shit in your bag. You just don't have deliveries to pick up and drop. You've replaced it with a six pack of beer. . . . The distinction between job and hanging out is very blurred in the end of this occupation.

A conversation I had with Joan was equally insightful. We were going to take a bus up to Boston for a race. In addition to my courier clothing—which was all rather worn, tattered, and covered in patches—I brought along what messengers in the subculture call "civilian clothes." Joan asked why my bag was so full, and I explained that while in Boston I would also be visiting old friends. I further clarified that I would not want to go out with these friends in what I was currently wearing. Joan looked at me rather confusedly and said, "Just be yourself." For Joan, there was no distinction between her work clothes and her leisure clothes. She always dressed like a courier because she was a courier. It was not just something she did; it was who she was. It was, to put it simply, her *self*.

Perhaps the best example of how messengers blur the line between leisure and work is their decision to ride when neither racing nor working. This choice will be discussed in much greater detail in the next chapter. For now, however, it should be noted that lifestyle messengers rarely tone down their riding. As Jordan explained, "Bike messengers generally don't take the slow way anywhere." Craig elaborated: "I am terrible. When I am in no hurry, I am more impatient because I feel that I can get away with it." In other words, even when money and prizes, or even the personal pride of outpacing another cyclist, are removed from the equation, Craig still feels compelled to ride like a messenger. That is, Craig, for no particularly rational reason, pushes the edge in traffic. In doing so, he brings the values of the alleycat into his mundane life and thus reminds himself of the sacred.

On this point, my field notes from September 6, 2002, are illustrative:

I rode back to Brooklyn with the Banditos [a crew of Latino messengers] and Jason [at midnight]. We took over the whole road. We didn't stop at a single red light—all the way from Fourteenth [Street] and Ninth Avenue [in Manhattan's Greenwich Village] to Broadway and Montrose [in Williamsburg, Brooklyn]. The Banditos did not care. They just rode right out in front of cars and expected them to stop. Several times Jason commented: "These guys are crazy."

We had no deadline to make, and nowhere in particular to be, but this was simply how the Banditos acted. Jason's comment was not directed at the Banditos' sentiment. He did not think we should stop at the lights either, but the flamboyance in which they carried it out was startling. Much of this ride lacked the finesse discussed in chapter 4 and instead looked more like a game of chicken. Regardless, it affirmed our intentions of handling ourselves in a particular way in traffic. In other words, we demonstrated our desire for nothing to stop our flow.

Yet, as I have explained, not all messengers are part of the subculture, and even those that are have varying levels of commitment. Matt and Justin provided two surprising examples. Matt, it should be remembered, claimed he was always fast and routinely took great risks in traffic. Justin not only loved to ride his bike but saw the occupation as his destiny. While both men lavished praise on the joys of the job, they also had starker boundaries between their work selves and their leisure selves than many of the other messengers I have discussed. As we rode to get food after work one evening Matt chastised me for riding too fast: "We can slow down. We're not working. I've decided I hate going fast when I'm not working." In a similar vein, Justin, criticizing other messengers, explained to me that when he is at home, he does not dress like he does for work: "I'm dressed to ride my bicycle professionally. When I get home and all this shit comes off, I put on a pair of, this is really funny, I put on a pair of super-nice Born clogs, and a pair of loose-fitting Levis, a T-shirt, and a sweatshirt. That's me at night."

Despite his veteran status, Justin has never raced in an alleycat. He claimed that racing, in any capacity, was not fun. Matt, at the time of our evening ride, had attended only one alleycat. By contrast, the Banditos, Joan, Kelsey, and Tanya are regulars at messenger races. Alleycats, of course, are not the only events that could qualify as messenger rituals, but they provide the clearest division between those that optimize the lifestyle as extreme integrators and those divergent from it. More than drinking after work (and other forms of socializing), alleycats sanctify the flow of urban cycling. It is not surprising, therefore, that those who have not attended races or have not raced in a long time are more disconnected from the lifestyle. We can see this in the division Matt and Justin make between leisure and work. However, it would be incorrect to claim that Matt and Justin were not part of the subculture. They are, but less so than others. Unlike Lester and Malcolm (from chapter 1), Matt and Justin socialize with messengers after work and talk about the job as more than just a paycheck. Nevertheless, since they are cut off from the transforming experience of alleycats (especially the CMWC), messengering is less of a lifestyle for them.

At the risk of pointing out the obvious, I should make it clear that lifestyle messengers are not one-dimensional robots always racing through the city. Clearly, there are times when even the most ardent members of the subculture slow down, take the long way around, and even stop at an intersection when they don't absolutely have to. Regardless, the messenger subculture extols the virtues of urban cycling on the edge. What makes messengering a lifestyle, and not just an occupation, is the degree that messengers carry the extremes of the occupation—specifically, aggressive, fast riding—into their nonwork lives and, consequently, see messengering as something more than work. Alleycats, as sentimental education, are the primary way this is accomplished. Matt and Justin highlight how engrossment in the labor of delivery is not a complete answer to the lure of delivering packages. It is through participation in the rituals, especially alleycats, that the job truly becomes more than a job. As Gertrude, a New York messenger, attested about races, "I live for these things! It is all I want to do."

To recap, the bike messenger subculture is fortified by alleycats. Races are a form of deep play. They transform lived emotions into affect-meaning. That is, individual experiences are connected to the collectivity. The values of the subculture are then internalized as objectively real. This process is compounded by the designation of sacred symbols, and these symbols serve a dual purpose. First, they transfer the affect-meaning of the ritual into nonritual life. The bicycle, for instance, becomes a symbol of the entire ritual experience, which, in turn, is taken as indicative of the occupation itself. The reality of the races can, therefore, be recalled through the image of the bike in everyday life. Second, symbols heighten the ritual experience both by increasing the anticipation of the coming event and by generating more emotions in the event. Thus they increase the effervescence that can be returned to mundane life, and the cycle continues.

In focusing on affect-meaning, I have sought to highlight the often-overlooked aspect of emotion in sociological analysis. However, the question of the lure of delivering packages is still not fully answered. Up to this point, the analysis has covered only people and their emotions, both individually and collectively. Lived experience, however, does not happen in a vacuum. It occurs in physical space. More importantly, the affect-meaning of urban cycling is just as dependent on its urban nature as it is on cycling. Thus our analysis must now turn to the setting in which the actions we have discussed occur.

THE AFFECTIVE APPROPRIATION
OF SPACE

Having discussed affect-meaning, we must now move to the physical context in which it occurs; we must *emplace* the lived experience of flow. Ultimately, the argument I am building in this book is about space, not place. Space is an abstract dimension of the physical world. That is, space involves direction, distance, shape, size, and volume. Place, on the other hand, is about the meanings attached to *specific* spaces.[1] We make use of space as we move through our environment, but the unique attributes of our environment are what conform them into actual places. Thus action is always emplaced, but the action itself is about the use of space.

I am concerned with how messengers appropriate space. To this end, we have been studying the generalized activities of the occupation and subculture that hold true in all places. The reasons for this spatial approach should already be apparent. In describing courier work and the messenger subculture, I have made occasional allusion to the specifics of certain places (e.g., taxis in New York and hills in Seattle), but our attention has been on how couriers traverse the *space* of the city. This will continue to be the focus of our discussion. However, before addressing the matter of how messengers appropriate space, it will be useful to provide a description of each of the cities I studied.

Imagining and Reimagining the City

New York City is an immense place. It comprises five boroughs: the Bronx, Brooklyn, Manhattan, Staten Island, and Queens. Most messenger work, though, is confined to Manhattan—an island thirteen miles long and two miles wide. While bike courier companies technically service the entire island (as well as nearby locations in Queens and Brooklyn), most messenger work is below 110th Street (the southern boundary of Harlem). Moreover, a bike messenger is unlikely to spend much time in the residential parts of the East Village and the Lower East Side. Midtown (the area encompassing Times Square, the Empire State Building, and Rockefeller Center, among many other sites) and Lower Manhattan (home to the Financial District) are the most frequent origins and destinations for deliveries. As a rider for Sprint, I regularly went to the Upper East and West Sides, but these areas produce less work than Midtown.

In terms of urban planning, much of Manhattan is on a grid—most rigidly in Midtown. However, even in the parts of the city that are geometrically on a grid, block numbers are not uniform from one avenue to the next. For example, the 300 block of Fifth Avenue is mated with the 800 block of Sixth Avenue. This can cause a great deal of confusion for the messenger, as there is no intuitive way to know the location of an address. Thankfully, the numbering on the cross-streets is a bit more standardized.

Overall, New York's defining features were set in stone long before the automobile became a viable means of everyday transportation. This, combined with the ever-increasing density of Manhattan, makes the city a unique place to ride a bike. There is an incessant tide of cars, trucks, mopeds, and pedestrians, which ebbs and surges with the timing of the traffic lights. Beyond its sheer volume, New York traffic is famed for the egocentric behavior of those composing it, and messengers, of course, are no exception. As we will see in this chapter, bike couriers find a sense of comfort in knowing other users of the road will not yield to a cyclist.

Compared to New York, Seattle is a seemingly simpler and safer city for the bike messenger. Most work is confined to the small downtown core (about a mile in each direction), and the streets there follow a uniform grid and numbering system. Outside of the downtown, though, the city can be confusing. Streets dead-end only to reappear miles later. For example, finding Roy Street in West Lake will not help a rider get to her destination on that same street in Capitol Hill. Most importantly, bike navigation in Seattle is defined by the hills. There are various flat spots (especially if you are traveling north or south downtown), but the city is built on a giant incline rising from the Puget Sound. As an illustration, take Fourth and Fifth Avenues. The Columbia Center, Seattle's tallest skyscraper, has entrances on both avenues. The Fifth Avenue side is a full four stories above the Fourth Avenue entrance. Yet six blocks to the north these avenues are at the same elevation. Similar variations also exist on other avenues. Such a drastic topography, clearly, influences how a rider will route himself, but avoiding hills comes at the cost of additional mileage and time.

San Diego (along with Los Angeles) epitomizes post–World War II urban sprawl and car dependency. San Diego actually covers more land area than all of New York City. People (even locals) often mistakenly assume that many of the city's neighborhoods are actually independent entities. It is a place carved up by massive canyons, speckled with small mountains, and crisscrossed by giant freeways. Center City in San Diego, however, is less than a mile in each direction and nearly flat. It also adheres to an easy grid. Aloha's riders routinely travel upward from the downtown core to the adjacent mesa of Hillcrest, but few other messengers need to make such trips. In fact, some San Diego messengers have even ridden BMX bikes at work. Were these riders covering greater distances or traversing rougher terrain, such a bicycle choice would be unimaginable. Perhaps most importantly, San Diego has remarkably pleasant weather. Rain is rare, snow is nonexistent, and temperatures rarely drop below 40 degrees or rise above 80.

In terms of social environments, New York is a city that seems to hate its messengers. While they are certainly lauded within bohemian circles, messengers are generally treated as pariahs. At major office towers couriers are forced to use service entrances and are scrutinized by security as they enter buildings. Seattle, as a whole, is far less hostile to its couriers. Messengers never have to use service entrances and rarely have to check in with security. The Washington Mutual Tower even hosts an annual "messenger appreciation day," giving out a free lunch and sponsoring a bicycle mechanic to check couriers' machines. A San Diego messenger's social experiences are a lot like those of messengers in Seattle, but there are no corporate sponsorships for lunch.

In many respects the places I studied can be conceptualized on a continuum. It is hard not to see New York as the most extreme city for messengers. It is true that New York messengers do not have to deal with

Seattle's hills, and endure fewer days of rain. But New York gets snow in the winter and has blistering hot days in the summer. Most importantly, as we have discussed, New York messengers have to deal with an absolutely insane amount of traffic, and face the greatest amount of social stigma. Conversely, among lifestyle messengers, New York couriers reign supreme in subcultural capital. As for Seattle, its traffic is less harrowing than that of New York, but compared to San Diego, the city's streets are densely populated and navigating them is intense. San Diego and Seattle have similar social environments (in terms of outsiders), but (as discussed in chapter 2) Seattle has a much more developed subculture. All the same, while San Diego lacks some of the harsher aspects of other places and the strength of a renowned subculture, it is still a city, and everything discussed in this book applies to its messengers as well. In all places, messengers dart through traffic, trying to meet their client's deadlines or just in an effort to have fun. Regardless of where it takes place, messengering is dangerous and exciting work.

Bringing in Space

Most social research is thoroughly aspatial. To paraphrase Clifford Geertz, sociologists don't study cities; they study *in* cities.[2] That is to say, researchers tend to treat the environments of social activity as inconsequential. Analyzing messengers solely in terms of flow and ritual is certainly informative, but such an approach misses one of the most distinctive aspects of both the courier's job and lifestyle—that it is *urban*. And, to be clear, the urban quality of messenger work is about space. Every city is a different place, of course. But, in every city, messengers make similar use of urban space.

As we saw in the introduction, bike messengers work in the downtown cores of major metropolitan areas. Their services are most useful in older cities, whose business districts, developed long before the primacy of automobiles, are prone to traffic congestion and continually hampered by insufficient parking. Outside of these areas, bicycle couriers are largely unknown, and their existence is considered, at best, quaint. Inside these major urban centers, however, the bike messenger's presence is an economic necessity as well as a cultural phenomenon.[3]

In order to understand the full sociological significance of messengering as an urban subculture we need to consider theorist Anthony

Giddens's approach to the problem of agency and structure. This problem revolves around the seemingly irreconcilable fact that every individual has a unique mind, personal desires, and a capacity for free will, yet society (regardless of the fact that it is made up of such individuals) persists in remarkably predictable ways. In other words, despite our capacity for agency, most of us behave in very structured ways nearly all of the time. As students we sit in class even if we find our professors boring; as customers we wait in line even when we are in a hurry (to list just two very pedestrian examples).

Traditionally, sociologists tended to think of structure as something constraining agency. The bored student would simply walk out of the classroom were he not worried about failing the course, and the impatient customer would cut in line if those in front of her would not complain. At the same time that the traditional view conceptualizes structure as constraining, it also assumes that within the boundaries of the structure there is no impediment to agency. In other words, the context of being in a classroom or waiting for service has not generally been understood as influencing our experiences of boredom, impatience, or anything else—just the socially approved ways of dealing with such experiences.

In Giddens's famous reformation of sociological theory, individual agency and the continuation of preexisting social structures are explained through a process he calls structuration.[4] For Giddens, subjective action can be explained only *within* the context of the objective structures from which it arose. In other words, structure and agency do not exist in opposition (either/or) but as a dialectic (one presupposes the other). In other words, for Giddens, structures do not simply constrain action; they also enable it. Alternatively, there is no freedom within the boundaries of structure; it constrains and enables *all* moments of action.

The clearest example of structuration is language. Language should be thought of as a set of rules and resources. That is, language is constituted of various words (i.e., resources) that must be organized in rather specific ways (i.e., rules) for anyone to understand their user's intent. At the same time, a proficient user of language does not follow a rule book or simply recite prearranged sentences. The user can arrange her words in unique ways and (within limits) even alter sounds or phrases to create new meanings. On one level, language is clearly a structure that constrains. I cannot write, "constrains is a that language clearly structure level on one," and expect anyone to understand me. At the same time, though, language enables. My thoughts—subjective as they may be—are actualized by my ability to express them *through* language. In fact, aside from those especially accomplished in the musical, performing, or visual arts, we are almost entirely dependent on language to express almost anything of even mild complexity, and all of us do so very routinely.

If agency and structure presuppose one another, the environment of social activity is anything but inconsequential. Like all other structures, the raw physical environment is "both the medium and outcome of the reproduction of practices."[5] In fact, in a very literal sense, the material world is a series of structural forms. Unfortunately, sociologists and lay observers alike tend to view material structures as static entities. However, just like social structures, the buildings, streets, rooms, and doors that surround us are sociologically relevant only when they are utilized in systems of interaction. The obdurate existence of four walls and a roof does not make a building a home. Such a structure becomes a home, and not an office or a prison, because of the social designation of those who use it, or do not use it. Thus the physical environment is also a set of rules and resources. A place is defined by rules. Rules are part of what designate one type of place as different from other sites. For example, we eat in dining rooms and sleep in bedrooms. Resources also define places. Not all dwellings have dedicated dining rooms or bedrooms, and even those that do vary in the size and the quality of these spaces.

In our everyday lives, therefore, we draw on the structural properties of a physical setting at the same time that we exercise our own agency. Kitchens, for example, were designed for preparing food, but that does not mean that all a person does in a kitchen is cook. It does mean, though, that the contours and context of a kitchen influence what else we can choose to use it for and how we will go about getting it done. Access to a kitchen, for instance, greatly facilitates being able to turn powdered cocaine into more profitable crack. Alternatively, a kitchen table is, perhaps, a particularly salacious spot for having sex. Of course, a kitchen does not make someone a drug dealer, nor does it inherently energize one's romantic life, but it is a space structured in a way that can constrain *and* enable such endeavors. The size and quality of one's stove and cookware will influence the quantity and rate of crack production, after all. And there are things than one can do on a table that one cannot do on a bed (or in a shower, the backseat of a car, etc.) and vice versa.

More to the point of the argument developed in this book, architectural theorist Iain Borden provides a wonderful illustration of the structuration of physical space in his analysis of skateboarding. Although he

Figure 18. San Diego messengers arriving at an alleycat checkpoint

uses different terminology, Borden shows that skateboarders draw on the rules and resources of the city, but their use of space is far removed from ordinary perceptions and official conceptions. That is, they use the rules and resources of the urban environment in ways unintended by urban planners. Specifically, rolling, grinding, and ollieing across otherwise utilitarian surfaces, skaters turn handrails, curbs, and steps into playthings.[6] Borden explains: "In the case of the handrail, the skateboarder's reuse of the handrail—ollieing onto the rail and, balanced perilously on the skateboard deck, sliding down the fulcrum line of the metal bar—targets something to do with safety and turns it into an object of risk."[7]

Like skateboarders, couriers are engaged in a dialectical relationship with the city's built structures. It is through their use of the city that messengers construct their social world and make sense of their lives. Bike couriers are at once constrained and enabled by the urban environment.

Specifically, the flow of the workday and the affect-meaning of alleycats are intertwined with the messengers' appropriation of urban space. That is, messengers are who they are—wild-riding madmen (and madwomen) living the life you may have dreamed of—precisely because space matters. The material world is not only the stage on which they act. More than something in the background, it is a dialectic component of messengers' lifeworld.

Playing with Space

Bike messengers play in (and with) urban space. As we have seen, streets and sidewalks, cars and pedestrians, are all conceptualized as part of a complex, shifting puzzle. It is an urban death maze. Solving the maze requires macro- and micro-routing to find the fastest trajectory between two points. This objective is not attained primarily through velocity produced through pedal power and aerobic capacity. Instead, it involves what Andy called skills with spatial capacity. It often necessitates riding in a manner that looks "fucking insane" to outsiders but comes from the confidence generated through experience in urban cycling.

Proscriptions versus Problems

Whereas skateboarders creatively use the functionally bland objects of the city, such as handrails and parking curbs, messengers play with the functional rules of city traffic. For bike couriers, traffic laws are used only as predictors of what *other* users of the city should be doing. Travis Culley remarks: "Red means red and green means green: I keep moving regardless."[8] Recounting a recent traffic citation, Jessica informed her friends: "I didn't know I'd even run [a red light]. I look at traffic. I don't pay attention to lights." Andy bluntly stated: "I don't give two shits about traffic laws." What Culley, Jessica, and Andy demonstrate is that messengers do not conceptualize traffic as a set of legal proscriptions. Instead, traffic is a set of problems—or, better put, dangers—that must be continually resolved.

To explain, traffic is typically thought of in terms of regulation. A good driver, it is said, follows the rules of the road, and the same also holds true for most people's understanding of what makes a good cyclist. By contrast, for messengers a good cyclist does not follow traffic laws; she avoids dangers. For example, a red light at an intersection signifies that one is likely to encounter more problems than if the light was green. The messenger may or may not be able to resolve this "problem" by fitting between the cross-flow of traffic. If she can solve it, laws be damned. If the rider cannot find a line through, she must stop. But stopping is always a source of frustration. This is why Jacky, Erik, and Cory proudly acknowledged their ability to flow through traffic. Matt described the approach: "I literally run more red lights than I run green lights. I've gotten to the point where I just straight up bomb [i.e., speed through] everything that goes. There'll be cars going through [an intersection], and I'm just like, 'Okay, I see a car going,' and then like boom [makes a hand motion implying forward motion], and even with pedestrians it's the same thing."

As they route themselves through the city, other objects and users of the city become obstacles and implements for messengers as they attempt to keep their flow. Pedestrians provide a good example of obstacles to messengers. Colliding with a pedestrian is dangerous for both walkers and riders. Of the numerous stories of such accidents, Calvin's week-long coma stands as a stark reminder of the dangerous nature of cyclist-pedestrian collisions. A basic courier mantra, therefore, is, "Avoid collisions; they slow you down."[9] One Seattle messenger, for example, collided with an elderly woman during his first month on the job. She sustained only minor injures but still required medical attention. In response, she sued the messenger's company, and when I left Seattle the case still had not been resolved.

Pedestrians are also implements of messengers, because jaywalkers can slow down cars and alter the flow of traffic to messengers' advantage. Nick refers to jaywalking pedestrians as "the human shield." Chuck, whom I was interviewing at the same time, explained: "Since they are jaywalking, you can be sure that no cars are coming." Nick quickly chimed in: "Or, if a car is coming, they'll hit them instead of you." Hence the human shield. Buses can provide the same effect ("bus shielding"). Both are examples of how messengers creatively (and in some ways counterintuitively) *use* the rules and resources of the city (in Giddens's sense of the terms) to ride against the rules of the city (in the legal sense of the term).

It must be remembered that this sort of knowledge is often tacit, and, even when used consciously, it is decided on in fractions of a second. In the case of pedestrian shielding, as a messenger speeds toward an intersection, he looks for indications of what may or may not occur as he crosses the plane of the opposing street. The presence of pedestrians helps the rider determine what other vehicles can or cannot do in the following few instances of time. As Erik previously explained, it is not a logical thing. Instead, the body seems to act instinctually. Further, as Matt noted, often it is only later that the rider consciously recalls the gravity of the specific dangers he faced.

The difference in orientation—to proscriptions versus problems—is demonstrated by worried and often angry motorists (or even cyclists and pedestrians) fretting over a rider who refuses to obey traffic laws. These concerns persist even when there is no danger present. In other words, the issue for many nonmessengers is following the letter of the law, not safety in itself. One night in Seattle, Nick blew through a stop sign as we were riding together. Accelerating, rather than slowing, as he approached the intersection, he slipped seamlessly between the cars. None of the drivers needed to hit their brakes. In fact, even if they had wanted to brake, few would have had reflexes quick enough. An extremely irate man yelled from his car: "You're going to get killed riding your bike like that." Nick ignored the warning (which was also a threat) and continued riding. A moment later he looked at me calmly and remarked: "No, actually, I'm not going to get killed riding like that. That's how you ride *not* to get hit." Cat explained this perspective: "Messengers know how to ride in urban traffic, and flow *with* traffic....I think that idea of 'we are traffic too' can hurt you more than help you....I try to stay out of the way.... I think if I rode and obeyed all the laws and treated myself as traffic, I'd actually be stopping the flow as opposed to going with it."

Betwixt and Between

The relationship of bike messengers to traffic is completely divergent from bicycle commuters' and recreational cyclists' relationship to traffic. All three types of rider are concerned with safety, but nonmessengers tend to follow the principles of vehicular cycling. From this perspective, bikers should behave like automobile drivers. In turn, cyclists should be given the same rights to the road as motor vehicles. This is what Cat means with her derision of "we are traffic too." Thinking in terms of problems, however, messengers conceive of bicycles as a sort of supra-traffic. In this conception, cars and pedestrians are required to follow the rules of the road, and cyclists are given clemency to fit between the cracks of the system. The messengers' view of themselves thus perfectly reflects a traditional view of agency and structure. That is, messengers

Figure 19. New York messenger in Times Square

believe that their cycling skills allow them the freedom to operate *between* the girders of the structure. For this reason, bike couriers often describe themselves as invisible or claim that they wish they could be invisible.

Herbert, an eccentric CLS administrative worker and former top rider for the company, provided a telling example: "I think a good cyclist remembers that he's invisible. He looks at the whole thing, at what's going on, and makes decisions based on that, whereas a regular street cyclist picks his line and stays with it, because that's all he knows how to do. You have to go around and through and up and down." Conversely, while Dan wants to be invisible, he felt that the motorists that did see him hampered his riding:

> My object is, one, be safe—not get myself killed—and two, if I could just be invisible, completely invisible to cars, and no one could see me in traffic.

> I don't want anyone to speed up or slow down for me. I don't want any-
> one to hesitate or worry. There are times that I know I could make an
> intersection…, but I won't because I know that, just by the fact that I'm
> hauling towards that intersection, I'm going to scare oncoming traffic.
> I know I can make it. I know I've got plenty of room to make it.

Dan's comments are doubly poignant because, as noted earlier, I interviewed him soon after a very serious collision that occurred precisely because a car coming from behind did not see him.

Two separate issues arise regarding invisibility. First, there is Herbert's
claim. In Herbert's description, urban cyclists should view the entire scenario laid out before them and slip in between the cars and people. This
is micro-routing. According to a Chicago messenger, "A nice metaphor
for it is, if you imagine like water falling over rocks in a stream. There is
a natural way to go, and you know, the path of least resistance, etc. So, if
there is a line of cars in traffic in a street that you're going down, there is
just kind of a natural way that you fall through."[10] Second, there is Dan's
explanation. Dan also wants to find the natural way to fall through, but
since cyclists usually are visible, the scenario they face changes based on
their efforts to manipulate their way through it. Dan is not simply worried about scaring people for altruistic reasons, although that might be
part of it. He is more concerned with the fact that if he scares people as
he hauls toward an intersection, the route he is planning—the gap in
vehicles he is prepared to traverse—can change unpredictably if some
drivers alter their speed when they see him coming.

A San Diego messenger formerly from Chicago explained: "I'd rather
drivers didn't see me. When they slow down, you can't plan for that." He
said this to compare Chicago, where drivers are less likely to alter their
speeds when they see a cyclist, to San Diego, where drivers will often stop
or slow down out of fear of hitting a cyclist. The point here is that even if
she does not want to be, a messenger is still part of traffic, and her behaviors influence what drivers and pedestrians can and will do on the road.
Further, as visible beings, cyclists' own actions often create the very situations they have *not* planned for (potentially leading to their injury).

In contrast to messengers, bicycle advocacy groups uniformly, and
for very obvious reasons, want to increase a cyclist's visibility. Their efforts are generally referred to as "bicycle awareness," and the goal is to
improve the attentiveness of motor vehicle operators to the presence
of cyclists on the road. Visibility, of course, is a good thing for cyclists *if*

they are going to follow the rules of the road, and act predictably while doing it. Namely, visibility is good for cyclists staying on the far right of the lane and stopping at red lights. Concurrent with the broad objective of bicycle awareness are efforts to enhance the bicycle infrastructure of cities. Specifically, bicycle advocacy groups want bike lanes. Bike lanes accomplish two things. First, they separate cars and cyclists. Second, they give legitimacy to bicycles. The latter is important because many motorists seem to believe that cyclists do not belong on the road, and even if their legal right to be there is acknowledged, it is often suggested that cyclists have no moral right to be on the road.[11]

I have been a cyclist for many years, and my personal examples of motorists disregarding my rights to the road are legion. While it is no surprise that I have irritated drivers when practicing a problem-oriented approach to urban cycling, I have been told to "get on the sidewalk" or "get off the road" countless times while simply riding in a straight line on the far right of the road. In more extreme cases, I have been threatened or had objects thrown at me. Perhaps most disturbing is the number of people who rant about bicycles getting in their way and slowing them down when they are driving. In reality, cars cause traffic congestion. It is absolutely incalculable the number of times a driver is slowed by another motor vehicle. On the other hand, the amount of time any one motorist has to slow down for a cyclist is minimal to nonexistent. Still, it is the cyclist that often burns in the driver's memory. These instances bring to the surface an underlying belief that bicycles do not truly belong on the road. Motorists, of course, complain incessantly about bad drivers, but cyclists, bad or good (however that criterion is defined), are lumped together as a nuisance for simply using the road. Bike lanes, however, make it clear that there is, at the very least, a three-foot strip in which bicycles undeniably belong. Conversely, by designating a place that bicycles belong, bike lanes also demarcate that bicycles do not belong anywhere else.[12]

Unlike cyclists seeking legitimacy, messengers occupy a liminal space: they invisibly fall through the gaps other users of the road have left. That is, messengers see themselves as riding "betwixt and between," to use a phrase made famous by anthropologist Victor Turner. Bike messengers want to be invisible because they do not want to be part of traffic. Justin, for example, stated: "I find the [bicycle] commuters who sit in traffic behind cars, in a lane of traffic, ... the most obnoxious. It's defeating the purpose of riding a bicycle in the city. The ability to move through traffic and not be part of traffic is the reason why [people should commute on a bicycle]." In other words, Justin has no interest in the political platform of bicycle advocacy groups. He wants neither awareness nor legitimacy. Instead, he wants the ability to manipulate his way through the city, and he wants to do this in ways neither conceived nor perceived by other users of the road.[13]

Regardless of what is written in the law, bicycles are always, at least somewhat, liminal. Drivers have the road; pedestrians have the sidewalk. Cyclists have neither. This deserves a bit of elaboration. Places where pedestrians are allowed to leave the sidewalk and enter the road are usually marked by a painted crosswalk. This is because roads are understood as the domain of cars. The painted markers of the crosswalk, therefore, are necessary to visually denote the proper places where this domain can be transgressed. Bike lanes are like crosswalks. They are little slivers of land conceded to foreigners in a vast territory they do not otherwise control. But bike lanes represent only a tiny fraction of the roads cyclists use. For the most part, even for riders that adhere to the principles of vehicular cycling, a biker is still in a liminal position. What vehicular cyclists want to do, however, is eliminate the ambiguity of the machine and give the bicycle a distinctly recognized and *regulated* right to the road.

In contrast, messengers do not want an end to their liminality. As Justin put it, it is "obnoxious." That is, it offends his sensibilities about what cycling in the city can offer. For Justin, the bicycle is a way around the rules of the road. Herbert takes a different view, commenting on the proposition of more bicycle lanes: "Any advantage for a bicyclist is a good thing. It would be a tool. It wouldn't be, 'You can only ride in the bicycle lane.'" In other words, for Herbert, a bike lane is just one more place to be betwixt and between as the rider finds her natural way to fall through.

Cities and Social Worlds

As we have seen, when messengers discursively rationalize their riding, they often emphasize safety. One bike courier, juxtaposing nonmessengers and messengers, noted: "They handle themselves seemingly more cautiously, but actually it is a little more dangerous." As Nick asserted, his riding style kept him from getting hit. Corporeal security, however, is only part (and in many ways only a small part) of the equation. Without a doubt, there are distinct dangers in the principles of vehicular cycling, but the problem-oriented, "invisible" method of messenger riding has its own very obvious hazards.[14] The frequency of messenger injuries underlines this fact.

Clearly, the messengers' style of riding is primarily concerned with speed and efficiency—in the short run. The micro-routing that couriers cherish arises from their liminality. Their style of riding is primarily about playing the game and pushing the edges of flow. At this point in the analysis, however, we need to look at how such emotions are emplaced. That is, we need to connect the joy of flow and the affect-meaning of rituals to how messengers move through the city. In other words, it is here that we can finally address the affective appropriation of space. To understand this is to incorporate physical structures into the sociological analysis. The courier's speed is not generated sui generis; it is the result of individuals acting *within* and *through* space.

The rule orientation of vehicular cycling applies in all situations—empty country roads and crowded city streets alike. The specific practices of riding in rural areas or urban areas may differ somewhat, but the principles are the same. The cyclist should follow the rules of the road and act predictably. By contrast, the messengers' style of problem-oriented cycling is only viable within the context of urban gridlock. Cat astutely made this point when trying to explain why a messenger's riding style is about more than time deadlines: "I think downtown riding is different than any riding almost anywhere else in the city. . . . I'm much more aggressive, but it's because I'm downtown. . . . I think it is more downtown versus non-downtown than clock versus off the clock."

Downtown is packed and congested, and there are cracks for the courier to fall through. Messengers downtown cannot ride like messengers outside the downtown core. Bicycles are liminal objects (or, at least, have the potential to be in a liminal position) in all situations, but this liminality is advantageous only in terms of relative speed in specific situations. Whatever puzzles are offered on suburban streets or rural stretches, they are not the challenges surmountable by the messengers' skills regarding spatial capacity.

The flow of urban cycling, therefore, is *enabled* by the city. Regardless of how messengers conceptualize themselves in traffic, the constraints of the city are integral to their actions. Which is to say, messengers are not pure agency invisibly falling through the structure. They are intertwined with it. In this way, the physical dimensions to Giddens's duality of structure start to come into focus. It is the very limitations of the urban environment—its gridlock and unavoidable inefficiencies in traffic engineering—that allow messengers to act back on the city and impose

Figure 20. Craig traveling the wrong way down Fourth Avenue in downtown Seattle

their own conceptions of space onto the city.[15] Being neither an automobile driver nor a pedestrian allows messengers certain freedoms, but only in the material context of the city. That is, the process of structuration involves more than social structures; it involves physical space as well.

To illustrate this, our analysis must move beyond descriptions and explanations of messenger practice and introduce the meanings couriers give to their actions. It is here that space becomes explicitly cultural. And it is here that we can understand the significance of emplaced action. To begin, the problem-oriented method of riding is not confined to the workday. To the contrary, the speed, daring, and creative outlook are carried over into the messengers' nonwork lives. When I asked Justin, for example, if he runs red lights when not working he replied: "Occasionally, sometimes." But, then, thinking it over, he remarked: "Fuck it. If I look around, and there's not a cop, yeah, I'm gonna go for it because I'm on a bike, you're in a car, I'm going to be gone before you get through that light anyway." Justin's approach to riding relates to what he calls "the rhythm and flow of the city" and what he sees as his inalienable right to manipulate his way through it. This goes back to Andy and his open disdain for the law. As Andy sees it, the rules were written for motor vehicles, and messengers possess talents that should not be confined to such codes of conduct. Here we might also recall Jessica's point about not even knowing she had run a red light.

The extremes of such non-work-related, edgework-oriented riding are illustrated in a Saturday I spent with a group of New York messengers. Crossing paths with me during a weekday, Stan suggested I hang out with him and his friends on the weekends. He explained: "[We] ride around and cause havoc." A few weeks later, I met up with this group for a ride to the Kissena Park Velodrome (from Brooklyn to Queens). On this trip, we rarely stopped for lights and generally infuriated drivers throughout the two boroughs.

At one point our wild riding prompted a physical standoff between our group and an angry driver. The incident started when Hugo, slightly separated from the main group, made a particularly rash choice in running a red light to catch up. One driver felt especially slighted by Hugo's actions. As Hugo rode back up to our group, he and the motorist were engaged in a heated argument. The driver was riding beside him, and both were issuing various threats. Hugo staked out his position rather succinctly by stating to the driver: "I never said it was your fault. I just told you to fuck off." In the end, it took Andreas brandishing his bike lock, a six-pound chain, as a weapon to convince the driver that he did not want to escalate things further. It was at this moment that I realized just how literal Stan's invitation had been.

Later, I also realized that the ride was also an audition. It was a test among a recent group of friends to size up each other's riding prowess. Toward the end of the day, Hugo proclaimed: "We now know that we are all riders." His point being, throughout the day, as we rode around causing havoc, everyone in our group had demonstrated they were urban cyclists. The day had been about showing a willingness to push the edge in traffic and having the prerequisite ability to do so. In the interest of accuracy, I should mention that both my bravado and my skills lagged far behind the rest of this group. Hugo may have proclaimed that we were all riders, but they were riders of a different caliber.

What my weekend with Stan and his friends underscores is the connection between how a messenger rides and the larger lifestyle that he is part of. The epitome of how messengers live and the cultural values surrounding how messengers ride is, of course, the alleycat. To repeat Kelsey's words from chapter 5, "It's what you do for a living, but it's not *just* what you do for a living." In this blurring, it is not just work and leisure that lose their bounds. As we have seen, the wild riding behaviors of messengers become indications of their innermost selves. Here we should recall Edward's claim regarding urban cycling: "This is our life." Edward said this while recounting the story of a messenger who was severely injured while racing and was condemned by outsiders for bringing his ill fate on himself. Edward would meet similar misfortune a few months after he repeated this story, but, as in Dan's case, Edward's own physical traumas (in this instance a shattered femur) did not alter his worldview.

At the risk of belaboring this point, it needs to be stressed that cyclists cannot ride around and cause havoc outside of cities—or, at least, not in the way Stan meant. When Hugo said that we were all riders he was not referring to our cardiovascular fitness or the suppleness of our pedal strokes. He was talking about each cyclist's ability to navigate the maze. And navigating the maze was what the day had been about. We were *urban* cycling. To remove the "urban" from our experience would be to remove the "mountain" from a mountain biking trip. In both cases, the rider is cycling. He is staying upright through the centrifugal force of two wheels propelled by his own biological energy. But it is the first word in the term that is definitive. Kelsey explained:

> When I'm just riding [outside the city], and I'm by myself, it's like unattached riding. I don't have to pay as much attention to what is going on. I don't necessarily have to be focused on where I am, where I am going.... I like to hop on the back country roads and just go ride and not have to stop, and not have to look where I'm headed, and just kind of stare off and, you know, be free—just enjoy my surroundings and where I am.... I've learned how to ride in traffic and around heavy groups of people, and get through without stopping.... It's a very different style.... [Urban cycling is] a lot more aggressive riding style, even though it is slower [than riding on back country roads].

Structuration in the City

It goes without saying that bike messengering is a strictly urban occupation. It is equally apparent that alleycats are a purely urban phenomenon.

Less obvious, however, is what such simple observations mean for the role of space in cultural theories about urban social worlds. Clearly, messenger practices are emplaced. This fact alone is unlikely to raise the reader's eyebrows, but it should. To go back to Giddens, the move from a dualism of agency and structure to duality within them has immense repercussions. As we have already discussed, structure is traditionally understood as a constraint. More so, it is understood as an external constraint. As such, structure is removed from agency—as if it could exist outside of human action. Conversely, by viewing structure as an external force, an agent's activities are freed from structure, insofar as they do not directly confront the structure. From this perspective, "the structural properties of social systems ... are like walls of a room from which an individual cannot escape but inside which he or she is able to move at whim."[16] Not surprisingly, this view represents the messengers' take on their actions. Summing up her younger, and wilder, years as a messenger, MAC stated: "There definitely wasn't any social rules, and that was very free."

Theoretically, however, for Giddens, this view is flawed. Agency and structure exist in a dialectical relationship; they presuppose one another. For the purposes of the present argument, the built environment must be understood as "an agentic player in the game," to quote Thomas Gieryn again. Just as skateboarders are connected to their use of architecture, couriers are tied to the city's structure. There are good reasons why MAC feels that there were no social rules and why Matt described his occupation by claiming: "We're pretty much just paid outlaws." Sociologically, however, these lay conceptions miss the duality inherent in courier practices. In terms of structuration, messengers are far less outside the law than inside it. The freedom MAC describes and the outlaw character Matt cherishes come from how messengers use the very strictures of traffic and the rules of the road.

There is also a second, bolder point to analyzing messenger practice as a form of urban structuration. Messengers not only utilize the rules and resources of the city, but in doing so they help reconstitute what the city is. As sentimental education, alleycats teach couriers to not give "two shits about traffic laws" but to wildly embrace the potential edgework of dodging cars. My weekend with Stan and his friends, for example, has new significance when thought of in terms of the ritual sanctification of urban cycling. Our riding was connected to the effervescence of alleycats and reified subcultural values as an objective reality. But such riding not only educates and reinforces shared identities through collective meaning.

This riding transforms the space in which it occurs. The utilitarian and rational rules of traffic are turned upside down and used for their own negation. By turning streets into racecourses (either in an alleycat, in making a paid delivery, or just in riding around town), messengers transform the arteries of commerce into the roots of play. It is precisely these sorts of events that radicals like Henri Lefebvre believe can overturn the oppressive cloak of rationalization permeating everyday life.[17]

The issue of liberation will be discussed further in the conclusion. For now the essential point is simply to stress that space matters. Physical structures, just like social structures, are intertwined with human agency. While messengers rarely alter the obdurate form of the city, the meaning of the design—how it is experienced—is drastically altered through their practices. To ignore this is to fall into the trap of environmental determinism. It is to concede that urban planners successfully dictate how the city's spaces are used. Instead, as sociologists we must conceptualize the built form of the city as interconnected with the actions occurring within the city.

At the same time, it should be emphasized that while agency and structure may presuppose one another, it is a mistake to assume that structuration requires parity in this dynamic. Messengers are in a dialectic relationship with the city, but the space they produce does not change the urban environment outside their specific interaction with it. Thus the point is not that messengers can appreciably transform the city for others. Messengers' riding styles may alter the tenor of the street. They can, for example, make the streets a little bit more dangerous, as their numerous detractors are quick to observe. They may also make the streets a little bit more romantic, as we see in their pop culture depictions and in Justin's and Rachel's childhood idolizations of the occupation. These, however, are not the sort of grand urban transformations attracting industries or leveling ghettos. Messengers are insignificant players in the death and life of great cities. But this does not negate the emplacement of the messenger subculture. The city is not simply a thing in the background of the messengers' social world. Urbanism is a way of life for messengers, but only to the degree that it is utilized by their creative use of structure. That is to say, messengers conduct an affective appropriation of the city, and, in turn, they find meaning in delivering packages.

As we have seen, the flow of urban cycling cannot be separated from the urban environment. Thus the affect-meaning of the messenger subculture is codeterminate with the appropriation of physical space. Generally absent from sociological analysis, space is an essential component in the theoretical issues of structure and agency. In the case of bike messengers, the individual actions of urban cyclists are based on the pursuit of flow and informed through the sentimental education of messenger rituals. It is in these actions that messengers creatively use and alter the structural arrangements of space. In doing so, messengers engage in what I call the affective appropriation of space.

THE MEANING OF MESSENGER STYLE

The year 2000 saw the release of fashion photographer Philippe Bialobos's *Messengers Style*. In its oversize, glossy pages, New York bike couriers, poised in perfect lighting, stand against blank white backgrounds. It is a scenario intended to bring the color and personality of each of the featured messengers into central focus. Three years before Bialobos's photographs were published, one journalist noted: "It was only a matter of time before the fashion world got hip to bike-messenger chic, a distinctive style that is equal parts hip-hop, skateboarder, and punk."[1] Indeed, in her introduction to *Messengers Style*, fashion historian Valerie Steele proclaims messengers to be "trendsetters," with their sporty clothes and athletically toned physiques. She concludes: "Strong, brave, fast, and free. No wonder we admire messengers and their style."[2]

Messengers and Style

Up to this point, my argument has focused on practices. We have seen how the lived experiences of messengers are embedded in the material environment. Of course, I have touched on style here and there.

Now, however, I want to confront messenger style head-on. Specifically, I want to provide a sociological account for Steele's admiration of messenger style. In her formulation, outsiders admire messengers and their style because it symbolizes what messengers *do* and what they *represent*. That is, the physical aspects of the job, being "fast" and "strong," are connected to the job's cultural values, being "brave" and "free." In line with Steele's terminology, messengers use their physical strength to speed bravely through the city, free from the rules and responsibilities of the average citizen. What Steele hints at in the conclusion to her introduction, therefore, is a semiotics of messenger style.

In Clifford Geertz's words, "The culture of a people is an ensemble of text, themselves ensembles, which the anthropologist strains to read over the shoulders of those to whom they properly belong."[3] I propose that the couriers' subculture, like all cultures, represents an ensemble of text, and by analyzing messenger style we can uncover how couriers' meanings are symbolically expressed. More importantly, by analyzing this text we can see a *particular* story of *affective spatial appropriation*.

Geertz's semiotic approach has already been utilized in the discussion of messenger races. Alleycats, as we saw in chapter 5, are not only rituals generating collective effervescence, but also a form of sentimental education. In other words, messenger races express a deeper set of subcultural values about the significance of flow over and above economic rationality. But the semiotics of the messenger subculture can be taken much further. It is not only alleycats (and other forms of collective after-hours socializing) that exude and instill the courier ethos. Perhaps more than anything, it is through style—the demeanor, argot, and image of a subculture[4]—that insiders and outsiders alike are informed of the messenger lifestyle.

Implicit in what follows is an understanding that subcultural styles must be understood as a symbolic component of practice. Further, I contend that practices cannot be separated from the meanings that inform them.[5] The question, therefore, is not only, as Geertz emphasizes, *what* is said, but also *how* and *why* it is said. To this end, the cultural analysis of bike messengers offered here connects the affective appropriation of space with its semiotic dimension. In a word, there is a homology between the messengers' actions and the messengers' symbols.[6] That is to say, messenger style is the meaningful expression of the lure of delivering packages produced by the flow of urban cycling.

Liminality: Strangers in the Urban Grid

As we saw in chapter 6, city planners are ambivalent about bicycles. Roads have been constructed for automobiles, and sidewalks have been put in place for pedestrians. Bicycles, however, exist betwixt and between, and in this liminal zone, cyclists have a freedom to maneuver that is denied to others. It is the very nonstatus of the bicycle, therefore, that allows messengers to perform their job. In negotiating their way through the ebbs and flows of "legitimate" traffic, messengers disregard traffic laws, and often this disregard is displayed quite flamboyantly. We see this in Justin's statement "Fuck it" and in Andy's lack of "two shits about traffic laws."

Not surprisingly, insiders and outsiders alike often describe messengers as outlaws. Matt, it may be recalled, referred to himself and his coworkers as "paid outlaws," and Fannin called himself a "paid criminal." Likewise, in differentiating himself from commuters and recreational cyclists, a former D.C. messenger commented to me: "They don't understand. You and I have experience with the outlaw side of cycling." Steve the Greek, a former rider turned company owner, actually explained his time as a messenger by dividing society into four categories: "There was civilians. Then you have the police—the paramilitary. Then you have criminals. Then you have outlaws. Bike messengers fall under the realm of outlaw."[7]

An outlaw may break laws, but the word "outlaw" is not synonymous with "criminal." The outlaw is characterized not by her specific crime, but by a disposition assumed to be dangerously incongruous with civil society. That is, outlaws demand autonomy at the expense of the greater good, or so their detractors claim. At the same time, outlaws are not totally outside society. The autonomy they demand can actually make them folk heroes—at the price of also being pariahs.[8] Outlaws are a particular form of what German sociologist Georg Simmel calls strangers. Strangers are neither natives nor aliens. They are estranged in their own homeland—"near and far *at the same time.*"[9] Strangers and outlaws are not synonymous. There are certainly strangers who are not outlaws, but there are no outlaws who are not strangers. In analyzing messenger style we can see how the more general character of the messenger's strangeness contributes to an outlaw image. In other words, using Simmel's conception of the stranger, we can connect the liminal space in which messengers ride with the outlaw character that messengers espouse.

According to Simmel, "The stranger is by his very nature no owner of land—land not only in the physical sense but also metaphysically as a vital substance which is fixed, if not in space, then at least in an ideal position with the social environment."[10] As we saw in chapter 6, cyclists, unlike drivers and walkers, have no land. Further, couriers, unlike other cyclists, are ambivalent about their landlessness. To own land (e.g., a bike lane) is to be confined to it, and messengers desire something very different from a rightful claim to a small strip of road. Instead, messengers relish their liminal position as strangers, and the opportunities it affords them, even if those opportunities are often outlawed.

Pedaling through the city, the bike messenger feels outside the bounds of ordinary society. Laws and regulations are rarely enforced, and the messenger can travel (more or less) where she desires, as fast as she dares. Travis Culley writes of his experiences: "I am free to move as I wish, piercing gridlocked intersections, snaking between cars, and running the wrong way up one-way streets. I get juiced by this." Conversely, when the messenger dismounts her bike and enters the client's office, she feels thrust back inside society, and she is forced to conform to laws and regulations. The lawlessness and feelings of freedom offered by bicycle travel stand in sharp contrast to the strict conformity the messenger faces when entering a building.

Culley, somewhat dramatically, writes of an elevator ride to make a pick-up: "I was in a steel box now, realizing that the world, like a projected film, runs across my neutral surface evenly. I was not in control here. I knew that. My heart gulped as it endeavored to know itself once again on this mythic descension into the modern world."[11] Of course, messengers, like all agents, are never free from structure. But the interconnection of agency and structure is an objective, theoretical point separate from subjective perception. Beyond the theorist's explanatory gaze, messengers feel that their actions remove them from structure. This was MAC's point, related in the previous chapter, about being free from social rules.

My field notes are filled with stories demonstrating the contrast between being inside and being outside (literally and figuratively). It should be noted that the sense in which I use the expressions "to be inside" and "to be outside" partially inverts their meaning in relation to subcultures. That is, to be outside buildings is to feel outside of social regulation, which means to be *inside* the subculture (and vice versa). This confusion is regrettable. Unfortunately, while the inside/outside distinction is an established one in the subcultural literature, the terms *inside* and *outside* (in their simple, literal definitions) perfectly capture the material and sensorial distinctions being made here. My field notes from June 23, 2002, illustrate this:

> I got frustrated several times today trying to find just where exactly I was allowed to enter the building. One guard made me turn around and walk a block around the building just so I could use the freight elevator (an elevator that was 10 feet away and in plain sight of where the guard was standing). To make matters worse, when the freight elevator arrived the elevator guy barked, "What do you want? Why don't you use the regular elevator?" I started to walk to the other elevator, only to have the guard start yelling at me again to go back to the freight elevator. The freight operator, in turn, looked at me as if the confusion was entirely my fault.

Five days earlier, though, I wrote about the exhilaration of being outside:

> When you catch a wave of traffic it is pretty awesome. All of a sudden you can just be flying through the city. You can cover serious distance in no time. I feel pretty safe in these situations, but, damn, there are so many things that could possibly go wrong. And at that speed it could get messy. Of course, that is half the reason it is thrilling. Your legs are just pumping as hard as possible, and your mind is racing, looking ahead for approaching dangers.

While urban cycling is, in itself, liminal, the other aspects of messenger work, especially entering buildings to make pick-ups and drop-offs, enhance this liminality. Messengers are continually thrust back and forth between feelings of freedom and conformity. In both situations, however, the messenger is still a stranger. She is someone who does not belong to either world. Just as bikes have a tenuous position on the road, landlords, business managers, and the employees they command are often unsure what to do with couriers in buildings (as the confusion over which elevator I should use underscores). Messengers are making deliveries, but they are not handling freight. They are part of the business day, but they are not businesspeople. In other words, other people, even those who regularly deal with messengers, do not know how to properly classify them. Perhaps inside, even more than outside, bike couriers are "*no longer* classified and *not yet* classified."[12]

The Semiotics of Messenger Style

Ultimately, messenger style must hold the "objective possibility" of portraying liminality.[13] Thus messenger style should be the style of a stranger, but not just any type of a stranger—a stranger with outlaw potential. Most importantly, styles should not be understood as accidental or circumstantial. Styles become styles (as opposed to individual particularities) because they "encapsulate a mood" that is understood to be objectively real.[14] At this point, the reality of the messenger subculture should be clear. Through a dialectical relationship with the urban environment, messengers generate flow that is collectively experienced in rituals producing affect-meaning. The question, then, is, how are these emplaced lived experiences encapsulated by messenger style? In the following sections I will analyze several aspects of messenger style: demeanor (acting rushed); argot (keywords); image (not wearing helmets, riding track bikes, and clothing *bricolage*). In each instance, the symbols of the courier lifestyle will be connected to liminality, which will be shown to be a specifically urban liminality utilized in the pursuit of flow on a bicycle.

Demeanor: Acting Rushed

As we have seen throughout this book, the outlaw image is most thoroughly cultivated in how messengers ride their bikes. A *Chicago Tribune* headline declared: "Pedestrians may swear at bicycle messengers, but companies swear by them."[15] As we now know, however, the way couriers ride cannot be reduced to their clients' timetables. Messengers commit their offenses because of the joy they find in pushing the edge. And messengers are not just fast on their bikes; they are fast off of them too. Whether pedaling or walking, couriers usually appear to be in a hurry. They are people with places to go, or so it seems.

As with riding, there is, most certainly, a practical component to a messenger hustling in and out of buildings. There are, after all, jobs that must be done. At the same time, couriers often hustle when they are not on a deadline. While there may be some vague flowlike elements to efficient building travel, no messenger, whether in casual conversation or in interviews, described his time inside a building as thrilling. If there is joy to be had in buildings, it comes from wanting a respite from the weather, or maybe socializing with other messengers or receptionists who might be inside. In these cases, joy comes from *not* being rushed. Most of the time, though, messengers appear to be in a hurry as they enter and exit buildings, and there is a symbolic component to being in a hurry. Rushing is what messengers idealize. This is what they are paid to do and what they play for. Acting rushed, therefore, sends a clear signal to all that one is doing "real" messenger work.

At the same time, rushing is more than a mere signal. That is, it does not simply indicate (correctly or falsely) that one is busy. Instead, it is deeply symbolic. In explaining why he wanted to be a bike messenger, Hultman stated: "I love bikes, and then there is that edgy element…of being a 'bad boy.' Having a reason to run lights, sort of. Having that kind of behavior justified a little bit. You can kind of be an asshole as you push your way through lobbies." Upon hearing this, Erik quickly interjected: "Elevator 'Close Door' button, I think that is very important." Erik's point was that as messengers, there is no social obligation to be polite by holding an elevator door for someone. In fact, just the opposite behavior applies: messengers should try to close the doors as fast as possible. Hultman added: "Close those things [i.e., elevator doors] as fast as you can. Growling at people, and then smiling as you turn around." In other words, to act rushed is about more than looking busy. Acting rushed separates messengers, in a specifically stylized way, from others, and messengers cherish this distinction. As a case in point, when Erik's girlfriend asked him the most important thing about being a messenger, he responded simply: "Hitting the 'Close Door' button on elevators."

Of course, businesspeople act rushed too. The symbolism of messengers acting rushed, however, does not come from simply walking fast, with eyes fixed in determination, or from frantically conveying information over a cell phone. Both couriers and office workers share these traits. The difference is that messengers embrace (indeed relish) an ethic of incivility. Further, in most cases a harried businessperson acts rushed by quickening her pace while still, more or less, attempting to display the comportment of a person under no serious duress. For the messenger, though, there are times when making mad dashes through lobbies and upstairs is not only necessary but also cool.

Messengers, therefore, place themselves outside normal conventions of civility, but they do it under the guise of performing their job. This is what Hultman means when he says that the behavior is justified (a little bit). As they push their way through lobbies, messengers exude a certain outlaw quality. They assert their autonomy over the convenience of others. Moreover, in buildings, messengers are strangers. They are individuals near and far—at the same time. That is, most other occupants of the city acknowledge the scripts messengers write: that couriers are rushing because of their job. This is especially true of those inside the buildings messengers usually service, even if they do not fully agree with some of the behaviors. In this sense, messengers are near. It is understood that "companies swear by them," so to speak. At the same time, the curtness to outright rudeness described by Erik and Hultman inevitably makes messengers seem far from others. Performing a job or not, messenger offenses can cause others to "swear at" the courier—which, as Hultman made clear, was his intention. He wanted to come off as a "bad boy."

Argot: Suits, Civilians, and Working

"I'm not sitting behind a desk": Messengers versus Businessmen

The symbolic value of acting rushed, which for messengers means portraying oneself as a stranger and a bit of an outlaw, is further illustrated by the term "suit." Suits are businesspeople. "Suit" is an obviously pejorative term. It reduces a person to an inanimate object. Further, this object is associated with a way of life couriers abhor. As Rick said of being a messenger, "I'm not sitting behind a desk being strangled." This is the quality-of-life issue described in chapter 2. That is, when couriers barge through lobbies and hit the "Close Door" button in elevators, they are being rude to a specific subclass of people—*business*people. It is assumed that these people, more than others, are jealous of the messenger's lifestyle. In being rude to businesspeople, the messenger emphasizes that he is, in fact, free in ways the office worker is not. This is why Hultman growls to their faces, but smiles when he turns around. In other words, being a bad boy is fun because one is being an outlaw while others are conforming to social norms. Further, suits are assumed to be especially resentful of the courier's freedom. Thus suits are blamed for encouraging enforcement of traffic laws and for supporting restrictive building policies. Being rude to businesspeople and referring to them as suits (although rarely in face-to-face interchanges) is thus equally an act of revenge. It takes back in subjective pride what is lost in objective power relations.

Of course, the meaning of the word "suit" is never articulated in this exact way. Suits are suits because they are "assholes" or "boring" or "stuck-up." Rick, a particularly aggressive messenger, for example, told a story of punching a man getting out of a cab. The man had not looked before opening his door, almost causing Rick to crash. In describing the incident, Rick explained: "He got out of the cab [Rick then pauses and sticks up his chin and motions toward his throat, adjusting an imaginary tie]. I got up in his face and sort of slapped him. 'Do you know what you just did?' He got out his cell phone to call the cops. Yeah, right. It's going to take at least five minutes for them to get there. I'll have dropped five packages by then. I hit him right in his face." Rick did not use the word "suit" in his tale, but the moral justification for his violence is evident in his gesture indicating the man was wearing a suit. That is as much as to say, the man was being a suit.

The crux of Rick's story is about the man's indifference, illustrated by the adjustment of his tie, to the injuries he might have inflicted on Rick. The term "suit," then, is the semantic complement to acting rushed. It emphasizes the difference between messengers and those they serve, and it delineates the appropriate target for messengers' behavior when they act rushed. It is useful to note that Rick told this story to a group of messengers relaxing after-hours. Thus it is a form of sentimental education: messengers bravely play the game of flow while suits are strangled behind their desks, or worse, endangering messengers through pompous indifference.

The outsider, of course, may observe a clear hypocrisy in the messenger's villainization of suits. Businesspeople act rushed, just like messengers, and businesspeople are assholes, just like messengers. Such ideological inconsistencies, however, are masked in everyday interactions of the social world and come to light only in the sort of etic analysis offered here. I have taken different stories, with different moral intentions, and told at different times and placed them side by side. Such inconsistencies can be found in any social world. As Victor Turner makes clear, symbols can be contradictory, and what people say about them can be inconsistent. It is the analyst's responsibility, however, to step back and attempt to make sense of them.[16]

"If I was a civilian": Messengers versus Outsiders

Messengers not only place a linguistic barrier between themselves and businesspeople. Couriers actually distinguish themselves from *all* other people. To go back to Steve's division of society, messengers, as outlaws, are separate from ordinary civilians. Steve explained: "A lot of people spit on you…which didn't bother me because as far as I was concerned I was part of a whole different culture."[17] Messengers regularly use the term "civilian" to distinguish others from themselves. As Lee, a former CLS rider who moved on to dispatch work, remarked, "People outside the community [are] referred to as civilians because there's that same camaraderie that cops [have]. You do something where you face adversity on a daily basis, and you have a tendency to stick together." Much of this adversity is defined in relation to messengers being strangers—that is, in messengers occupying an ambivalent place in society and willfully going against social conventions by being outlaws.

In describing the worst part of her job, for example, Cat pointed out: "Sometimes I don't like the way people treat me....I've had these encounters in elevators and on the streets. People yell at you, and they say things at you, and I think if I wasn't a messenger they wouldn't say those things to me. If I had a suit on...they wouldn't say things to me....I feel like people say things to me that they wouldn't say if I was a civilian." Of course, urban life, for all people, involves dealing with the anger, indifference, and rudeness of others. Cat, though, felt that being a messenger increased such treatment by others. This is a perfect example of how messengering is dirty work (see chapter 3). However, in denoting themselves as *not* civilians, messengers make it clear that their strangeness is not confined to the workday. It is not an identity that can be stripped off on the weekend. The treatment Cat received, or felt she received, is endemic to her self, and using the word "civilian" (like using the word "suit") is a form of sentimental education for all those who hear it. With their stories and words, therefore, messengers construct their subculture around being strangers—of a particular sort.

"I didn't work there": Work versus Ride

While the words "civilian" and "suit" educate messengers about themselves in relation to the rest of society, the words "ride" and "work" educate messengers about their life within the subculture. "Ride" and "work" are both used synonymously for "messenger work." A telling example of how these words are used occurred during my first weeks working as a messenger. Adam, the six-year veteran contemplating retirement introduced in chapter 4, and I were discussing his year-long stay in Los Angeles, and I did not understand the meaning applied to the terms:

JEFF: So did you ride in LA?
ADAM: No, I did not work in LA.

JEFF: Were you going to school in LA?
ADAM: No, I moved out there for a job in graphic design.
[later in the conversation]
JEFF: You didn't ride your bike when you were out there?
ADAM: Of course I did.

In this conversation Adam thought I was asking if he worked as a messenger in LA. Conversely, I was confused as to why he started talking about working in graphic design when I was talking about riding bikes. Later, when I attempted to ask Adam why he had not ridden his bike in LA, he was completely confused as to why I assumed he had not. Likewise, when I told New York messengers I lived in Boston for a year they would ask if I "worked" in Boston. I would get funny looks when I told them about my job at a community newspaper. Eventually I learned to tell people, "I lived in Boston for a year, but I did not work there." In such a statement it is understood that I had a job, but I had not worked as a bike messenger.

What does conflating riding with working tell us about messenger meaning? Among lifestyle messengers, we have seen how the spheres of work and leisure are highly integrated. Messengers spend their non-work hours in largely the same manner that they spend their work hours: speeding through the city on bikes. Since messengers spend a great deal of their leisure time riding, reducing work to "riding" is indicative of the messenger lifestyle colonizing the logic of work. In other words, messengers do not so much work as they simply ride their bikes, whether they are riding their bikes to a party or to make a delivery. Identifying the boundaries individuals construct between their occupational time and leisure time is crucial to understanding how identities are constructed. Thus messengers can be seen as constructing identities that conflate their work and leisure selves. By using "ride" and "work" synonymously, messengers demonstrate not only an integration of work and leisure, but also liminality. The rationalization of labor assumes the clear demarcation of work and leisure time, but, for the courier, riding for work and riding for fun all becomes just *riding*. Thus messengers define their activities outside of cultural classifications. They are no longer classified and not yet classified. In other words, they define themselves as strangers. This is why the poor treatment described by Cat strikes at the heart of her identity. She *is* a bike courier, and not a civilian.

Image: Helmets, Bikes, and Clothes

"I've learned a lot about how to ride": Not Wearing Helmets

We already know that messenger behavior cannot be explained by simple economic motives. Instead, messengering has been shown to be a game of flow, sometimes played at the edges of survival. The symbolic importance of risk (or, more accurately, the symbolic importance of risk management) is expressed in the refusal to wear a helmet. While many messengers do wear helmets, at least occasionally, the vast majority do not wear them consistently.

A conversation I overheard at the Warriors Fun Ride was indicative of how helmets are understood within the subculture. The wife of one of the race organizers was talking to someone about a competitor's girlfriend: "She wanted him to wear a helmet.... It is the one night he wants to hang out and have fun with his boys, and do you know how much shit he would get for that?" On another occasion, a well-respected veteran rode into Tompkins Square Park wearing a helmet. Another veteran courier loudly yelled, "Rookie!" The insult was a joke, but there was a meaning behind it.

Veteran couriers, it is assumed, do not need to wear helmets because they know how to handle themselves in traffic. Rookies, on the other hand, do not. For example, when Alex, the punk-rock Portlander, moved to New York he originally wore a helmet. In his first weeks as a courier he got into two serious accidents. One accident sent a pedestrian to the hospital. In the other accident, Alex collided with a car, and his bicycle was completely destroyed. The latter accident also broke his helmet in two. The helmet, by all counts, spared him from a serious head injury. Possibly, it even saved his life. After this second accident, though, Alex decided to *stop* wearing a helmet. When I questioned him about what I felt was rather strange logic Alex replied: "Yeah, but I've learned a lot about how to ride in New York since then."

There is no functional reason that messengers abstain from helmet use. Some messengers claim that helmets are too hot for the summer months. However, these couriers did not wear helmets in the winter. The general courier disdain for helmets is purely symbolic. Riding without a helmet conveys confidence, justified or not, in one's skills and experience. Further, such skills and experience implicitly involve knowledge of the environment. To ride without a helmet is to assert not only an ability

Figure 21. Portland messenger with large architectural rolls

to handle one's self, but an ability to deal with others. Specifically, it shows an ability to deal with the danger of cars.

At the same time, messengers readily admit the risks inherent in their job, and they candidly discuss the injuries and deaths of their friends and coworkers. Dan, for example, the seriously injured courier who stated that *all* riders will eventually have an accident, was ambivalent about helmets. This was true even in the days immediately following his injuries. He observed: "I don't like wearing a helmet. I understand there's a reason for it. In fact, if I'd been wearing my helmet a couple of weeks ago I would have been saved from a lot of these injuries. But I just don't like wearing a helmet. Call me stupid, whatever. I don't know....It's not a fashion thing. It just feels better to be not wearing a helmet. It's as simple as that." Or, in Rachel's words, "When I wear it, it gets in my way; it bothers me. I can't flip my sunglasses up. I can't wear the hat I want to wear. Which, I suppose, could be misconstrued as vanity, but...I don't feel that's why I don't wear a helmet. Truly, it's just an inconvenience to me, and the times that I wish I was wearing a helmet, it's too late."

On the surface, these quotes about helmets seem to indicate indifference, and when asked to discursively justify their behaviors, messengers
tend to waffle between acknowledging dangers and simply disregarding
them. To write off messenger ambivalence as indifference, however, is to
miss how helmets are symbolically rooted in practice. A comparison can
be made with motorcycle clubs; anthropologist Daniel Wolf notes: "The
outlaw considers their face-it-head-on-and-tough-it-out approach towards
danger and discomfort to be another line of demarcation between themselves and the citizen. . . . Bikers face their vulnerability with a cavalier attitude, a style they feel has a lot to do with the courage to face risks and
endure uncertainty."[18] In refusing to wear helmets, messengers assert
a face-it-head-on-and-tough-it-out image that differentiates themselves
from more timid cyclists, and civilians more generally. This is why the
rider at the Warriors Fun Ride would get shit for wearing a helmet and
why an otherwise respected veteran wearing one was called a rookie.

More importantly, for messengers, not wearing a helmet is a visual
representation of their "natural" fit with the urban environment. That
is, people require protection from elements beyond their control. For
example, a hiker packs a raincoat because he cannot prevent rain. A
construction worker wears a hard hat because she cannot be certain
something will not fall on her head. Conversely, messengers show their
control by shunning such protection. Whether any messenger actually
possesses this control is a totally separate issue. At the semiotic level,
messengers resolve the danger of urban cycling by simply removing their
helmets.

To not wear a helmet is to be at home with the liminality of cycling.
There are objectively agreed-upon dangers to riding in the city, but to
not wear a helmet is to render them subjectively irrelevant. As explained
in chapter 6, couriers' problem-oriented cycling strategically utilizes the
bicycle's liminal status. And they consider this method a safer way to ride.
Thus in being strangers who can successfully handle liminality messengers are justified, at least in their own minds, to ride helmetless.

In recent years I have noticed several prominent New York couriers, many who previously did not wear helmets, donning them. I see
the move as an effort to achieve greater legitimation of messengering
among the public. To wear a helmet is to reverse everything said in this
section. First, a helmet wearer is making it clear to outsiders that she
has thought about and cares about her personal safety. Second, a helmet wearer is indicating that her present environment *is* a threat to her

safety. Thus messengers wearing helmets draw attention to the dangers of their occupation, especially the attention of outsiders. This move by some within the messenger subculture, therefore, can be seen as an effort to make messengering less strange. It allows messengers to be taken as legitimate workers doing a dangerous but necessary job. In terms of stated ideologies, this is what messengers have always espoused. I think that the adaptation of helmet wearing comes from the realization, by a minority of publicly prominent New York couriers, that to make their stated ideology understood by nonmessengers, some aspects of courier style must also be changed.

"Rebels without brakes": Riding Track Bikes

In terms of risk management, messengers do more than push the edges of flow without helmets. Many are pushing the edge on bicycles without brakes. Messengers ride several types of bicycles. Road bikes and mountain bikes are the most common. Track bikes, however, are considered the archetypical machine. Messengers pride themselves on their track-bike riding skills. Not only does their work experience allow messengers to feel they possess talents hipsters lack; couriers also contrast their skills with those of elite track racers (i.e., professional-level cyclists competing on the velodrome in the sport for which track bikes were specifically designed).

Efren, for example, joked about track racers: "They don't know how to skid [i.e., control their speed by forcing the rear wheel to stop spinning]! They couldn't ride in traffic. They'd be scared!" Indeed, on a recreational ride in Athens, Georgia, I met a former track Olympian who said as much. Despite his ability to race on a velodrome at the highest levels of international competition, this man had ridden his track bike on the street just once. He explained that he found the experience far too dangerous to ever repeat. Conversely, Calvin, who worked on a fixed for nearly three decades, commented: "If anyone says anything to me about riding fixed they are just jealous because they can't do it." And, certainly, many people do not understand how riders can control fixies. As a man in an elevator asked me, "Are you one of those crazies who rides without brakes and gears?" Emphasizing the fears of outsiders, a group of messengers who regularly trained for alleycats in New York referred to themselves as Los Guerreros Sin Frenos—Rebels Without Brakes.

Figure 22. New York messenger showing the quintessential style of a courier on a track bike

The exoticism of riding fixed on city streets is quickly disappearing. While many people choose to ride with a brake, the mystery of the track bike has nearly dissolved within the larger social world of bicycling. However, this was not the case during the time of my fieldwork in New York.

In chapter 2 I listed several functional reasons messengers use track bikes. Jack Kugelmass, the anthropologist who conducted the first ethnography of bike messengers, argues that messengers adopt track bikes specifically because they are harder to ride.[19] While I believe that the practical advantages to a track bike are more relevant, there is a great deal of truth in Kugelmass's claim. For instance, several messengers and I occasionally rode our track bikes around Central Park before or after work. Central Park is one of the few places in Manhattan where a cyclist can ride *not* as an urban cyclist. In the warmer months, it is always crowded with bike riders doing laps for exercise. Many of these people are serious athletes with top-of-the-line racing machines. One day as we stopped to rest, Alex commented: "Man, we'd be so much faster if we had gears." The physics of such a claim, at least on relatively flat terrain, is questionable, but it is (correctly or not) considered true among most cyclists.

Alex, however, was not advocating that we trade in our fixies for multigeared machines. Quite the opposite, he was implying that we were working harder than the other cyclists in the park. Similarly, in places like Seattle and San Francisco, which are hilly and wet, there are numerous disadvantages to riding fixed. A Seattle messenger who rode a track bike told me: "This is a stupid city for riding fixed. It's a city with seven hills."

As with helmets, the messengers who chose to ride fixed display a face-it-head-on-and-tough-it-out image that clearly extends beyond rational concerns of income into the realm of subcultural meaning. And, as with refusing to wear helmets, choosing to ride fixed is an assertion of comfort and control within the liminality of city riding. That is to say, to ride the most minimalistic of cycling machines in arguably some of the most dangerous and technically challenging of conditions is to assert that one is undeniably confident in one's abilities. To ride a track bike is also to fully embrace the outlaw side of messengering, as the legality of track bikes on city streets is often questionable.[20]

Further, as with acting rushed, riding fixed is a near and far activity, to use Simmel's words again. While outsiders may understand the practical advantages of riding fixed, the choice to do so still seems more than a bit crazy. Track bikes, therefore, enhance the strangeness of messengers for outsiders, who often cannot understand why a messenger would choose to ride a brakeless bicycle. Indeed, as the quote from the Seattle messenger shows, even some track riders themselves appear perplexed by their own decisions. This is because the decision is a symbolically infused practice often at odds with the economic rationalizations messengers use to discursively justify their actions.

"I still don't look like a cyclist": Clothing *Bricolage*

In general terminology, clothes and style are synonymous. To speak of style is, more than anything, to speak of how one dresses. In analyzing how couriers choose to dress, the other aspects of messenger style—demeanor, argot, and image—come together. Moreover, just as with the rest of messenger style, messenger clothing is interconnected with messenger practice. As we will see, the *bricolage* of messenger clothing is codetermined by the actions of messengers in liminal space.[21] As noted at the beginning of this chapter, messenger style is distinctly urban—fusing hip-hop, skateboarder, and punk styles. What it is not is "cycling chic." That is, it is not the tight spandex shorts and bright polyester jerseys of professional competitive cyclists. While the business districts of New York are filled with couriers, one is hard pressed to find a messenger working in complete spandex cycling kits. Commuters and recreational riders may proudly ride in full cycling regalia, but the messenger look is something very different.

Messengers do wear cycling clothing. Cycling shoes, gloves, jerseys, and caps, for example, are frequently seen, but the use of these items is consciously (and cautiously) monitored. As a case in point, Jason admitted he originally wore cycling shorts to work because he was excited about being a bike messenger. Reflecting back, though, he shook his head, commenting: "I looked like a dork! You can't walk into a bar after work dressed in spandex." Many messengers do wear cycling shorts or cycling pants in the winter. These items, in addition to clinging to the rider's legs, have a padded chamois and special seam construction, all of which help to reduce chafing and saddle sores. The messengers who wear such clothes, however, usually wear regular, loose-fitting shorts or pants over them. This allows for the comfort of cycling shorts without looking like a cyclist. An interaction I had with Klaus provides a telling example. Stopping to talk at a messenger center, I commented on the frigidly cold weather. Dressed in baggy black Carhartt work pants and jacket, Klaus gave me some advice: "I don't really like cycling gear, but in the winter it is warm." He then pulled up his jacket to show a cycling windbreaker worn underneath. Klaus concluded by proudly stating that even though he wore cycling clothing, "I still don't look like a cyclist."

Implicit in Klaus's disclaimer is the belief that looking like a cyclist is bad. This point is equally illustrated by Justin. Justin, as noted earlier, dressed to ride his bike "professionally." He did own standard cycling clothing, and he would wear it when doing road rides on the weekend. Dressing as a professional messenger, however, meant not dressing like a professional cyclist. Like Klaus, Justin covered his cycling clothing when working.

The messenger's disdain for standard cycling gear was driven home by a group of couriers socializing after work. While drinking beer, one messenger casually flipped through a cycling mail-order catalog. Pondering the images of models posed in their cycling kits, he asked the

Figure 23. San Francisco messengers socializing between jobs

group: "Why don't they have pictures of [the models] on bikes, because that is what you do when you wear those clothes." To this, another messenger retorted: "No, they don't. They're in a coffee shop…online." Everyone laughed. The original messenger then said mockingly: "Look at me! I'm hella rich." While they couched their humor in class terms—people that can afford to look like they ride versus people that actually ride—the two men making the jokes rode very expensive machines built with high-end components. These messengers were not opposed to spending money on cycling but followed a specific stylistic code for how that money was spent. Small displays of cycling paraphernalia, like cycling shoes and cycling caps, denote an acceptable appreciation of bicycling. An overt display, such a full cycling kit, is considered detrimentally silly.

While street clothes are far more common among messengers than cycling gear, many of these items have been modified. Like Jason, Dan looked back on his rookie days as a time of stylistic naïveté. Dan's transgression, however, was not in looking too much like a cyclist, but in looking too much like a civilian: "I walked into that job, and I got a really good deal [i.e., making a good commission at a good company], and I remember the first day I started, I was really green. I think back on it, I think I was wearing the stuff that I had. It wasn't very functional, and to a certain extent it wasn't very 'happening,' if you will. I looked kind of stupid." Dan was wearing the clothes he usually wore, but, in hindsight, his clothing choices appeared foolish—foolish precisely because bike messenger style is urban, but it is not a mirror reflection of other street styles. Clothing is modified for functionality, and this functionality then becomes symbolic ("happening," in Dan's words) of the messenger lifestyle more generally.

One example of how civilian clothes are modified to make them both functional and happening is the cutting or rolling of pants just above the ankles. Even if all that was required would be to roll down one's pant leg, I rarely saw messengers do this—even if they would not be riding their bikes for hours. Of course, as we have seen, wearing messenger clothes when one is not working is perhaps the best indicator of the lifestyle messenger. In addition to rolling up their pants, bike messengers often have patches sewn onto the seat of their pants. The number of hours a messenger spends riding causes incredible wear on the rear section of pants. To prolong the life of their clothes, many couriers reinforce the thinning fabric with patches. Two of the messengers I met, Alex and William, were actually very skilled tailors. Alex had constructed his own messenger bags, and William participated in sewing circles held by a group in Tompkins Square Park. While both Alex's and William's patches were expertly sewn, an intentional effort was made to draw attention to the alterations. Alex had sewn large star patterns to the seat of his pants, and William used bright, contrasting colors to reinforce several pairs of his army surplus shorts. Likewise, Andreas used neon green fabric to mend his dark blue jeans.

At the surface level, messengers use patches to denote their work experiences. Patches signal that a rider has had enough time on the road to have worn out his pants.[22] As they do with rolled and cut pants, many messengers wear their patched pants when they are not riding bicycles. Ian, the owner of Dragonfly, for instance, wore his patched pants when going out to drum up new clients. On these ventures, he claimed he made a conscious effort to look presentable by civilian standards. His collared shirts and sweaters, however, were entirely offset whenever he turned around by the black patches sewn onto the rear of his light blue jeans.

Overall, the *bricolage* of messenger clothing is about more than pure functionality or the mere signaling of experience. Courier clothing, more than anything, is a symbolic representation of the liminality of messenger work. To elaborate on this: in usual terminology a suit is work clothing, and spandex is leisure clothing. Messenger clothing, however, is a style that is neither purely work nor purely leisure. Instead, it serves both functions simultaneously. In this sense, it represents the integration of the courier lifestyle. Further, as we have seen, couriers (like Simmel's strangers) are considered, by themselves and by others, as inside and outside society. Courier fashion, therefore, is not only about integration; it is also about ambivalence.

Cycling apparel is within; it denotes competence. Cycling caps or cycling shoes, for instance, conjure the images of dedicated professional cyclists. Conversely, patched and cut-off pants negate such a clear image. They are from without. These symbols denote an imperfect fit: fabric that has fallen apart too soon and inseams that were designed too long. Of course, I am not arguing that patches, cut-off pants, or other forms of clothing modification are inherently outside of mainstream fashion. Rips, tears, and patches often adorn haute couture. I am arguing, however, that all styles offer themselves to be read. The modifications messengers make to their clothes, when juxtaposed with cycling apparel, provide a reading that cannot be subsumed under the simple rubric of hip-hop, punk, or skater fashion. Therefore, we can understand messengers as *bricoleurs*.

Messengers could just dress as cyclists (as a few do). Or messengers could just dress in ragged street wear (as some do). For lifestyle messengers, however, neither style accurately speaks to the subculture. Thus they have introduced "noise" into the system.[23] They are neither ordinary citizens occupying the city nor recreational cyclists aping the style of professional racers. They are something in-between and, at the same time, something totally different. Within the messenger subculture's stylistic displays, therefore, we see a novel assembly of symbols that require a unique reading, and this reading comes from practice. It comes from using a bicycle to flow in the urban grid.

Sociologists have long cataloged the various styles of the people they study. Unfortunately, researchers rarely link symbols to the practices of the social worlds they are studying. By combining a semiotic analysis with a theory of practice, messenger style can be understood as the symbolic dimension to the affective appropriation of space. In other words, there is a homology to messenger style. The demeanor, argot, and image of the subculture all express a liminal strangeness. It is important to stress that this homology does not arise from a static structural position. An analysis of messenger style is not simply about decoding systems of sign relations. Instead, messenger style comes from the lived experiences of individuals, enabled and constrained by their environment. It is a style derived from the game of flow realized through the bicycle's liminal position in the city. The lure is found in practices, but the practices, in turn, are semiotically expressed by subcultural style.

What we as sociologists gain in this analysis is a fuller understanding of agency and structure. In chapter 6 emotional practices were connected to physical space, allowing us to see how lived experiences are dialectically related to the structures in which they occur. Likewise, in this chapter, style was connected to the same dialectic between emotional practices (i.e., agency) and structure. Thus a practice-based semiotics helps explain the lure of delivering packages. Actions, specifically the flow of urban cycling, are part of a larger cosmology. They are a set of meaningful styles reflected in and reflecting emotionally significant practices. Understanding the homology between messenger practice and messenger style helps illuminate this duality.[24]

In the argument I am making about messengers, style informs. It is sentimental education. At the same time, the subculture is not, in the final analysis, reductive to its semiotic dimension. The affect-meaning of messengers is, more than anything, a *lived* reality. In the conclusion, we will move from the semiotic realm back to the materiality of practice to show the potential political significance of the lived experience of messengers.

CONCLUSION
The Politics of Appropriation

This book has addressed the question, "What's the lure of delivering packages?" On the surface this question is pretty simple to answer. Messengering work is, as Fannin put it, "the biggest non-job I've ever had"; or, as Jordan described it, "the most fun job I will *ever have in my life,* without a doubt." Such replies, however, do little more than fashion the question into a statement.

Emotions, Space, and Cultural Analysis: A Recap

What I have attempted to do throughout this book, is answer the question of "the lure of delivering packages" from a sociological perspective. I have explained why messengers have such affective ties to their job, and why they participate in a subculture based on the occupation. To do this I have combined two often-divergent strands of social theory: emotions and space. Emotions and space combine through lived experience in a process of affective spatial appropriation. Because of the affective appropriation of space, messengers relish a job that is dirty, exceedingly dangerous, low paying, stigmatized, and strenuous. When viewed from afar, it appears to be anything but satisfying, yet messengers make it so. For the lifestyle messenger the job is the foundation for authentic identity.

Affect-Meaning

The affective appropriation of space starts with emotions. Put simply, dodging cars and pedestrians while attempting to chart the most efficient course through the city is anything but boring. It is mental and physical labor performed in a highly unpredictable environment. As Kelsey explained in chapter 4, "[Messengering] uses every skill I have on the bike and uses them all. It takes everything I can do to make it all happen, and make it happen quickly and smoothly." When Kelsey says that messengering takes everything he has he means that he is engrossed by messenger work. Instead of clockwatching, a primary indicator of alienation, Kelsey is totally submerged in his labor. Such dedication, though, is not exhausting. It is invigorating. As Stanley Aronowitz notes, "In creative work as well as genuine play exhaustion is not deadening. The activity, like deep sexual pleasure, enlivens the senses and elevates the person."[1] Mihaly Csikszentmihalyi calls this elevation flow. Flow's creative, spontaneous action is an optimal experience, and it is intrinsically enjoyable. To be in a state of flow is to be in a state of play. And, as we saw in chapter 4, delivering packages is a game that bike couriers play throughout the day.

Messengering, however, is more than a game of delivery. Beyond making the labor process a game, messengers also make a game *of* the labor process. That is to say, outside of work, couriers take part in competitions that replicate certain aspects of their job, as we saw in chapter 5. As Jordan observed, "An alleycat boils down your job, like the game aspect of your job, and it is fun to be good at a game." Specifically, alleycats remove all of the tedious requirements of the job, like waiting on clients and riding in elevators, and leave only the outer extremes of flowing through urban traffic. This turns flow into edgework. Further, the ritual of alleycats prioritizes the excitement and thrills of urban cycling in what Clifford Geertz refers to as models *of* and models *for* reality. Most importantly, alleycats function as Durkheimian rituals. That is, alleycats generate collective effervescence attaching couriers to their subculture.

Taken together, the flow of messenger labor and its consecration in the ritual of racing go a long way toward explain the lure of delivering packages. Emotions appear to arise from our innermost being. More importantly, the emotional engrossment of delivering packages is not only lived through an individual's subjective experience. Alleycats collectivize the emotions generated in urban cycling. In doing so, the ritual of racing imbues the optimal experience of flow with affect-meaning. With affect-meaning, lived experience feels objectively real. This is what Geertz calls the "really real," and it is the theoretical underpinning of Durkheim's study of society. With the generation of affect-meaning, delivering packages can be profoundly alluring—so alluring that messengers base their lifestyle around it. To be succinct, affect-meaning is the foundation for the subculture.

Spatial Appropriation

While affect-meaning explains *why* there is a lure in delivering packages, it does not explain *how*. To address this issue our analysis turned from emotions to space. The physical contours of the material world have long been the sole province of geography, a domain few sociologists have shown an interest in entering. Space, however, is an integral aspect of the social world. This point is one of the major, but often overlooked, contributions of Anthony Giddens's theory of structuration. Physical structures, like all other structures, constrain and enable action. In chapter 6, we explored the importance of the material world for the lived experience of messengers. Cat captured its importance in describing riding her bike downtown as compared to other parts of Seattle: "I think downtown riding is different than any riding almost anywhere else in the city....I'm much more aggressive, but it's because I'm downtown." For Justin, what makes urban cycling *urban* is attending to "the rhythm and flow of the city." All of which is to say that messengering is a specifically urban phenomenon, and, in order to understand couriers, sociologists must not lose sight of the fact that their subculture is emplaced.

Through practices like what Nick called "the human shield," messengers often counterintuitively use the rules and resources of the city (in Giddens's sense of the terms) to produce the flow of urban cycling. Moreover, cyclists are able to creatively manipulate their way through the city because of the liminal position bicycles occupy within the urban infrastructure. Unlike automobile drivers who have the road or pedestrians who have the sidewalk, cyclists exist betwixt and between. This is a status at once liberating and limiting. It is limiting because it is dangerous and because it is often unclear what legal rights a cyclist has. It is also liberating because with no official place in which she belongs, the cyclist is free to maneuver where she can fit. Josh, for example, described this experience as "water falling over rocks in a stream...the path of least resistance." In this way, messengers appropriate the space of the city. Like skateboarders, messengers use the material structures of the urban environment and the rules governing their use for their own purposes. In doing so, they transform urban space into a site of play.

In the final analysis, what the affective appropriation of space shows us is how the physical world is of major consequence for social research. The messenger subculture can be realized only within dense city traffic. It is there, and only there, that messengers can generate the affect-meaning of urban cycling. Space and the ways in which social agents use this space, therefore, are not tangential to the process. To the contrary, couriers actively engage with the environment by appropriating it for their own ends. Borrowing from Henri Lefebvre, messengers *live* through space, and they do so affectively. That is, emotions and space are lived together. We saw the subcultural relevance of affective spatial appropriation in the analysis of messenger style in chapter 7. Combining the concepts of Victor Turner and Georg Simmel, we identified a liminal strangeness in messenger style. Couriers act rushed, *bricolage* clothes, conflate working and riding, shun helmets, ride brakeless bikes, and trash-talk "suits." To adequately understand the meaning of messenger style requires more than a semiotic decoding. Instead the cultural analyst must step beyond the purely discursive realm. The symbols couriers wield are inexorably linked to the emotionally charged and spatially situated practices that sustain them. Messenger practice and messenger style form a homology that is derived from messengers' unique manipulations of their *spatial* position as they flow through the urban grid.

Closure and Aperture

In chapter 7 we saw the cultural significance of affective spatial appropriation, and in many ways, the discussion there represents the theoretical conclusion to my sociological argument. Here, I want to bring up a separate matter. Instead of culture, I want to discuss politics. Or, more accurately, I want to use culture to analyze politics. To be perfectly clear, however, my primary academic goal with this work is to improve the theoretical tools for understanding culture, and I have attempted to achieve this through the incorporation of emotions and space in the analysis of an urban subculture.

These things said, sociology is a discipline that should not (and, for that matter, cannot) be separated from the political. In these final pages, therefore, I want to work through the political implications and possibilities of a cultural analysis incorporating emotions and space. To do this, we need to ask not only why the bike messenger subculture exists and how it exists, but also whether it *should* exist. I want to show that considering the affective appropriation of space can do more than improve cultural analysis. It can also help us understand the conditions of human liberty, and, in this sense, the study of bike messengers becomes a study of the politics of everyday life.

Politics of the Allure

Concurrent with messengering's allure is the occupation's danger, and hidden beneath the mystique of the subculture is a job with many hardships and minimal economic return. Beyond the questions of why and how, therefore, is the question of should. Should companies be allowed to continue profiting off the backs of messengers without giving more in return? Should couriers so willingly consent to this exchange? Well over a decade ago the Teamsters tried to unionize the New York City bike courier industry. The initiative failed. At the time, an article in the *New York Times* referred to the occupation as "the sweatshop of the streets." In the article a bike courier asks rhetorically: "How can messengers be happy?"[2] In chapter 4, Cat confided that her nonmessenger friends did not understand her attraction to the job. As she put it succinctly, "they don't get it." As messengering is a hazardous and strenuous job performed for little pay and no benefits, perhaps there is little to get. Or worse, perhaps it is messengers who really don't get it.

Manufacturing Consent

Michael Burawoy's labor process as a game is an attempt to explain why some workers "don't get it." Conducting ethnographic research among piece-rate machinists at a factory he called Allied Corporation, Burawoy asks: "Why do workers work as hard as they do?"[3] An unabashed Marxist, he thinks the working class should be fighting for a systematic redistribution of wealth—for control of the means of production. Yet the working class in the United States has failed to live up to its revolutionary potential. In fact, Allied's machinists voluntarily work harder than necessary.

Importantly, Burawoy does not assume that an individual's dedication to his or her work arises inherently from an ideological agreement with the owner's wishes. In other words, individuals do not conceptualize their relationship to the labor process based on what is promoted by management, taught in classrooms, preached from pulpits, or printed in newspapers. Likewise, individuals do not inherently identify with the ideologies of labor organizers either. Company newsletters, schools, churches, and media outlets may profess the ideologies of the owning class, and union leaders may espouse their antithesis. But the daily practices of individuals do not simply mirror ideological content, regardless of what that content may be. That is to say, discursive ideology alone cannot explain worker motivation.[4]

Ultimately, Burawoy argues that worker motivation can be explained only by looking at the actual process of production. Specifically, the workers at Allied play a game of making out. In this game they produce more than the minimum output required for a specific job and thus earn a higher rate for the parts produced. Playing the game results in pride and prestige and also alleviates boredom. In a word, it makes the workday fun or at least bearable. At the same time, playing the game means the machinists work harder. In Marxist terms, they provide more surplus labor, and in providing more surplus labor they generate greater surplus value (i.e., higher profits for the owners). Not surprisingly, Burawoy is highly critical of labor being constituted as a game. Beyond whatever economic, mental, or social rewards the game offers Allied's employees, the ultimate beneficiaries are the managers and owners. They are the ones truly profiting from the workers' added effort.

This is not to say that, as a worker, Burawoy did not take part in the game. He did, and he readily acknowledges enjoying its challenges and rewards. As a Marxist, though, he views such games as a particularly insidious aspect of the overall perpetuation of capitalism. Specifically, at the same time that the game adds to surplus labor, it further obscures that surplus labor by making the rules of the game appear natural and inevitable. That is, through the daily practices of the shop floor, the game is not only played but also thoroughly consented to. The rules of the game are an ideology *lived* in practice, and those rules benefit capital at the expense of labor. Specifically, they involve hard work and submission to the task at hand.[5]

Burawoy does not deny that various aspects of the game contradict the regulations management passes down. For example, workers set upper limits on how much they will produce when playing the game. Specifically, workers conspire to ensure output never exceeds 140 percent of the company's set minimum. The machinists know that if they play the game too well, management will raise the minimum. However, for Burawoy, the necessity of such covert tactics on the part of workers only further obscures the game's true function of greater exploitation. In other words, workers consent to the game because it appears to be in their interest. That is, it is fun, and they are paid at a higher rate, and the more the game contradicts managerial edicts, the more the game appears to be under worker control. But, borrowing from critical theorist Herbert Marcuse, Burawoy claims that enjoying the game is nothing but repressive satisfaction.[6] It is a satisfaction coming from choices made within the strict limits of a system over which the individual has only minimal control. That is, Allied's machinists gain satisfaction from the game only by first consenting to a system in which their survival requires laboring for another's profit. The game, by obscuring the workers' position within the system, therefore, reifies capital at the same time that it reproduces it.

Pedaling Consent

There is one glaring difference between the machinists Burawoy studied and bike messengers. Unlike the employees at Allied, most piece-rate messengers have no base rate. Going into the day, Allied's workers know that they will at least earn a predetermined minimum. The goal, of course, is to beat this rate. Few commission riders have such a guarantee. Their employment ensures them nothing but the right to *potentially* make a living. In Burawoy's analysis, "Participation in the game is predicated on two limits of uncertainty in outcomes: on the one side, workers have to be guaranteed a minimum acceptable wage and, on the other side, management has to be assured of a minimum level of profit."[7] Commission riders forgo the first limit on uncertainty and thus nullify management's need for the second. If Burawoy found the game of making out disheartening at Allied, one can only assume he would find the game of delivery horrifyingly egregious. And that is why, of course, there is an argument to be made that couriers work in a sweatshop on wheels. Moreover, the behaviors of hourly riders are even more outrageous.

These workers consent to a game in which they are given no material rewards for playing.

As applied to messengers, Burawoy's argument appears to be drastically understated. For Burawoy, the practices of the shop floor produce an adherence to capitalist ideology. This ideology, however, is situational. It exists within the factory; workers do not carry it home with them or vice versa. Bike couriers, as we have seen, do bring their work home. As Kelsey remarked in chapter 5, "It's what you do for a living, but it's not *just* what you do for a living. It becomes way more than that." In the messenger subculture, the manufacturing—or, more accurately, the pedaling—of consent spins beyond the workday into the realm of leisure, and then returns intensified.

As a case in point, CLS hired both bike messengers and walking messengers. Its bike messengers performed on-demand deliveries while its walkers performed route deliveries. Walkers followed a daily pick-up and drop-off schedule, much like that of the U.S. Postal Service. Several years ago CLS raised the starting wage for its walkers, but not its riders. Undeniably, bike messengers must physically exert themselves more than the walkers. On-demand delivery, because of the macro- and micro-routing skills required, also involves a much higher degree of mental operation. And, obviously, bikers incur *far* more risk throughout the day. The reason for the walkers' raise was simple economics. CLS needed walkers and was having trouble filling positions. CLS also needed riders, but it never had trouble finding them. This discrepancy, of course, is caused by the game of delivery. Bikers play a game that walkers, moving slower and following fixed routes, cannot.

When asked, CLS's messengers always insisted they should be paid more than the walkers. It is a claim that holds much merit. The potential joys found in playing the game, however, along with the mystique of the subculture that glorifies it, enabled management to comparatively reduce the riders' wages. In Burawoy's analysis, the game can result in lost earnings only if it is played too ambitiously. Workers must conceal their actual proficiencies or else management will change the numbers required for making out. The issue at CLS, however, was different. Seattle, along with many other smaller messenger markets, simply had more people willing to be bike messengers than there were slots to fill. This, however, was not simply the result of an overall depressed labor market. To the contrary, would-be bike couriers at CLS were turning down better-paying and easier jobs as walkers.

It is worth noting here that walking messengers at CLS had roughly the same freedoms from managerial oversight as the bikers. In some cases they may have had more. One walker, for example, claimed he had enough time in between his morning and afternoon routes to spend several hours at home in the middle of each day. Also, like bike messengers, walkers did not have a dress code. Regardless, many people preferred to be bikers. The job was tougher and paid less, but they still wanted it. In fact, they wanted it *because* it was harder. It offered the chance to have flow at work, and they would take a pay cut to have that.

Oppression and Liberty

Burawoy's Marxist critique of the game clearly holds merit, especially for those of us interested in promoting more equitable forms of social organization. To the extent that workers willfully consent to (or even enjoy) laboring under harsh conditions, the most cutthroat aspects of capitalism go unchallenged. Further, Burawoy's analysis of how such consent is produced through lived experience makes his book a modern classic, both in terms of ethnography and social theory. At the same time, I want to propose that his analysis, illuminating in so many crucial ways, is blinded to the full implications of lived experience by a dogmatic concern with the extraction of surplus labor. For Burawoy, the principal crime of capitalism—the grand chains with which it has shackled humanity—is the extraction of surplus labor. Until the day that workers, organized as a class for themselves, no longer consent to surplus labor, humanity cannot be free. This may be true, but it by no means follows that with an end to surplus labor humanity is free.

Exploitation and Power

Oppression is not only about extracting and controlling surplus labor. It is about power more generally. Power is having the ability to act otherwise in a given situation.[8] To lack power (i.e., to be oppressed) is to lack that option. For example, professors have more power than students within the lecture hall. Professors decide what materials will be covered and, on a whim, may end class early or modify sections of the course with no negative repercussions. At the same time, power is always multidirectional. Only by complete physical containment does a person truly lose the capacity for action (e.g., being bound in a straitjacket or having a gun literally pointed at your head). As Giddens points out, "in all other cases—that is, in all cases in which human agency is exercised within a relationship of any kind—power relations are two ways."[9]

Returning to the college example, students are by no means powerless within the lecture hall. As most professors readily concede, many students are experts in subterfuge. From checking e-mails and passing notes during class to cheating on exams, students have numerous methods for acting otherwise. And to these more subtle practices can be added the option of forthright rebellion or complete withdrawal from the course. In other words, regardless of the drastic power imbalance, students are far from powerless, and this is true no matter how authoritarian or bullheaded a professor may attempt to be.

This brings us to the issue of exploitation. Exploitation can be positioned as the systematic organization of power relationships in a manner contrary to an individual or group's own interests for the benefits of another individual or group. In other words, not all inequalities of power result in exploitation. In the case of college, students are certainly subjected to an organized set of power relationships. However, it would be difficult to argue that college students are uniformly exploited, because the power relationships are not clearly contrary to their interests (although tuition increases and campus police policies may potentially be characterized in that way). A similar point could be made about the power difference between parents and their children; it is only under very extreme circumstances that the charge of exploitation is leveled against parents.

Burawoy sees the game as exploitative because producing surplus labor is against the workers' interests.[10] While Burawoy admits the game offers "a critical freedom" to Allied's workers, he believes its value is negated by the workers' consent to harder labor.[11] Conversely, I want to assert that regardless of management's agreement with most aspects of the game, workers are still exercising their own control over the workday. That is, workers have power in playing the game.

What Burawoy misses in his focus on surplus labor is the multidirectional aspect of power. He depicts workers as more or less powerless because they collude with management. Power is assumed to be nonexistent if workers do not directly struggle against the financial interests of management. Burawoy is correct to conceive of the piece-rate system as a managerial strategy intended to increase profits. What he fails to see is the dialectical nature of power. Coexisting with strategies, therefore, are what Michel de Certeau calls tactics. Tactics are "the ingenious ways in which the weak make use of the strong."[12] Thus a consideration of exploitation is only part of any serious attempt to understand oppression. We must also consider power as an individual process of events-in-the-world. When one thinks in terms of power, the game cannot increase oppression but only reduce it, because workers are able to exercise agency over their labor.

Alienation

In making such a claim about power we enter the long debate over the relative importance of Karl Marx's early work and his later writings. In his later writings Marx focuses on how surplus is allocated within society. Specifically, workers must gain control over the means of production. This will allow the productive powers of society to be geared toward collective, rather than private, gains. In his earlier writing, Marx focuses on the concept of alienation. Here the emphasis is less on the means of production and more on the *practices* of production. For Marx, humans are inherently productive. That is, human life requires conscious, creative activity. From cooking foraged food over a fire to fabricating high-tech widgets on the assembly line, people are in a nearly continual state of producing. Such creation is our very "species-being."[13] Alienation arises from an inability to see one's productive potential. The alienated individual feels stripped of her agency. In this state there is no joy, only frustration and boredom.

For Marx, selling one's labor for an hourly wage supersedes an individual's ability to see their creative process in acting on the world. Wage labor is alienated labor that deadens us in exhaustion because we feel motivated only from outside. Play, as noted in chapter 4, is the antithesis of alienation. In play the individual connects her actions to events-in-the-world. A player, in other words, understands her agency. Games are about asserting one's power in a situation (e.g., being able to hit a baseball or knowing the answer to a trivia question). Thus, in creative, playful labor, we feel invigorated because our actions are connected to our own volitions.

Therefore, we must understand exploitation as only one component within a larger classification of oppression. Power relationships can be systematically organized against an individual's interests, but at the same time, that individual may still have the ability to exercise agency. This is the critical freedom described by Burawoy. Unfortunately, he does not acknowledge just how critical it is. Indeed, what is the value of one's labor if it alienates rather than satisfies? Is an equitable share of the surplus adequate compensation for an entire work-life defined by drudgery? Certainly, workers deserve greater access to the surplus of society, but the realities of actually existing socialist societies clearly indicate that beyond capitalist exploitation is the oppression of monotonous, boring labor in itself. In this regard Certeau's tactics are of no small consequence. *Tactics empower.* They give creative control back to the individual in a plethora of ways, and this power is an integral component of human liberty.

The Message of Liberty

There is no denying that messengers are exploited. At the same time, messengers are not alienated.[14] To the contrary, their labor—as physically strenuous as it may be—is invigorating. Macro- and micro-routing, as a series of tactics, give messengers creative control of the labor process. In this sense, messengering is anything but oppressive. At the same time, of course, the discussion of oppression does not end with the acknowledgment that some workers may find enjoyment in their labor. After all, Burawoy would simply label this repressive satisfaction. The real liberty of messenger work comes not from affect in isolation, but from its connection to flow in the urban grid. It is in its *materiality*, therefore, that the affective appropriation of space achieves its biggest coup against oppression.

Capitalist cities are predicated on commerce. They function as control nodes for global, national, and regional economies.[15] Whatever else a city might be, it is first and foremost a space of strategy. The urban environment is planned and developed in a manner intended to facilitate the accumulation of surplus. In Henri Lefebvre's terms, cities are increasingly the province of abstract space. In abstraction the potential uses of space are reduced, leaving only the planner's conceptions. That is, business districts are places for business, shopping districts places for shopping, and residential areas places to reside. Most importantly, every place is planned to optimize profit. The contingencies and possibilities of urban life are thus negated: "Within this space, and on the subject of this space, everything is openly declared: everything is said or written. Save for the fact that there is very little to be said—and even less to be 'lived,' for lived experience is crushed, vanquished by what is 'conceived of.'"[16] In other words, abstract space is about alienation, not just the alienation of labor, but an alienation from the material world.

The alienation of abstract space is counteracted through spatial appropriation. That is, just as games illuminate the power of the player's actions, spatial appropriation illuminates the individual's power in the physical constitution of the world. In what Certeau calls "an ensemble of possibilities" (or what I call macro- and micro-routing), couriers take control of their relationship to the material environment.[17] This control is a political counterpart to the messenger's problem-oriented cycling. Instead of taking the rules and resources of the city as a set of forces restraining one's options (e.g., stopping at red lights or giving pedestrians the right of way), messengers are *enabled* by the opportunities the rules and resources provide.

Again, none of this is to deny that couriers supply surplus labor. Nor is this to claim bike messengers do not have legitimate grievances about the conditions under which their labor is produced. They most certainly do on both counts. The problem is that most efforts at labor reform threaten to *disempower* couriers and realienate the workday. That is, working to improve the safety of the messenger threatens to increase her alienation by circumscribing essential elements of the game. To clarify, danger itself is not the most essential part of the game (although it is required for the extremes of edgework), but systematically reducing danger in the occupation would inevitably result in a reduction, if not the elimination, of the game. Riders would need to be subject to greater regulations, and conditions of the labor would need to be standardized to whatever extent possible. In other words, companies, or a riders' union, would need to actively suppress riders' tactics and impose a set of officially sanctioned strategies.

One example of this conundrum is insurance. Medical insurance could insulate messengers from some of the financial dangers that accompany their work. The problem, however, is that insurance companies will not underwrite individuals in such an injury-prone occupation without extremely high premiums and/or a guarantee that the riders they are insuring will not be injury-prone. In general, there are three basic insurance models for the occupation: (1) the messenger company simply does not cover its riders (this is the option most small companies choose, as few small companies can afford to pay insurance premiums); (2) the messenger company formally covers its riders but in practice seeks to limit claims for injuries (this was the option chosen by Sprint

Courier; claims are limited by blacklisting or firing workers who report injuries); (3) the messenger company truly covers its riders (CLS provided this coverage; at the same time, and not surprisingly, it also actively sought to monitor and regulate, to at least some degree, its riders' behaviors; for that reason many Seattle messengers viewed CLS negatively: the job involved a lot of "hand holding," as more than one messenger described it).

In chapter 1, we noted that the affective appropriation of space challenged purely cognitive and aspatial notions of liberty. Following the preceding discussion of alienation, the reasons for this should be coming into focus. Bike messenger labor can sound atrocious because, as liberal, reform-minded individuals, we want workers to be free from the dangers and hardships messengers face. To be sure, the steps taken to move beyond the horrors of an unregulated market are a measure of a nation's progress. In contrast to the early days of industrialism, Western societies today have made workplaces safer and limited the number of hours individuals labor each day. Such unpleasantness has been shipped overseas or else has been hidden from government regulators. On the other hand, labor itself has not necessarily become any less alienating. If anything, many have argued alienation has increased.[18] This is clear in the pejorative sense in which the word "work" is often used. Work is what people call the activities they do not want to do. It is what they must endure to achieve something else. Despite all the promises offered by reformers, there is a limit to the correlation between safer and easier labor and happier laborers.

In messengering we see labor that is not alienating. But the price is greater danger and hardship. Too often, especially in low-end service jobs, we discuss the qualities of an occupation simply in terms of its simplicity. We make comments like "It's easy money." Such statements underscore just how alienating we expect our work to be. We have increasingly given up hope of finding much satisfaction in work. So we cherish its simplicity. By contrast, we do not play games because they are easy; we play them to be challenged. Similarly, the satisfaction an individual gets from messengering is not liberation from the exigencies of his labor. It is most certainly not easy money. Messengering does not offer liberation from physical exertion or risk. Instead, it is liberation to act creatively. Throughout the workday, messengers have myriad chances to act otherwise. They have control over their production. Most importantly, by looking at the material environment, we can see the challenges of macro- and micro-routing as countering the alienation of the material world. In their appropriation of space, couriers (monetarily) open new possibilities in the abstraction of the city.[19]

Thankfully, the reduction of alienation does not have to be accompanied by greater exploitation. In contrast to traditional attempts at labor reform, which require greater regulation of workers, some messengers have come up with alternative ways to improve their position as workers. The messengers I am referring to seek to limit or eliminate their production of surplus labor without realienating the workday. They do this by forming collectives. These messengers share in the administrative duties of the operation and divide the profits. This is possible because the messenger industry lends itself to small companies operating with very little overhead cost.

Unfortunately, collectives are a far more viable option for bike messengers than they are for machinists, who would have to pool millions of dollars to start their own factory. Further, increasing government regulation of the messenger industry and the industry's consequent reforms raise the cost of doing business. Smaller companies are squeezed out, and it becomes increasingly difficult for collectives to operate legally. Of course, the quandary here is that, generally speaking, government regulations are an essential measure to protect workers. In the case of messengers, however, regulations threaten to kill with kindness everything riders cherish about their job.

Putting It in Perspective

The liberation offered by messengering, in many respects, is exceedingly small. Our discussion of alienation says nothing about how class, gender, and racial inequalities (or many other forms of oppression) are perpetuated. Moreover, messengering and other high-skilled physical occupations are a viable option only for a small and shrinking portion of the population, and the idealized situation of small collectives is not a reasonable model for other industries to emulate. Social philosopher André Gorz thinks that labor in modern societies is, of necessity, alienating. He asserts that complex social organization requires too much rationalized production for all activities to be nonalienating. The solution, according to Gorz, is not to attempt a utopian unification of existence, but to minimize the amount of time any one individual spends performing boring, unsatisfying work. That is, we need to accept a certain degree of alienation, since drudgery can never be eliminated. Yet if society's resources were reallocated to equitably increase every individual's autonomy, exploitation would be diminished significantly.[20]

All of these things said, important political implications for messengers remain. To go back to the question "Should it be?" there appears to be no one clear answer. Messengering is not alienating, and that is a good thing. That individuals can find the work enjoyable enough to almost be characterized as "a calling" is remarkably positive, especially when compared to the crushing monotony many individuals feel performing paid labor. On the other hand, employers unduly profit from the lure of delivering packages. Collectives are a possibility for some bike couriers, but the overall trend seems to be toward bigger companies (relative to the overall contraction of the industry). Even for those working for larger companies in clearly exploitative situations, however, the flow of the workday and the edgework of races provide something more. Beyond the usual confines of labor issues, messengering confronts the abstraction of space. Impractical as the messenger model may be as any sort of global solution to oppression more generally, it is a lifestyle that empowers the individual. Further, unlike most lifestyles, it is not avocational. As such, it is a job that allows individuals to realize their power as agents in the moment-to-moment enactment of tactics. In this regard, messengering most definitely "should be." Regardless of its flaws, and no matter how it could be better, messengering stands as a testament to the affective satisfaction individuals find in appropriating space, and to the ability of tactics to operate beneath and alongside the official strategies of the powerful.

To dismiss the lure of delivering packages as mere repressive satisfaction misses the vital importance of creation in human life. Again, messengers are not harbingers of revolution, but in their lifestyle we can see integral components for a meaningful reorganization of everyday life. Yes, workers deserve material equity, but they also deserve creative control. When this control is given, work no longer feels like a four-letter word. Instead, it feels like play. And, this is the reason that time and time again messengers tout their job as one they love.

To go back to the night of the Warriors Fun Ride, there was no identified enemy. No one talked of unions or better wages. It was not an explicitly political event. Regardless, every one of us, as we sped through the streets, took part in making a different world for ourselves. It was not a world of capitalist abstraction; we cut an alternate cosmos from the asphalt and steel surrounding us. When couriers exclaim that messengering is the best job ever they are referring to moments epitomized by the Warriors. These are moments of creative, spontaneous action—moments when the material environment no longer controls but is controlled. These moments are perfected in alleycats, but they are not experienced in the leisure sphere alone. The messenger lifestyle integrates the courier's life. To borrow from Aronowitz again, "the soul cannot be healed unless divided labor is reintegrated, unless the lost 'instinct of workmanship' is found within the ordinary sphere of labor rather than becoming an 'avocation.'" This is the political significance of the messenger's subculture; it is a style that counters the oppression of everyday life. As Mary exclaimed, "I cannot believe I get paid for this shit."

APPENDIX A
Theoretical Outline

In the introduction, I claimed, following a long line of sociological research, that job tasks are generally disconnected from what can be considered authentic action. Although occupational sociologists continue to clamor about the importance of work in people's lives, it is taken for granted that, in contemporary times, most individuals (to at least some degree) divest their real selves from their work roles. And, it is safe to say, for many people this divestment is thoroughgoing. Generally speaking, work is a means to a paycheck, which is a means to actualizing who one really is. That is, one endures work to finance avocational interests (e.g., being a devoted father, model-airplane builder, or scuba diver). The inauthentic quality of most occupations contrasts sharply with the authenticity of messengering. Messengers, like most people, find meaning in their lives, but for messengers that meaning derives not from avocational pursuits, but from a fusion of work and leisure.

As we have seen throughout this book, the first step toward understanding the disconnection or connection, between job tasks and authenticity is a sociological analysis of emotions. To put it simply, feelings of authenticity are realized through emotional involvement. The conditions under which authenticity is generated (e.g., doing Sudoku for pleasure or solving complex problems for pay) are irrelevant. Second, as we have also seen, individual emotions can be imbued with affect-meaning through rituals. Third, emotions (both individual and collective) are always generated through the body and therefore are always emplaced in the material world. By including space in the analysis of emotions, the otherwise ethereally cerebral subject of social research is incarnated back into the physical setting in which all interaction actually occurs. This means that space itself is part of the sociological research agenda. It is not just the backdrop to action; it is dialectically connected to action.

My goal in this appendix is to expand on the ideas informing my concept of affective spatial appropriation. Throughout the rest of this book I have attempted to keep my argument accessible to the general reader. Here, I will delve into more esoteric territory and provide a more detailed discussion of how emotions and space can be integrated within the sociological literature.

Affect in Action

Emotions present themselves as totally separate from cognitive thought. They appear as unmediated biological sensations arising from within a person's inner being. Sociologist Arlie Hochschild explains: "The concept 'emotion' refers mainly to strips of experience in which there is no conflict between one and another aspect of self; the individual 'floods out,' is 'overcome.' The image that comes to mind is that of a sudden automatic reflex syndrome."[1] Of course, appearances aside, emotions are neither unmediated nor purely biological; instead, cultural schemas inform them.[2] Culture defines what we find offensive, frightening, or enjoyable, and emotions, once generated, are further managed through various techniques (from surface acting to more ingrained methods of redefining one's role within the situation). Hochschild, for example, famously details how individuals reflexively work with their emotions to meet social expectations.[3]

Emotions as Lived Experience

Much of the sociological literature of emotions deals with specific emotions. Thomas Scheff has developed an entire microsociological model based on the experiences of pride and shame.[4] Jack Katz explores the

interactional roots of anger, humor, and shame. Katz's approach is notable for its phenomenological orientation. While Katz focuses on certain
emotional displays (e.g., laughing at reflections in a distorted mirror or
crying in police interrogations), he provides a more general theory of
how emotions are experienced collectively as a set of phenomena. Katz
asserts: "[Social research] is far from sensual and richly phenomenological because analysis ignores *how the person bodily lives* the matter being
analyzed."[5] For Norman Denzin, emotions are a process of being-in-the-
world. That is to say, emotions are lived experience. Denzin elaborates:
"What is phenomenologically decisive in these feelings is the uncovering
and revealing of the person to herself. These feelings announce themselves and make their presence felt by the person."[6] And Katz remarks
further: "Instead of thinking about transcendent significance, the person
registers the implications of the action in progress in a sensual appreciation. One commonly *feels* situations."[7] Thus emotions are embodied
experience—what Denzin calls self-feeling.

It is this embodiment that gives emotions an undoubted realness.
Denzin explains: "The emotional experience, in the form of embodied
self-feeling, radiates through the person's inner and outer streams of
experience. During its occurrence emotional experience is lived as absolute reality."[8] Loïc Wacquant refers to these lived experiences as "sensual logic."[9] Pierre Bourdieu's renowned understanding of class-based
distinctions rests on the notion of habitus,[10] a set of emotive bodily
dispositions. Habitus is not a discursively organized map of the social
world. Rather, it is the practical organization of self-feeling, which consistently reinforces social hierarchies. Ultimately, affect defeats purely
cognitive reason in the formation of the self and in the constitution of
meaning. Bourdieu remarks: "Practical belief is not a 'state of mind' ... ,
but rather a state of body." As he puts it, "The body believes in what it
plays at."[11]

"I," "Me," and Flow

It should be clear by now that affect, as I am using the term, is not about
specific emotions, but about the embodiment of lived experience. All experience, of course, has an affective component, but some experiences
are saturated in emotions (e.g., sex and skydiving) while others are less
so (e.g., filing taxes or flossing teeth). In order to understand the emotional significance of certain activities, our discussion must go back to

the sociological foundations of the self. For Émile Durkheim, "Two consciousnesses exist within us: the one comprises only states that are personal to each of us, characteristics of us as individuals, whilst the other comprises states that are common to the whole of society."[12] George Herbert Mead describes these two states as the "I" and the "me." The "me" is the socialized aspect of the self. It is the internalization of the generalized other—the product of an internalized conversation between the self and the expectations of one's community. By contrast, the "I" exists only in the moment of action. It is the individual's creative responses to situations. Mead points out: "The 'I' reacts to the self which arises through the taking of the attitude of others. Through taking those attitudes we have introduced the 'me' and we react to it as an 'I.'"[13]

Together, the "I" and the "me" form the individual's personality, but they exist as separate aspects of the mind. This is because the human mind is a reflexive entity that can be both subject and object. Self-consciousness is made possible by the ability to consider one's self impersonally. For this reason, the "me" is absolutely essential to identity. However, it is the spontaneous action of the "I" that feels authentic to the agent. It is the "I" that appears to be our true self. Mead explains: "It is there that novelty arises and it is there that our most important values are located. It is the realization in some sense of this self that we are continually seeking."[14] The "I," therefore, is Denzin's self-feeling; it is the "I" that threatens to flood out the "me" in interaction.

To actualize the "I" is to be subsumed in the moment of activity. It is to momentarily halt the self-reflexive process. As we have seen, this is what Mihaly Csikszentmihalyi refers to as flow, and it involves the tasks of an individual being perfectly matched by her skills. Under these conditions, the individual becomes *engrossed*. Csikszentmihalyi refers to flow as optimal experience, and it tends to be discussed as a joyful, positive state. Arguably, however, moments of blind rage are equally engrossing, although far less positive.[15] Whether positive or negative, flow appears as optimal because, lost in the movements of the "I," actions appears utterly authentic. That is, they feel instinctual. Of course, it should go without saying that the "instinctual" quality of flow—like the seemingly biological determination of emotion, more generally—is merely an illusion. Flow is not, in reality, presocial; it is completely dependent on the "me" for informing the possible options of the "I."[16]

Rituals as Collective Flow

It would be quite easy to conceptualize flow as if it were entirely individualistic. Building from Mead's work, though, an individual's ability to experience flow is *not* completely individualistic. For example, a lone woman kayaking through the rapids may be engrossed in optimal experience, but the "I" that overcomes her is still inseparably tethered to her "me." Thus even solo experiences of flow result from sociological processes.[17] Moreover, the most profound experiences of flow are thoroughly collective. As explained in the introduction, the sociological significance of emotions goes back to Durkheim. For Durkheim, emotions are at the very core of social organization. Studying the religious practices of Australian aborigines, Durkheim argues that interpersonally generated emotions—what he calls collective effervescence—produce social solidarity. It is in solidarity that the social state of the self becomes privileged, and this is what bonds the community together. The linchpin in Durkheim's model is ritual; rituals produce collective effervescence, and therefore it is rituals that maintain society.

As detailed in chapter 5, it is in rituals that the sacred is distinguished from the profane. More importantly, in Durkheim's theory, rituals are both collective *and* effervescent. They must be ecstatic events: "The very act of congregating is an exceptionally powerful stimulant. Once the individuals are gathered together, a sort of electricity is generated from their closeness and quickly launches them to an extraordinary height of exaltation."[18] Thus the ultimate power of ritual is to take the individual experience of flow and transform it into a collective effervescence that is at once trans-situational and thoroughly rooted in immediate perceptions.

Musical performances, and most clearly rock concerts, illustrate this point. On the one hand, the event is completely formulaic. With only minor variations, the band performs songs already written, and those in attendance behave in equally predictable ways (e.g., singing along and dancing, sometimes quite violently). However, for those engrossed in the concert, all these actions (even when acknowledged by the participants as more or less interchangeable with activities of previous shows and future ones) appear as something generated afresh, in *that* moment. Merely attending a rock concert, of course, does not ensure that one will be launched into extraordinary heights of exaltation, but under the right circumstances it is possible. It all depends on engrossment and stepping beyond reflexive awareness of the performance.[19]

Durkheim's boldest claim about ritual is that religion generates its power not from its ideological content, but from the communal emotions of ritual activity. Of course, it should be noted that the Durkheimian perspective on religion is totally removed from issues of divinity and the content of scriptures. Instead, religion is the most elementary form of social solidarity. In other words, it is the bond that directs individual egos to the assumed needs of the collective. I use the term "religion" throughout this book only to the extent that I am surmising Durkheim's theories on rituals (and those influenced by him). These theories, in the end, are about modern, secular societies.

It is by acting in unison, regardless of the discursive justifications of those actions, that the embodied experience—that which feels most real—is connected to the group. The desires of the ego are subsumed by the group, but the individual does not consciously bend to the will of the community. Instead, the individual and the community become one. This does not deny the significance of discursive explanations. However, rituals communicate far more than what is contained in myths or written in scriptures.[20] For example, a rite of passage may mark a person's change in status, but any cognitive shift is preceded by a collective emotional experience. In modern times, the hollowness of many rites of passage arises precisely from a failure of the ritual to generate effervescence—leaving only rational discourse to justify their continuation (e.g., highschool graduation marking the transition from childhood to adulthood). In such instances, the event—lacking in communal ecstasy—often seems stale and insignificant.

On the other hand, in successful rituals, flow provides affect-*meaning* by connecting otherwise individual self-feeling to the larger collective. In this process the individual feels energized—not only in rituals, but also in mundane life fortified with sacred symbols. To quote Durkheim again, "The man who has obeyed his god, and who for this reason thinks he has his god with him, approaches the world with confidence and a sense of heightened energy." Most importantly, "This stimulating action of society is not felt in exceptional circumstances alone. There is virtually no instant of our lives in which a certain rush of energy fails to come to us from outside ourselves. In all kinds of acts that express the understanding, esteem, and affection of his neighbor, there is a lift that the man who does his duty feels, usually without being aware of it."[21] This solidarity is *the* source of meaning for humanity.[22] It is only by connecting with the collective—that which is greater than the individual—that the actor can feel purpose in action and belief. To explain this a bit further, private emotions feel authentic; collective emotions feel supranatural. They grip the person as something moral yet mighty precisely because what is felt so intimately is simultaneously expressed by the larger group.

Emplacing Emotion

As discussed in chapter 6, most of social theory is thoroughly aspatial. Sociologist Herbert Gans gives a paradigmatic explanation of this mind-set: "Bad design can interfere with what goes on inside a building, of course, and good design can aid it, but design *per se* does not significantly shape human behaviour." Reacting against what he considers to be myopic professional training and class bias on the part of urban planners, Gans insists that the environment cannot overcome the *social* structures shaping one's life: "What affects people, then, is not the raw physical environment, but the social and economic environment in which that physical environment is used."[23]

Spatial Structuration

At the same time, over the last three decades, a growing number of sociologists have shown an increasing interest in space. At its heart, a sociological interest in the raw physical environment revolves around questions of structure and agency. Anthony Giddens's work, in particular, has spurred interest in sociospatial theorizing.[24] As we have seen, in Giddens's theory, agency and structure presuppose one another. This is what he calls the duality of structure. As a duality, structures are rules (i.e., meaningful schema) and resources (i.e., physical materials) used by individuals within systems of social interaction. As such, structures are virtual. They do not exist in time and space. It is systems (i.e., reoccurring patterns of social interaction) that have an actual presence. This is a major deviation from typical sociological models. Structural properties organize systems, but structures themselves exist only in the instance of their reproduction by acting individuals.

Giddens calls the process of mediation between agents and structures (realized in systems of interaction) structuration. Giddens elaborates: "To say that structure is a 'virtual order' of transformative relations means that social systems, as reproduced social practices, do not have 'structures' but rather exhibit 'structural properties' and that structure exists, as time-space presence, only in its instantiations in such practices and as memory traces orienting the conduct of knowledgeable human agents."[25] That is, structures allow for the institutionalization of social practices (i.e., systems) across time and space, but structure itself is an absent totality. According to Giddens, "practices are the situated doings of a subject...; structures, on the other hand, have no specific socio-temporal location, are characterized by the 'absence of a subject,' and cannot be framed in terms of a subject-object dialectic."[26] In this way, social structures and physical structures function like a language. This point is elaborated in chapter 6.

William Sewell criticizes Giddens's claim that resources can be virtual.[27] By definition, they are physical materials. Giddens attempts to stymie this critique: "Some...resources (such as raw materials, land, etc.) might appear to have a 'real existence' in a way which I have claimed structural properties as a whole do not....But their 'materiality' does not affect the fact that such phenomena becomes a resource...only when incorporated within the process of structuration."[28] For example, gold is physically real, but the uses for gold are contingent on the maintenance of specific systems of human relations. As a *resource,* therefore, gold is virtual; its value has very little connection to its presocial properties (i.e., its molecular makeup).

Lived Space

Giddens's duality of structure is related to what Henri Lefebvre calls the production of space.[29] For Lefebvre, physical, mental, and social spaces must be conceived together; the environment in which we think and act is a product of our thoughts and actions. On one level, this is an obvious point, given the biological limits of our species. If nothing else, what makes us human is our need to alter the world in order to survive in it. In other words, we are a tool-using species because without tools we would quickly die of starvation or exposure in even the most hospitable of climates.[30] At the same time, even as we build the world to suit our needs, the world we build also acts back on us. In Bourdieu's analysis of the Kabyle house, for instance, structural oppositions between male and female—as realized through each sex's logical associations with wet and dry, dark and light, culture and nature—help transfer cultural beliefs into cultural practices (and vice versa).[31] That is, the physical organization of the home is intertwined with the maintenance of a specific Kabyle habitus—one that appreciates a certain type of naturalized oppositions of men and women. Lefebvre notes: "Space is at once the result and the cause, product and producer."[32]

The production of space has three dimensions; space is perceived, conceived, and lived. Space is an experienced set of material practices—a mother cooking in the family kitchen, for example. Meanings are also given to these practices—the mother becomes the nurturer, while the father becomes the wage earner. It is important to remember here that these practices exist in a space—a house divided into sex-segregated roles.[33] The first two dimensions offer themselves to a rather static reading; conceptions of space simply become the perceptions of space. This gives the cultural order a naturalized appearance. However, because space is not only determining but can also be determined, users can appropriate it against intended conceptions. Lefebvre refers to this as *lived* space.

There is a very large rift between Gans and Lefebvre. Gans has actively worked against efforts at developing a spatially sensitive sociology, while Lefebvre is adamant that social issues are inseparable from spatial concerns. Given these theoretical misgivings, it is more than somewhat surprising to note that Lefebvre's focus on lived space is, in fact, analogous to Gans's attack on urban planners. Both theorists understand that space can be appropriated in unintended ways. Lefebvre points out: "The user's space is *lived*—not represented (or conceived). When compared with the abstract space of the experts (architects, urbanists, planners), the space of everyday activities of users is a concrete one, one which is to say, subjective."[34] This is precisely Gans's point about urban reform. The projects of urban planners (i.e., those who conceive city neighborhoods) are often too far removed from the social realities of those who use their creations. That is to say, youth outreach centers, libraries, or parks cannot, by their mere presence, appreciably alter the social life of a neighborhood in the ways that planners intend. In other words, the projects rarely result in decreased crime or increased cultural capital.[35] But the failure of such projects to produce *intended* results is not the same thing as the projects having *no* effect.

The difference between Gans and Lefebvre comes from the latter, attending to the duality of structure and conceptualizing physical space as part of the social world. That is, class, race, gender, and age influence how space is lived, but the place itself cannot be disconnected from this process: "Social relations... have no real existence save in and through space. *Their underpinning is spatial.*"[36] Thus Thomas Gieryn works to remind sociologists: "Everything we study is emplaced; it happens somewhere and involves material stuff."[37]

In geographer Allan Pred's study of southern Sweden, for example, alterations of land-use patterns precipitated by the nineteenth-century enclosure movement directly relate to contemporaneous changes in social relationships.[38] That is, emplacement means more than pointing out the obvious: all action exists in space. Rather, it means that spatial and social relationships are intertwined. To exist in space means that alterations to space alter the rules and resources individuals can draw upon in their lives. In Gans's research, the youth center in Boston's West End, instead of inoculating teens against their mischievous ways, simply became a proving ground for working-class values (against the stated bourgeois ethic of the center).[39] In Sweden, enclosure dispersed townships and changed farming techniques, completely transforming the distribution of power within communities as communal organizations became less effective and some landed peasants became direct overseers of village labor.

Following Gans, and other hard-nosed social scientists, the playground or the road to the supermarket are nothing but a physical limit to human agency. Beyond what physics prohibits, people, it is assumed, go about their lives unencumbered. For Giddens and Lefebvre, however, all structures, whether they are social or physical, function as rules and resources utilized in interaction. The raw physical environment not only encumbers our lives or aids in the ease of movement; it also enables us (in the fullest sense of the term). This is the essential point in Bourdieu's analysis of the Kabyle house; the material world (perceived, conceived, and lived) is part of the habitus. It is inscribed at the same time that it inscribes cultural values. Geographer Edward Soja refers to this as the sociospatial dialectic. In his words, "[The] social relations of production are both space-forming and space-contingent."[40]

Affective Appropriation

If sociologists have been ambivalent about giving space a chance, geographers have been militant about it. Most famously, David Harvey advocates for a geographical imagination connecting individual biographies and geographical positioning.[41] But research into the sociospatial dialectic (regardless of the discipline—anthropological, geographical, or sociological) tends to be derived from aggregate, historical data. Three very notable examples include Pred's work on Sweden, Soja's analysis of Los Angeles, and Harvey's case study of Paris.[42] Pred's specific concern is the unintended outcomes of spatial practices, and Soja refers to "affective geographies."[43] Regardless, large-scale, historical projects (by their very nature) can make only abstract reference to lived experience.

Sociologist Michael Bell uses ethnographic data to understand the moral boundaries residents of an English exurb establish between nature and society.[44] In no small part, these boundaries are marked by emotional attachments to specific places, and these emotions are no doubt lived through material space, often against institutional conceptions and presumed perceptions. At the same time, Bell's analysis is theoretically disconnected from any concern with the sociospatial dialectic. In fact, most ethnographies that are place-sensitive address neither emotions nor structuration. For example, Caroline Fusco's study of locker rooms takes great pains to detail the built environment.[45] She even interviewed the locker room's architect. All the same, there is no attempt to explicate how agency and structure are mediated through space.

If social interaction is intertwined with the material environment, emotions and space (ipso facto) are connected, and this connection must become a focus of sociological analysis. This is not an assertion of the blatantly obvious: individuals become attached to their homes, their hometowns, or their favorite places away from home.[46] Instead, I am claiming that affect-meaning not only happens *at* some place, but is produced *through* space. That is, emotions involve not only the embodiment of lived experience, but also lived space (in Lefebvre's sense of the term).

With Iain Borden, for example, we see that skateboarding is not only the reinterpretation of space. The skater's lived experience can happen only through an engagement with the space being used. Thus skaters are not unfettered agents, ollieing on top of the city's structure. Instead, skateboarding is realized *within* such space: "In terms of skateboarding's relations to architecture, its production of space is not purely bodily or sensorial; instead, the skater's body produces its space dialectically with the production of architectural space." The skater reads the surface of space to find lines of movement, and the body *interfaces* with the physical structure—producing "a dynamic intersection of body, board, and terrain." It is in this interaction (and only at this intersection) that skaters can produce space on their own terms (terms that have been, in part, constructed by previous conceptions of space). Borden observes: "Above all, it is the engagement with architecture that is important…, such that the moving body treats architecture as but one projector of space to be interpolated with the projection of space from itself."[47]

The implications of the affective appropriation of space for cultural analysis are potentially profound. In the case of bike messengers, discursive explanations are plausible (i.e., reframing, recalibrating, and refocusing their dirty labor) but fail to explain why messengers have such strong subcultural identities. Aspatial but affect-oriented explanations of messengers (i.e., analyzing messengers solely in terms of flow and ritual) are informative but miss one of the most distinctive aspects of both the job and the lifestyle—that it is urban.

Throughout the book I have shown with empirical data that messenger labor requires flow, that alleycats function as rituals, and, ultimately, that couriers appropriate the city. It has been my primary contention that the messenger subculture cannot be adequately understood without the inclusion of both emotions and space. Chapter 7 demonstrated this point by providing a practice-based semiotics of messenger style. There we saw the interconnection of emotions, space, and culture. In other words, affect-meaning—generated through the appropriation of the material environment—dialectically informs courier symbols (i.e., the demeanor, argot, and image of messenger style).

At this point in the discussion, a caveat is necessary. Messengers, like Borden's skateboarders, generate emotions by manipulating the space of the city. In this sense, they are space workers; they are paid because they can efficiently travel through urban gridlock. Thus analyzing emotions through the appropriation of physical space is far more relevant for bike couriers than, for example, stamp collectors (who generate emotions, I presume, by researching the history of various forms of postage and diligently collecting and cataloging rare stamps). Therefore, one of the aspects making messengers sociologically valuable—their unique relationship to the city—also makes them less representative. However, because all social activity is emplaced, the affective appropriation of space is a generalizable aspect of the human condition. Messengers may do it uniquely (in a risky, masculine manner), but there are obvious cultural lessons to be learned from how they do it and the significance they attribute to their practices. Addressing the affective appropriation of space helps to anchor sociological analysis concretely back in the material world. The beliefs and practices of social worlds—so often treated as purely arbitrary in research—can be incorporated into a sociospatial dialectic and thus account for the power of culture more thoroughly.

APPENDIX B
Expanded Discussion of Method

At least since Bronislaw Malinowski published his study of the Trobriand Islanders in 1922, anthropology has considered participant observation an essential component to understanding the Other.[1] It is always worth remembering, however, that Malinowski had no intentions of conducting such in-depth research. He had, in fact, only planned to spend a brief period of time on the Trobriand Islands. However, as a Polish national studying at the London School of Economics, he was prevented from returning to England by the outbreak of World War I. Papua was, in a sense, an internment camp, and the young anthropologist was begrudgingly sentenced to academic stardom. Around the same time as Malinowski's study, an ethnographic tradition was also developing in the University of Chicago's department of sociology. From Nels Anderson's research on homeless men to Edwin Sutherland's classic study on the professional thief, sociology, like anthropology, has a long history of observing and participating in curious and unknown social settings.[2] This methodological appendix will elaborate how my research on bike messengers builds from the ever-growing tradition of ethnography.

Ethnography and Knowledge

Over the last several decades, social researchers have increasingly acknowledged the interconnection of practice and belief. And ethnographers have moved away from the ideal of "detached involvement" as an epistemological issue.[3] Whereas early ethnographers believed that personal distance was an essential component of "objective" research, contemporary ethnographers increasingly advocate what could be called attached involvement.[4] This attachment is generated through active participation in the social world under study.

For example, instead of merely observing behaviors, anthropologist Richard Nelson proposes that ethnographers must learn and master the tasks required in foreign cultures.[5] Nelson, who worked among Eskimos, goes so far as to claim that seal hunting cannot be adequately described without first successfully hunting a seal. With such active participation, Nelson argues that formal interviews are not necessary. Instead, because the researcher engages in everyday life, informal conversations can be used to elicit information. Anthropologist Daniel Wolf describes this as "being there." As he asserts, "combining participation and observation is the most effective way of achieving an understanding of a culture as it is experienced and lived by its participants." Further, Wolf goes on to claim: "An ethnographer who removes himself—the 'I'—from the ethnography only creates the illusion of objectivity."[6]

More recently, sociologist Loïc Wacquant's ethnography of a boxing gym in South Side of Chicago stands as a testament to the role of active, attached involvement in the process of knowing. Wacquant goes so far as to claim a "total 'surrender' to the exigencies of the field."[7] That is, Wacquant submitted himself entirely to the lifeworld of the gym: informants became friends, and fieldwork transformed itself into recreation and personal release. Proclaiming that he had never previously entertained the idea of becoming a pugilist, Wacquant spent three years training and sparring at his field site.

It is only by repeatedly and regularly stepping into the ring and experiencing "the taste and ache of action" that Wacquant could gain the trust of his informants. But, far more importantly, it is only by participating in "the carnal dimension of existence" that the world of the boxer is understood.[8] Wacquant asserts that the *embodiment* of the social world within the individual is what informs the individual about the meanings he attributes to his social world.[9] A researcher ignorant of these sensual processes misses the essence of the object of her investigation. Thus "it is imperative that the sociologist submit himself to the fire and action *in situ;* that to the greatest extent possible he put his own organism, sensibility, and incarnate intelligence at the epicenter of the array of material and symbolic forces that he intends to dissect."[10]

Studying Messengers

There is a difference between trying something to say one has done it and really doing something—becoming fully immersed in an activity as an intrinsic part of one's life. This point is one of Pierre Bourdieu's key critiques of traditional anthropology: "The anthropologist's particular relation to the object of his study contains the making of a theoretical distortion inasmuch as his situation as an observer [excludes him] from the real play of social activities by the fact that he has no place (except by choice or by way of game) in the system observed and has no need to make a place for himself there."[11] This is also the organizing methodological principle for Wacquant's study of boxing. In a similar vein, sociologists are quick to point out the failing of many journalists comes from "reporting" from the field instead of participating in it.

Total Surrender

Through a series of factors—none of which were the result of intentional epistemological foresight on my part—I entered the field in a state of total surrender. I came to study bike messengers after completing one year of graduate studies at the University of Georgia. At the time, neither Athens, Georgia, nor graduate school seemed to be a good fit for me. I read Travis Culley's oddly titled memoir of his time as a courier, *The Immortal Class,* and decided to drop out of graduate school. Truthfully, it was a decision much of the faculty appreciated. I made arrangements to move to New York, where I planned to start working as a messenger. Before I left Georgia, however, one of the professors there, Jim Dowd (seeing some sort of potential in me), suggested that I not drop out. Instead, he proposed I take a leave of absence, and during that time do the fieldwork for a master's thesis. It seemed like a pretty good idea. Besides, I figured I could always stay in New York if I did not want to come back.

The result is the book you are holding. I did go back to the University of Georgia and eventually to University of California, San Diego, for my doctorate. I bring up this autobiographical information because it situates me, in important ways, in the field. I am not a bike messenger cannibalizing his past—putting an academic spin on my previous life. I moved to New York and took copious field notes. I got Institutional Review Board approval before I left Georgia. In other words, I was always cognizant of and attentive to my role as a researcher.

At the same time, when I started the research, I was not sure if I was really going to go back to complete my master's degree. In this sense, my difficulties in graduate school were really a blessing. I had the training to go out in the field and do productive work, but I was also unsure of my desire to be a sociologist. Thus I was able to fully immerse myself in the occupation and be sincerely engaged with the messengers I met. At least at first, my field notes were little more than diary entries—inspired by the sociological imagination. Later, in San Diego and Seattle, I entered the field completely accepting my position as an ethnographer. But my initially tenuous position as a graduate student gave me a unique and valuable perspective for my rookie year. This is a perspective that (again, through no great forethought of my own) saved me from the theoretical distortions critiqued by Bourdieu.

Field Notes, Interviews, and Other Sources

Couriers' favorite topic of discussion (and often, it seems, their only topic of discussion) is messengering. To be a fly on the wall at a messenger gathering is to hear countless anecdotes, histories, and philosophies of messenger life. Many veterans, or even other rookies looking to assert the knowledge they have gained, are eager to help educate others about the ways of messenger life. Being an inquisitive rookie at messenger gatherings (as opposed to a fly on the wall) allows one—in very unobtrusive ways—to ask probing questions or request clarifications. This, as we have seen, is Nelson's approach to research, and in such situations—insiders talking to insiders—there is less bravado, shock talk, or hyperbole than when messengers talk to journalists. This is not to say there are no self-aggrandizing exaggerations in these situations, just that there are fewer. It is in these organic situations that the subculture is actually lived, and because I was accepted as a legitimate member of the messenger world, I was treated as an insider, with no need to put on airs around me.[12]

The bulk of my data comes not from working as a courier, but from hanging out as one. However, the former is a prerequisite for the latter. As stated in the introduction, I integrated myself into the messenger world. I did my best to make myself available for all sorts of social events—group rides, talking after work, parties, and races. I unobtrusively took notes throughout these gatherings and compiled them in my field notes when I got home. My formal interviews revealed little new information, but they did allow me to capture verbatim, elongated responses to my questions. I supplement my ethnographic work with historical and contemporary documentation. In the course of my research, I read as much of the literature produced by the bike messenger subculture as I could find. The most notable examples of this literature are the New York Bike Messenger Association's ten issues of *Urban Death Maze,* a desktop-published magazine produced from 1998 to 2001. I also used books, articles, and documentaries produced by outsiders for mainstream audiences. As chapter 2 makes clear, the *New York Times* provides a wealth of historical data on how the public has viewed the occupation.

Being a Messenger

I moved to New York in what I considered to be excellent physical condition. I had been an avid bicycle commuter for over a year. I had also spent several years working out quite heavily in the gym. This conditioning, however, proved to be inadequate. During my first few weeks of work I did very little other than ride, eat, and sleep. Within a few short weeks the constant pedaling required by the job also managed to put severe strain on my knees. My exceptional fatigue and aching knees were exacerbated by my desire to convince my dispatcher that I was a willing and capable messenger. In other words, for my first two weeks at Sprint I came into work by eight in the morning and worked until seven in the evening.

It was during these early days that I cultivated what is commonly referred to as a "courier appetite." For breakfast I would generally eat three to four bowls of cereal and maybe one or two peanut-butter-and-jelly sandwiches. During the day I would eat one to two bagels and around five bananas. An average dinner might consist of four sandwiches, a large sweet potato, and a bowl of vegetables. And the nights I did not fall asleep immediately after dinner—usually still sitting on the couch, dishes sprawled out before me—were a rarity.

The main thing I learned as a messenger, of course, was how to ride in traffic. When I moved to New York I was completely overwhelmed by the crush of cars. I still have a very vivid memory of the first time I squeezed myself between two buses riding side by side, and realized (as the sunlight became blocked by what seemed to be giant canyon walls made of glass and steel) that only a few inches separated me from disaster. Quickly, I learned to relish the thrills of riding in these situations. Slowly, I gained the skills to do so in a reasonably safe manner.

When I reflect back on my time as a messenger, though, I think less about urban cycling and more about the weather. Those February mornings riding over the Williamsburg Bridge with the frigid wind battering my fingers into icy misery were tough to endure, and I will never forget seeing messengers like Stan on the coldest of days not even wearing gloves. Many of my coworkers appeared to be utterly impervious to winter.

I also think a lot about public space. Increasingly, our built environment leaves no room for people who are not paying customers. In between jobs, a messenger is little more than a vagabond. You have to seek out places to sit without being accused of loitering. You also have to figure out where there are toilets you can access. Constantly roaming through the city (while drinking a fair amount of water), I had to learn which restrooms would not be locked or where employees might unlock them for me. Thankfully, San Diegans and Seattleites are somewhat more gracious to messengers. In New York, however, even a messenger's own clients might refuse them restroom access—which speaks volumes about the stigmatization of messengers there.

And Finally...

I started my research when I was 25. At that age, moving to New York and working as a messenger was a dream. I cannot imagine undertaking a more fun and exciting ethnography. The occupation itself was fulfilling, and I enjoyed going to bars after work and just hanging out with my fellow couriers. Traveling for races was even more fun. As a 30-year-old, however, my time in Seattle was more prosaic. I still enjoyed working as a messenger, but I was more interested in waking up early on Saturday to go on a long bike ride than I was in staying out late on Friday night. While many of the messengers I know are older than me, I cannot (nor do I have the desire to) keep up with their lifestyle. In the end, I guess

I am a square, perhaps even more than I'd care to admit. I am more content analyzing experiences than I am in the incessant carnival that surrounds much of the messenger subculture. This, I suppose, is a variation on that old adage—something to the effect of "Those that can do, do. Those that can't do, write books about those who can."

The days and years I spent as a messenger were great times, but they were arduous as well. I have nothing but respect and admiration for the men and women who have toughed it out on the streets and continue to do so day in and day out earning far less than they deserve. Outsiders fail to grasp the messenger subculture because they have never been part of it, and they look for simple explanations to either glamorize it, demonize it, or simply disregard it. My approach has—more than anything else— sought to overcome such pitfalls. Overall, I hope that in these pages I have done the messenger subculture justice—that even through the interpretive gloss of sociological analysis, couriers can see themselves and their world reflected in these pages.[13]

NOTES

Introduction

1. Peter Cheney, "Bicycle Couriers in Love with Life on Mean Streets," *Toronto Star,* March 27, 1993; Eli Sanders, "Keeping Downtown Rolling: Flouting the System and Serving It, Messengers Deliver" *Pacific Northwest: Seattle Times Magazine,* August 29, 2003, 2; Danita Smith, "Fast Company: Wheel Tales of Manhattan's Bike Messenger," *New York Magazine,* January 13, 1986, 40; Bob Levy, "Hope amid the Spokes and Wheels," *Washington Post,* September 4, 1989; Felicia R. Lee, "Coping: And You Think Crime Is Down?" *New York Times,* March 4, 2001.

2. Advertisement for the Cycle Messenger World Championships, *Urban Death Maze* 7 (2000): 21.

3. On doctors, see Donald Light, *Becoming Psychiatrists: The Professional Transformation of Self* (New York: W. W. Norton, 1980); on military officers, see James J. Dowd, "Hard Jobs and Good Ambitions: U.S. Army Generals and the Rhetoric of Modesty," *Symbolic Interaction* 23 (2000): 183–205.

4. See Robert Dubin, *Central Life Interests: Creative Individualism in a Complex World* (New Brunswick, NJ: Transaction Publishers, 1992).

5. See Richard Sennett, *The Corrosion of Character: The Personal Consequences of Work in the New Capitalism* (New York: W. W. Norton, 1998).

6. See André Gorz, *Farewell to the Working Class: An Essay on Post-Industrial Socialism,* trans. Michael Sonenscher (London: Pluto Press, 1982). Gorz discusses what he calls the heteronomous sphere—the deadening labor required to keep complex societies functioning—and the autonomous sphere—engaging, self-directed activities.

7. Should the reader be unfamiliar with these bits of pop culture, in *American Beauty* the main character, totally disillusioned with his life, quits his financially secure white-collar job and regains a sense of purpose by smoking marijuana, buying a muscle car, and lusting after his high-school daughter's best friend. In *Fight Club* the main character despises his middle-class job and its materialistic lifestyle so much that he moves into a squat and devotes himself to organizing an underground boxing club—which eventually transforms into a terrorist organization. In *The Office,* workers do not even attempt to hide their boredom. They rarely do any work, and they are instead continually sidetracked by their own social antics or (more commonly) the misguided efforts of their boss.

8. Max Weber, *The Protestant Ethic and the Spirit of Capitalism* (Upper Saddle River, NJ: Prentice Hall, 1958), 182.

9. See Ferdinand Tönnies, *Community and Association (Gemeinschaft Und Gesellschaft),* trans. Charles P. Loomis (London: Routledge and Paul, 1955).

10. Karl Marx and Friedrich Engels, "Manifesto of the Communist Party" in *The Marx-Engels Reader,* ed. Robert C. Tucker (New York: W. W. Norton, 1978), 476; Max Weber, "Religious Rejections of the World and Their Directions" in *From Max Weber: Essays in Sociology,* ed. and trans. H. H. Gerth and C. Wright Mills (New York: Oxford University Press, 1946), 357; Émile Durkheim, *Suicide: A Study in Sociology,* trans. John A. Spaulding and George Simpson (New York: Free Press, 1951), 212.

11. See Anthony Giddens, *The Consequences of Modernity* (Stanford, CA: Stanford University Press, 1990); and *Modernity and Self-Identity: The Self and Society in the Late Modern Age* (Stanford, CA: Stanford University Press, 1991).

12. Stanley Aronowitz, *False Promises: The Shaping of American Working Class Consciousness* (New York: McGraw-Hill, 1973), 61. Also see Roger Caillois, *Man, Play, and Game,* trans. Meyer Barash (New York: Free Press of Glencoe, 1961).

13. Émile Durkheim, *The Elementary Forms of Religious Life* (New York: Free Press, 1995), 419.

14. See Kenneth Allan, *The Meaning of Culture: Moving the Postmodern Critique Forward* (Westport, CT: Praeger, 1998).

15. I am paraphrasing Randall Collins, "On the Microfoundations of Macrosociology," *American Journal of Sociology* 86 (1981): 995: "The social structure is not a set of meanings people carry in their heads.... The structure is in the repeated action of communicating, not in the contents of what is said."

16. See Thomas J. Gieryn, "A Space for Place in Sociology," *Annual Review of Sociology* 26 (2000): 463–96.

17. Pierre Bourdieu's analysis of the Kabyle house provides the best-known empirical example of this issue. See Pierre Bourdieu, "The Kabyle House or the World Reversed," in *The Logic of Practice,* trans. Richard Nice (Stanford, CA: Stanford University Press, 1970), 271–83; see also Miles Richardson, "Culture and Urban Stage: The Nexus of Setting, Behavior, and Image in Urban Places" in *Human Behavior and Environment: Advances in Theory and Research,* vol. 4, ed. Irwin Altman, Amos Rapoport, and Joachim F. Wohlwill (New York: Plenum Press, 1980), 209–41.

18. See Allan Pred, *Making Histories and Constructing Human Geographies: The Local Transformations of Practice, Power Relations, and Consciousness* (San Francisco: Westview Press, 1990); Edward W. Soja, "The Spatiality of Social Life: Towards a Transformative

Retheorization," in *Social Relations and Spatial Structures,* ed. Derek Gregory and John Urry (London: Macmillan, 1985), 90–127.

19. Gieryn, "Space for Place," 466; also see Derek Gregory and John Urry, introduction to *Social Relations and Spatial Structures* (London: Macmillan, 1985); Allan Pred, *Place, Practice, and Structure: Social and Spatial Transformation in Southern Sweden: 1750–1850* (Cambridge, UK: Polity Press, 1986).

20. It must be mentioned that *subculture* is a contested term. However, I am not interested (at any point in this book) in being embroiled by debates in subcultural studies. Following conventional usage, bike messengers are part of a subculture because their practices, symbols, and values mark them as distinct and separate from other members of society in the United States. In regard to the argument I develop, the real issue is not subcultures, but how the inclusion of affective spatial appropriation improves cultural analysis. How does it explain the lure of delivering packages? How does it help untangle classic (and pervasive) theoretical problems surrounding meaning?

21. I borrow this expression from Dick Hebdige, *Subculture: The Meaning of Style* (New York: Routledge, 1979), 18.

22. See Henri Lefebvre, *The Production of Space,* trans. Donald Nicholson-Smith (Oxford: Blackwell, 1991); Bourdieu, "Kabyle House."

23. Michel de Certeau, *The Practice of Everyday Life,* trans. Steven Rendall (Berkeley: University of California Press, 1984), xvii.

24. See Henri Lefebvre, *Everyday Life in the Modern World,* trans. Sacha Rabinovitch (London: Penguin Press, 1971).

25. Some of my employers were unaware I would be conducting research when they initially hired me. Thus I use pseudonyms when discussing certain companies.

26. Richard G. Mitchell, Jr., persuasively illustrates this point when he contrasts his interactions with survivalists and the sensational portrayals found in newspaper and television accounts. See Richard G. Mitchell, Jr., *Dancing at Armageddon: Survivalism and Chaos in Modern Times* (Chicago: University of Chicago Press, 2002); also see Loïc Wacquant, *Body and Soul: Notebooks of an Apprentice Boxer* (New York: Oxford University Press, 2004).

27. I do not include any information that I consider unflattering or sensitive. All the same, some informants read their quotes with a very self-critical eye. It was often the individuals who were, in my estimation, the most articulate and insightful who, in hindsight, found their own statements troubling. This can probably be attributed to the strength of the messenger subculture. In all cultures, many of the strongest norms and deeply held values go unstated. When these norms and values are spelled out, few people feel they can capture their (sub)culture's depth with words. And, failing to fully describe it in words, these speakers open themselves to the criticisms of others.

1. The Job

1. See Don Oberdorfer, "62 Missile Crisis, via Western Union," *Washington Post,* November 18, 1989.

2. These estimates are derived from Peter McKillop, "The Uneasiest Riders: Manhattan's Streets Are Aswarm with 'Bikers,' a Death-Defying New Breed of Urban

Messenger," *Newsweek,* November 25, 1985, 28; Rebecca "Lambchop" Reilly, *Nerves of Steel: Bike Messengers in the United States* (Buffalo: Spoke and Word, 2000); Danitia Smith, "Fast Company: Wheel Tales of Manhattan's Bike Messenger," *New York Magazine,* January 13, 1986, 38–43.

3. Gregory Downey, *Telegraph Messenger Boys: Labor, Technology, and Geography, 1850–1950* (New York: Routledge, 2002).

4. See Saskia Sassen, *Global City: New York, London, Tokyo* (Princeton, NJ: Princeton University Press, 1991).

5. David Harvey, *The Conditions of Postmodernity: An Inquiry into the Origins of Cultural Change* (Cambridge, MA: Blackwell, 1990); see also Sharon Zukin, *Landscapes of Power: From Detroit to Disney World* (Berkeley: University of California Press, 1991).

6. See Edward W. Soja, "Economic Restructuring and the Internationalization of the Los Angeles Region," in *The Capitalist City: Global Restructuring and Community Politics,* ed. Michael Peter Smith and Joe R. Feagin (New York: Blackwell, 1987), 178–98.

7. See John Friedmann, "The World City Hypothesis," *Development and Change* 17 (1986): 69–83; Sassen, *Global City.*

8. Urban theorist Manuel Castells's discusses what he calls the informational mode of development and the restructuring of cities. Of particular relevance is his analysis of New York City in the 1980s and its dramatic expansion in the service sector (especially in relation to information processing). See Manuel Castell, *The Informational City: Information Technology, Economic Restructuring, and the Urban-Regional Process* (Malden, MA: Blackwell, 1989).

9. See, for example, Frances Cairncross, *The Death of Distance: How the Communications Revolution Will Change Our Lives* (Boston: Harvard Business School Press, 1997).

10. See Allen J. Scott, John Agnew, Edward W. Soja, and Michael Storper, "Global City-Regions," in *Global City-Regions: Trends, Theory, and Policy* (New York: Oxford University Press, 2001), 11–30.

11. Willam Geist, "Fastest Is Best as Messengers Pedal in Pursuit of a $100 Day," *New York Times,* December 2, 1983.

12. See Frank Green, "Bike Messengers Roll with Changes: Six San Diego Companies Still Doing Business in Internet Age," *San Diego Union-Tribune,* February 16, 2006; also see Steve Hendershot, "The Business of Speed: Racing against E-mail and Fax Machines," *Crain's Chicago Business,* July 9, 2007; Vanessa Ho, "The Plea of a Dying Breed: Don't Kill the Bike Messenger," *Seattle Post-Intelligencer,* February 26, 2008. To put these changes in historical perspective, see Robert E. Tommasson, "Fax Displacing Manhattan Bike Couriers," *New York Times,* March 19, 1991.

13. There are no statistics specific to bike messengers. There are only official data on the delivery industry as a whole (which include not only local driving couriers, but national and international freight shippers as well). Further, bike messenger companies are often secretive about their information. Thus there are no hard numbers for how many messengers are actually working in any city. For places such as Chicago, New York, and Washington, D.C., where there are a large number of couriers (many working on a sporadic basis), it is nearly impossible to know exact numbers. The numbers I rely on come from estimates made by journalists or local couriers and/or my own data.

14. Quoted in Green.

15. See Downey.

16. Given that messengers are often servicing people in the creative industry, it is not surprising that some clients would readily embrace the more outlandish parts of messenger style. See Richard Lloyd, *Neo-Bohemia: Art and Commerce in the Postindustrial City* (New York: Routledge, 2006).

17. See Sacha Pfeiffer, "Suit Argues Couriers Are Not Contractors," *Boston Globe,* March 7, 2007; see also Tommasson.

18. For example, see Selwyn Raab, "Teamsters Seeking to Form Bicycle Messengers' Union: Complaints Are Rife in a Tough, Risky Job," *New York Times,* October 30, 1994.

19. Another, very particular practice in Seattle involved messengers merely placing their U-lock on the chainstays of their bike, but not actually locking it to anything. The reason for this was never made clear to me.

20. Reilly, 29.

21. Quoted in Geist.

22. Damien Nesbit, a New York messenger, writing about an alleycat in "Motherfuckin' Monstertrack Race Report," *Urban Death Maze* 6 (2000): 20.

23. See Jack Tigh Dennerlein and John D. Meeker, "Occupational Injuries among Boston Bicycle Messengers," *American Journal of Industrial Medicine* 42 (2002): 519–25.

24. Kid, quoted in Peter Sutherland's documentary, *Pedal* (New York: Power-House Books, 2006).

25. See John Doyle, Phillip Messing, and Clemente Cisi, "Door Crash Kills Bike Messenger," *New York Post,* November 19, 2004.

26. For example, in St. Petersburg, Florida, a city known for its high fatality rate among cyclists, Mayor Bill Foster and city council member Karl Nurse have promoted a project called "Operation Share the Road." The operation, however, is not meant to reform the often deadly behaviors of automobile drivers. Instead, its focus is on ticketing bicycle scofflaws. As Nurse explained, "It would be a friendly gesture if [cyclists] try to remember that they're not the only people on the road." See Andy Boyle, "St. Petersburg Police Ticket 16 Bicyclists as Safety Campaign Begins," *St. Petersburg Times,* August 28, 2010.

27. Jack M. Kugelmass, "I'd Rather Be a Messenger," *Natural History* 90 (1981): 72.

28. Tom Leander, "Backpedaling," *New York Times,* July 21, 1984.

2. The Lifestyle

1. See Alex J. Berkman, "Foot Power Gives Them a Leg Up: Shoe String Approach Has Some Messengers Pedaling to Success," *Daily News,* April 20, 2009; also see Snap's website: http://snapdeliverynyc.wordpress.com.

2. For more information, visit the website www.careercourierthemovie.com.

3. Eric, quoted in Peter Sutherland's documentary *Pedal* (New York: Power-House Books, 2006).

4. British sociologist Ben Fincham makes an identical point in his article "Generally Speaking People Are in It for the Cycling and the Beer: Bicycle Couriers, Subculture, and Enjoyment," *The Sociological Review* 55 (2007): 189–202.

5. Michael Wood, "My Brilliant Courier: Scarred Knees, Bloody Palms," *The Independent,* August 16, 1994.

6. For readers unfamiliar with cycling terminology, the term "geometry" refers to the angles found on a bicycle frame. A frame's geometry greatly affects how the bicycle will handle when ridden. A hub is the center of a bicycle wheel and contains the axle and bearings. The hub is connected to the rim of the wheel by spokes. Most bicycle rear hubs are designed to accommodate a freewheel or a freehub. The sprocket or sprockets that comprise part of the bicycle's drivetrain are screwed onto the threads of a freewheel hub's body or slotted onto the freehub. The remaining parts of the drivetrain consist of the chain and the crankset (i.e., the chainwheel and cranks that are turned via the bicycle's pedals). The word "free" in the names of both types of hubs refers to the fact that the gearing attached to the hub can spin independently of the wheel—thus allowing the bicycle to coast. By contrast, a fixed-gear hub is not free, and the sprocket cannot spin independently of the wheel. Derailleurs are the mechanisms that move the chain onto different gears on most multigeared bicycles. There are front and rear derailleurs, allowing shifting at both ends of the drivetrain (i.e., the sprocket cluster attached to the hub, and the chainwheels attached to the crankset).

7. The semiotics of this first design are really quite fascinating. On one level the message on the shirt means exactly what it says: messengers are in no position to be giving legal advice. However, as regulars within the court filing room, messengers actually have a great deal of knowledge about the court's bureaucratic procedures. This is a source of great pride for many messengers (especially since lawyers, who often are totally removed from this part of the legal process, sometimes lack such knowledge). Thus, as most couriers understand the shirt's message, it indicates that the wearer has knowledge the reader wants, but he will refrain from providing it. In this sense the shirt is defiant.

8. See David Graham, "Wide Eyed," *Toronto Star,* June 18, 1998.

9. See Rob Walker, *Buying In: The Secret Dialogue between What We Buy and Who We Are* (New York: Random House, 2008).

10. If you are unfamiliar with bike polo, visualize regular polo but replace the horses with bikes, and instead of collared shirts, white trousers, and riding boots imagine punk-rock and heavy-metal T-shirts, cut-off camo shorts, and dingy sneakers.

11. William Geist, "Fastest Is Best as Messengers Pedal in Pursuit of a $100 Day," *New York Times,* December 2, 1983.

12. Jack M. Kugelmass,"I'd Rather Be a Messenger," *Natural History* 90 (1981): 67.

13. A new action movie about bike messengers, *Premium Rush* (starring Joseph Gordon-Levitt), is slated to be released in 2012.

14. See respectively: Philip Bozzo's letter to the editor, "Law-Flouting Couriers" *The New York Times,* December 16, 1983, A34; Worm and the Apple, "Red Light for Reckless Bikes," *The New York Times,* December 9, 1983, A34.

15. Sarah Lyall, "For Manhattan Couriers, Brakeless Bikes Are the Way to Go," *New York Times,* June 14, 1987; Walter Goodman, "Screen: 'Quicksilver,'" *New York Times,* February 14, 1986; Benjamin Ward, quoted in Alan Finder, "New York to Ban Bicycles on 3 Major Avenues," *New York Times,* July 23, 1987.

16. Bob Levy, "Do Messengers Own Their Bikes?" *Washington Post,* September 4, 1987; Levy, "The Squirrel That Got Biked to Death," *Washington Post,* November 2, 1991.

17. The Worm and the Apple, "Barreling Bikes and Blind Buses," *New York Times*, July 3, 1984; Ed Koch, quoted in Finder; The Worm and the Apple, "Barreling Bikes and Blind Buses"; Joyce Purnick, "Koch Approves Bill Regulating Bicycle Messengers," *New York Times*, July 7, 1984; Kirk Johnson, "Bicycle Ban on 3 Midtown Avenues Is Delayed for a Week by Judge," *New York Times*, September 1, 1987.

18. See "Assault by Bicycle," *New York Times*, November 21, 1997.

19. See Beth Daley and Jason Pring, "Outcry over Bicycle Couriers: Civic Leader Still in Coma after Being Struck," *Boston Globe*, November 7, 1997; Zachary R. Dowdy, "Chamber Urges Firms to Use Licensed Bike Couriers Only," *Boston Globe*, November 14, 1997.

20. Rudy Giuliani, quoted in Michael Cooper, "On Sidewalk, Fatal Collision with Bicyclist," *New York Times*, November 20, 1997; Kit R. Roane, "Bicyclists Are Police Priority after a Fatal Crash," *New York Times*, November 30, 1997.

3. Men's Work and Dirty Work

1. See, for example, Paul Willis, "Shop Floor Culture, Masculinity, and the Wage Form," in *Working-Class Culture: Studies in History and Theory*, ed. John Clarke, Chas Critcher, and Richard Johnson (London: Hutchinson, 1979), 196. Writing of arduous factory work, Willis observes: "Manual labor is suffused with masculine qualities and given to sensual overtones. The toughness and awkwardness of physical work and effort...takes masculine lights and depths and assumes a significance beyond itself....The brutality of the working situation is partially reinterpreted into a heroic exercise of manly confrontation with 'the task.'" Also see Irene Padavic, "The Re-Creation of Gender in a Male Workplace," *Symbolic Interaction* 14 (1991): 279–94.

2. See Michael Kimmel, *The History of Men: Essays in the History of American and British Masculinities* (Albany, NY: State University of New York Press, 2005).

3. On this point, see Gary Alan Fine, "In the Company of Men: Female Accommodation and the Folk Culture of Male Groups," in *Manly Traditions: The Folk Roots of American Masculinities*, ed. Simon J. Bonner (Bloomington: Indiana University Press, 2005), 72. Reflecting on his numerous studies involving male-dominated groups, Fine remarks: "In general, men do not object to women participating in their groups out of some hostile or mysterious misogynist urge. It is not biology per se that is at issue, but rather the cultural and folk traditions that surround gender in society."

4. For example, this does not appear to be the case in construction work or firefighting. See Susan Eisenberg, *We'll Call You If We Need You: Experiences of Women Working Construction* (Ithaca, NY: ILR Press, 1997); Carol Chetkovich, *Real Heat: Gender and Race in Urban Fire Service* (New Brunswick, NJ: Rutgers University Press, 1998).

5. See Cynthia F. Epstein, "Encountering the Male Establishment: Sex-Status Limits on Women's Careers in the Professions," *American Journal of Sociology* 75 (1970): 965–82.

6. See Lisa Adkins, "The New Economy, Property, and Personhood," *Theory, Culture, and Society* 22 (2002): 111–30; Jane Kenway, Anna Kraack, and Anna Hickey-Moody, *Masculinity beyond the Metropolis* (New York: Palgrave Macmillan, 2006).

7. See Blake E. Ashforth and Glen E. Kreiner, "How Can You Do It? Dirty Work and the Challenge of Constructing a Positive Identity," *Academy of Management Review* 24 (1999): 414–34.

8. William E. Thompson, "Handling the Stigma of Handling the Dead: Morticians and Funeral Directors," *Deviant Behavior* 12 (1991): 403–29; William E. Thompson, Jackie L. Harred, and Barbara E. Burks, "Managing the Stigma of Topless Dancing: A Decade Later," *Deviant Behavior* 24 (2003): 551–70.

9. Seymour Martin Lipset, Martin A. Trow, and James S. Coleman, *Union Democracy: The Internal Politics of the International Typographical Union* (Glencoe, IL: Free Press, 1956); William J. Sonnenstuhl and Harrison M. Trice, "The Social Construction of Alcohol Problems in a Union's Peer Counseling Program," *Journal of Drug Issues* 17 (1987): 223–54. The same could also be said of architects and railway workers: see Graeme Salaman, *Community and Occupation: An Exploration of Work/Leisure Relationships* (London: Cambridge University Press, 1974).

4. Playing in Traffic

1. See George Ritzer, *The McDonaldization of Society: An Investigation into the Changing Character of Contemporary Social Life* (Thousand Oaks, CA: Pine Forge Press, 1993).

2. For a study specifically about McDonald's, see Robin Leidner, *Fast Food, Fast Talk: Service Work and the Routinization of Everyday Life* (Berkeley: University of California Press, 1993). For a discussion about the increasingly alienating character of modern labor, see Richard Sennett, *The Corrosion of Character: The Personal Consequences of Work in the New Capitalism* (New York: W. W. Norton, 1998).

3. See Michael Burawoy, *Manufacturing Consent: Changes in the Labor Process under Monopoly Capitalism* (Chicago: University of Chicago Press, 1979).

4. See Mihaly Csikszentmihalyi, *Beyond Boredom and Anxiety: The Experience of Play in Work and Games* (San Francisco: Jossey-Bass Publishers, 1975).

5. Social psychologist George Herbert Mead refers to this authentic state of the self as the "I." See George Herbert Mead, *Mind, Self, and Society: From the Standpoint of a Social Behaviourist* (Chicago: University of Chicago Press, 1962). The "I" is the source of creative, spontaneous action, and Mead distinguishes it from the "me." Whereas the "I" exists only in the moment of action, the "me" arises from the internalized expectations of one's community. The "I," of course, is not instinctual. It is shaped through socialization. But the actions of the "I" feel instinctual because the individual does not consciously reflect on how others will judge the appropriateness of her response.

6. See, for example, Robert Blauner, *Alienation and Freedom: The Factory Worker and His Industry* (Chicago: University of Chicago Press, 1964); Donald F. Roy, "Work Satisfaction and Social Reward in Quota Achievement: An Analysis of Piecework Incentive," *American Sociological Review* 18 (1953): 507–14; Roy, "Banana Time: Job Satisfaction and Informal Interaction," *Human Organization* 18 (1959): 158–68; William E. Thompson, "Hanging Tongues: A Sociological Encounter with the Assembly Line," *Qualitative Sociology* 6 (1983): 215–37. The same can also be said of some white-collar

work. Caitlin Zaloom, for example, describes the emotional excitement generated during financial trading. See Caitlin Zaloom, *Out of the Pits: Traders and Technology from Chicago to London* (Chicago: University of Chicago Press, 2006).

7. See Stanley Aronowitz, *False Promises: The Shaping of American Working Class Consciousness* (New York: McGraw-Hill, 1973); Robert Caillois, *Men, Play, and Games,* trans. Meyer Barash (New York: Free Press of Glencoe, 1961); Viktor Gecas, "In Search of the Real Self: Problems of Authenticity in Modern Times," in *Self, Collective Behavior, and Society,* ed. Gerald M. Platt and Chad Gordon (Greenwich, CT: JAI Press, 1994), 139–54.

8. Eddie Williams has been a New York courier since the 1980s, and he has published his own photographic account of the messenger subculture: *Bike Messengers Life: New York City* (Madrid: La Fabrica, 2006).

9. Kid, quoted in Peter Sutherland's documentary *Pedal* (New York: PowerHouse Books, 2006).

10. Travis Hugh Culley, *The Immortal Class: Bike Messengers and the Cult of Human Power* (New York: Villard, 2002), 97.

11. See Stephen G. Lyng, "Edgework: A Social Psychological Analysis of Voluntary Risk Taking," *American Journal Sociology* 95 (1990): 851–86.

12. Lyng notes: "In contrast to the aims of normal, day-to-day behavior, the immediate goal of one's actions in edgework cannot be regarded as trivial. The point is survival, and most people feel no ambivalence about the value of this goal" (881). However, Lyng attempts to draw a strong distinction between his theory of edgework and Csikszentmihalyi's flow. If flow is at the threshold of boredom and anxiety, Lyng posits edgework as crossing well into the territory of anxiety. In fact, anxiety is the edge that is pushed. On one level, Lyng is certainly right. The flow generated in a challenging game of chess or a tense match of tennis should be differentiated from that created in activities in which a person is flirting with his own death. However, this is a difference of degree not kind. Lyng is correct to draw attention to the fact that edgeworkers find release in activities outsiders would find highly stressful, if not terrifying. This may seem to be far beyond the happy medium of flow, but it is really just a more intense version of the same experience. While Lyng's respondents use adjectives like "stressful" and "anxious" to describe their experiences, their ability both to survive and to desire repetition prove that edgeworkers are, in fact, simply engrossed in tasks perfectly matched by their skills. Therefore, I subsume edgework within the larger concept of flow. The denotation of edgework as a distinct type of flow is useful because it acknowledges that flow is a broader, generic process. Flow (whether it is edgework or something less dangerous) is generally enjoyable, and always authentic.

13. See Aronowitz, 62.

14. Burawoy, 89.

15. Lyng, 861.

16. See Jason, "The Line," *Urban Death Maze* 2 (1999): 9.

17. Steve the Greek, quoted in Sutherland.

18. Eric, quoted in Sutherland.

19. In 2008, Jason helped open the Second Chance Saloon in Brooklyn. The bar serves inexpensive drinks, hosts generous weekend barbeques, and maintains a stellar punk-rock jukebox. The staff and clientele are often current or former messengers.

20. Don Cuerdon, "I Was a New York City Bike Messenger: Five Days as a Rough Rider in the Big Apple's Hard Corps," *Bicycle Magazine,* March 1990, 84.

21. Aronowitz, 132.

22. Aronowitz, 132.

5. The Deep Play of Alleycats

1. Émile Durkheim, *The Elementary Forms of Religious Life,* trans. Karen E. Fields (New York: Free Press, 1995), 232.

2. See Roy Rappaport, *Ritual and Religion in the Making of Humanity* (New York: Cambridge University Press, 1999).

3. Victor W. Turner observes: "Ritual...periodically converts the obligatory into the desirable." Victor W. Turner, "Symbols in Ndembu Ritual," in *The Forest of Symbols: Aspects of Ndembu Ritual* (Ithaca, NY: Cornell University Press, 1967), 30.

4. This point is elaborated in great detail by Rappaport.

5. See Jeffrey C. Alexander, "Cultural Pragmatics: Social Performance between Ritual and Strategy," *Sociological Theory* 22 (2004): 527–73.

6. To quote Durkheim, "The man who has obeyed his god [i.e., society], and who for this reason thinks he has his god with him, approaches the world with confidence and a sense of heightened energy" (*Elementary Forms of Religious Life,* 211). Further, Durkheim's understanding of ritual directly connects to Mead's theory of the self; see George Herbert Mead, *Mind, Self, and Society: From the Standpoint of a Social Behaviourist* (Chicago: University of Chicago Press, 1962). For both theorists, there is a tension between personal desires and required social roles. Following Mead, the self arises in part from internalizing the role of the other, but ego's behavior is always a process of *mediation* between individual spontaneity and extraindividual norms. There are times, however, when the "I" and "me" can reach perfect agreement. This is what rituals achieve by collectivizing flow, and in the process the "I" and "me" fuse. Mead explains: "There is a sense of common effort in which one is stimulated by the others to do the same thing they are doing. In those situations one has a sense of being identified with all because the reaction is essentially an identical reaction" (273). Like Durkheim in describing religion, Mead refers to this state as "exaltation," and the exalting fusion of the "I" and "me" gives action an absolute purpose.

7. Clifford Geertz, "Religion as a Cultural System," in *Interpretation of Cultures: Selected Essays* (New York: Basic Books, 1973), 112.

8. See Randall Collins, *Interaction Ritual Chains* (Princeton, NJ: Princeton University Press, 2004).

9. Clifford Geertz, "Deep Play: Notes on the Balinese Cockfight," in *Interpretation of Cultures,* 449, 443, and 449.

10. Johnny, quoted in Peter Sutherland's documentary *Pedal* (New York: Power-House Books, 2006).

11. Durkheim, *Elementary Forms of Religious Life,* 212. This particular passage refers to what Durkheim calls the "demon of oratorical inspiration."

12. This is what Geertz ("Religion as a Cultural System") calls a model *of* reality.

13. This is Geertz's model *for* reality. See Geertz, "Religion as a Cultural System."

14. Collins, *Interaction Ritual Chains.*

15. "The Biker's Creed," *Urban Death Maze* 6 (2000): 11.

16. See Peter Donnelly and Kevin Young, "Reproduction and Transformation of Cultural Forms in Sport: A Contextual Analysis of Rugby," *International Review for the Sociology of Sport* 20 (1985): 19–38.

17. See Peter L. Berger and Thomas Luckmann, *The Social Construction of Reality: A Treatise in the Sociology of Knowledge* (New York: Anchor Books, 1966).

18. See Geertz, "Religion as a Cultural System." It is through rituals that the world as it is actually lived and the world as it is religiously imagined become one. That is, rituals are models *of* and *for* reality.

19. Durkheim, *Elementary Forms of Religious Life,* 215.

20. See Christena Nippert-Eng, *Home and Work: Negotiating Boundaries through Everyday Life* (Chicago: University of Chicago Press, 1996).

6. The Affective Appropriation of Space

1. On these points, see Thomas Gieryn, "A Space for Place in Sociology," *Annual Review of Sociology* 26 (2000): 465: "Space is what place becomes when the unique gathering of things, meanings, and values are sucked out.... Put positively, place is space filled up by people, practices, objects, and representations." While the argument developed here is about space, not place, I am arguing that actions and meanings must be *emplaced* (i.e., connected to the physical environments in which they occur).

2. Clifford Geertz, "Thick Description: Toward an Interpretive Theory of Culture," in *Interpretation of Cultures: Selected Essays* (New York: Basic Books, 1973), 22: "The locus of study is not the object of study. Anthropologists don't study villages (tribes, towns, or neighborhoods...); they study *in* villages. You can study different things in different places.... But that doesn't make the place what it is you are studying."

3. In one of the early statements of what would become the Chicago School of urban research, Robert E. Park notes: "The small community often tolerates eccentricity. The city, on the contrary, rewards it. Neither the criminal, the defective, nor the genius has the same opportunity to develop his innate dispositions in a small town that he invariably finds in a great city." Robert E. Park, "The City: Suggestions for the Investigation of Human Behavior in the Urban Environment," in *The City,* ed. Robert E. Park, Ernest W. Burgess, and Roderick D. McKenzie (Chicago: University of Chicago Press, 1967), 41. As we have seen, bike messengers fit this depiction perfectly. They are one of the countless cultural variations proliferating within a metropolis unfettered by the mores of the *Gemeinschaft.* Urbanists have long chronicled the social worlds that make cities fascinating, fearful, and frustrating places. Largely absent from this literature, however, is a serious engagement with *physical* space. And this last point may require some clarification. Ethnographers have done an excellent job in depicting the environments they have researched. Gerald D. Suttles' *Social Order of the Slum: Ethnicity and Territory in the Inner City* (Chicago: University of Chicago Press, 1968), for example, wonderfully describes Chicago's Near West Side and the meanings the various places in the neighborhood have for its residents. The same can be said of Mario Luis Small's more recent work, *Villa Victoria: The Transformation*

of Social Capital in a Boston Barrio (Chicago: University of Chicago Press, 2004). Detailing the physical landscape and explaining the cultural values attributed to it, however, is not what I mean by a serious engagement with physical space. Instead, as we will see in this chapter, and as I will expand in the theoretical appendix, I am advocating for a sociological analysis of the material world that conceptualizes it as dialectically *interconnected* with human agency. It is certainly possible to read Suttles or Small (or the work of any number of urbanists) from such a perspective. However, this is not the stated goal of their research. Place is ever present in their analysis, but it is not shown to be inseparable from the social actions they describe.

4. See Anthony Giddens, *The Constitution of Society: Outline of the Theory of Structuration* (Berkeley: University of California Press, 1984).

5. Anthony Giddens, *Central Problems in Social Theory: Action, Structure, and Contradiction in Social Analysis* (Berkeley: University of California Press, 1979), 5.

6. To clarify these terms: skateboarders move by rolling their boards across the ground or other surfaces, they do tricks in which they grind their trucks (i.e., the metal axles connecting the wheels and attaching them to the board) across a surface (e.g., a curb or the top of a skate ramp), and they can also make their boards jump off the ground to get onto curbs and other objects or simply as a trick unto itself—this is called ollieing.

7. Iain Borden, *Skateboarding, Space, and the City: Architecture and the Body* (New York: Berg 2001), 192.

8. Travis Hugh Culley, *The Immortal Class: Bike Messengers and the Cult of Human Power* (New York: Villard, 2002), 189.

9. Ray, quoted in William Geist, "Fastest Is Best as Messengers Pedal in Pursuit of a $100 Day," *New York Times,* December 2, 1983.

10. Josh, quoted in Thomas Mucha and Mark Scheffler's video report, "Entrepreneurs in Action: The Need for Speed; Efficiency Theories and Occupational Hazards of a Bike Messenger," *Business Chicago Powered by Crain's,* July 9, 2007, http://link.brightcove.com/services/player/bcpid980748097.

11. See Dave Horton, "Fear of Cycling," in *Cycling and Society,* ed. Dave Horton, Paul Rosen, and Peter Cox (Burlington, VT: Ashgate, 2007), 133–52; Bob Mionske, *Bicycling and the Law: Your Rights as a Cyclist* (Boulder, CO: VeloPress, 2007); David B. Perry, *Bike Cult: The Ultimate Guide to Human-Powered Vehicles* (New York: Four Walls Eight Windows, 1995).

12. On these points (and many more), see Tom Vanderbilt, *Traffic: Why We Drive the Way We Do (and What It Says about Us)* (New York: Alfred A. Knopf, 2008).

13. For Victor W. Turner, "liminality may perhaps be regarded as the Nay to all positive structural assertions, but as in some sense the source of them all, and, more than that, as a realm of pure possibility whence *novel* configurations of ideas and relations may arise." Victor W. Turner, "Betwixt and Between: The Liminal Period in *Rites de Passage,*" in *The Forest of Symbols: Aspects of Ndembu Ritual* (Ithaca, NY: Cornell University Press, 1967), 97.

14. See Robert Hurst, *The Art of Urban Cycling: Lessons from the Street* (Guilford, CT: Falcon, 2004).

15. See Turner, "Betwixt and Between." In Turner's anthropological writing, novel configurations do not arise from a void, but from a dynamic tension between

two structural positions. For example, they arise during the transitional period between being a boy and a man.

16. Giddens, *Constitution of Society,* 174.

17. See Henri Lefebvre, *Everyday Life in the Modern World,* trans. Sacha Rabinovitch (London: Penguin Press, 1971); Lefebvre, *The Production of Space,* trans. Donald Nicholson-Smith (Oxford: Blackwell, 1991); see also Michel de Certeau, *The Practices of Everyday Life,* trans. Steven Rendall (Berkeley: University of California Press, 1984).

7. The Meaning of Messenger Style

1. Hannah Allam, "Messenger Chic Is Now a Fashion Statement / The Workplace: They Operate by the Seat of Their Bikes," *Minneapolis Star Tribune,* August 6, 1997.

2. Valerie Steele, introduction to *Messengers Style,* by Philippe Bialobos (New York: Assouline, 2000), 3. As an aside, it is bizarre how social commentators often let their assumptions about things distort their actual perceptions of them. In the introduction to this book we saw the following quote from *New York Times* writer Felicia Lee: "Some of these boys look good in tights." Truthfully, hardly any of these boys wear tights. Likewise, Steele assumes that the physical demands of the job must result in athletically toned physiques. But truthfully this is rarely the case. Jason, for example, referred to one of the most revered messenger crews from Boston as "fat drunks" who "brought folding chairs to races." Messengers can lack athletically toned physiques and still be fast, because a messenger's speed is about micro-routing not outright cardiovascular fitness.

3. Clifford Geertz, "Deep Play: Notes on the Balinese Cockfight," in *Interpretations of Culture: Selected Essays* (New York: Basic Books, 1973), 452.

4. Mike Brake, *Comparative Youth Culture: The Sociology of Youth Cultures and Youth Subcultures in America, Britain, and Canada* (Boston: Routledge and K. Paul, 1985).

5. Theorists often contrast semiotic approaches to culture with practice-based approaches. Semioticians, by the very nature of their analysis, conceptualize cultures as forming *systems* of meaning. Thus the researcher's job is to decode these systems by explicating how a cultural phenomenon also functions as a sign phenomenon. See Umberto Eco, "Social Life as a Sign System," in *Structuralism: An Introduction,* ed. David Robey (Oxford: Clarendon Press, 1973). Such analyses tend to ignore the process by which a society actually produces and reproduces culture. In Geertz's eloquent description of the Balinese cockfight, for example, one cannot help but notice that the thoughts and practices of Balinese men and women are nearly absent. As readers, we learn about how roosters function as surrogates for the status of men, but we learn virtually nothing about the individuals actually involved in the ritual. The same can be said of sociologist Dick Hebdige's famous study of British punks, *Subculture: The Meaning of Style* (New York: Routledge, 1979). Hebdige posits punk as a disruption to bourgeois hegemony, but he gives us no account of everyday life in the subculture. On these various points, see Ann Swidler, *Talk of Love: How Culture Matters* (Chicago: University of Chicago Press, 2001). The practice-based semiotics I advocate here is predicated on the interdependence of systems and practice. That is to say, I am

interested in uncovering "the pragmatic *relations* between signs and the organizations of practice"; see Richard Biernacki, "Language and the Shift from Signs to Practice in Cultural Inquiry," *History and Theory* 39 (2000): 309; see also Willam H. Sewell, Jr., "The Concept(s) of Culture," in *Beyond the Cultural Turn*, ed. Victoria E. Bonnell and Lynn Hunt (Berkeley: University of California Press, 1999), 35–61.

6. See John Clarke, "Style," in *Resistance through Rituals: Youth Subcultures in Post-War Britain*, ed. Stuart Hall and Tony Jefferson (London: Hutchinson and Company, 1976), 175–81; Paul E. Willis, *Profane Culture* (Boston: Routledge and K. Paul, 1978).

7. Quoted in Peter Sutherland's documentary *Pedal* (New York: PowerHouse Books, 2006).

8. See Don H. Shamblin, "Brotherhood of Rebels: An Exploratory Analysis of a Motorcycle Outlaw Contraculture" (PhD diss., State University of New York at Buffalo, 1971).

9. Georg Simmel, "The Stranger," in *On Individuality and Social Forms*, ed. and trans. Donald N. Levine (Chicago: University of Chicago Press, 1971), 148.

10. Simmel, 144.

11. Travis Hugh Culley, *The Immortal Class: Bike Messengers and the Cult of Human Power* (New York: Villard, 2002), 189, 35.

12. Victor W. Turner, "Betwixt and Between: The Liminal Period in *Rites de Passage*," in *The Forest of Symbols: Aspects of Ndembu Ritual* (Ithaca, NY: Cornell University Press, 1964), 96.

13. Clarke, 179.

14. Hebdige, 122.

15. William H. Duvall, III, "Pedestrians May Swear at Bicycle Messengers, but Companies Swear by Them," *Chicago Tribune*, November 3, 1991.

16. See Victor W. Turner, "Symbols in Ndembu Ritual," in *Forest of Symbols*.

17. Quoted in Sutherland.

18. Daniel R. Wolf, *The Rebels: A Brotherhood of Outlaw Bikers* (Toronto: University of Toronto Press, 1991), 52–53.

19. See Jack M. Kugelmass, "I'd Rather Be a Messenger," *Natural History* 90 (1981): 66–73.

20. In New York, cyclists can get tickets for not having an operable hand brake. In Seattle, cyclists are rarely cited for not having brakes, but it has happened. Oddly, in San Diego, a city with no history of deadly messenger collisions or pubic outcry against messengers for any reason, one police officer made it his mission to try and eradicate brakeless track bikes from downtown. For many years this officer targeted messengers and routinely gave out tickets for bicycles being operated without a brake. One San Diego messenger challenged his citation in court by demonstrating that a fixed gear, while technically brakeless, is still stoppable. The messenger won his case. However, the same police officer continued to ticket messengers riding fixed (including the messenger who had won the case).

21. *Bricolage* is a French word that implies the clever use of tools and resources immediately available to resolve problems. A *bricoleur*, therefore, is somewhat like a jack-of-all-trades, but in French there is an element of deviousness to the term. Members of the Centre for Contemporary Cultural Studies at Birmingham University brought this term into popular usage within the analysis of subcultures. See, for example, Clarke and Hebdige.

22. Mountaineers also sew patches on their clothes to denote past climbing experience. See Richard G. Mitchell, Jr., *Mountain Experience: The Psychology and Sociology of Adventure* (Chicago: University of Chicago Press, 1983).

23. See Hebdige.

24. All of this said, a very large disclaimer must be attached to this chapter. As Stanley Cohen makes clear, the researcher's attempt to explain the meaning of style can easily slip into a realm of complete theoretical conjecture. Criticizing semiotic approaches to subculture, he remarks: "This is, to be sure, an imaginative way of reading the style, but how can we be sure that it is also not imaginary?" Stanley Cohen, "Symbols of Trouble: Introduction to the Second Edition," in *Folk Devils and Moral Panics: The Creation of Mods and Rockers,* 3rd ed. (New York: Routledge, 2002), lix. And Hebdige, while believing he had correctly cracked the punk rocker's code, acknowledged: "It is highly unlikely…that the members of any of the subcultures described in this book would recognize themselves reflected here" (139). In the end, I cannot prove that the analysis I offer here is accurate, and I worry that most messengers will feel I have taken too many liberties in reading over their shoulders. Perhaps I have, but I do not want the analysis provided in this chapter to be taken as definitive truth. Instead, I hope that both messengers and nonmessengers alike will allow me some leeway in my interpretations. As semiotician Umberto Eco has observed, styles have significance. That is what makes them styles and not simply raw material. After all, as humans we shroud all our actions and objects in meaning. At the same time, this meaning is often below the level of discursive consciousness. To take the symbols of affect-meaning and hammer them into a coherent and logical set of words is to alter the very nature of their meaning. Something that is lived cannot always be translated into something thought. For Geertz, cultural interpretations are always fictional. They are a translation of raw human experience into a codified genre. In this sense, literature and science are the same. The semiotic analysis offered here, therefore, is "something fashioned." Clifford Geertz, "Thick Description: Toward an Interpretative Theory of Culture" in *Interpretations of Culture: Selected Essays,* 14. As such, this is not real life but an etic reconstruction of messenger life. Within the theoretical paradigm used in this book the analysis in this chapter is "correct." Affect-meaning is not only emplaced, but emplaced emotional practices are interconnected with cultural meaning in what Biernacki calls a pragmatic relationship between practice and signs. However, such explanations may ring false to many who live the lifestyle. But, wrongheaded as it might seem to those within the subculture, for the sociologist interested in the subculture the homology between practice and symbols must be explored.

Conclusion

1. Stanley Aronowitz, *False Promises: The Shaping of American Working Class Consciousness* (New York: McGraw-Hill, 1973), 62.

2. Danny, quoted in Robert Lipsyte, "Coping: Voices from the 'Sweatshop of the Streets,'" *New York Times,* May 14, 1995; see also Selwyn Raab, "Teamsters Seeking to Form Bicycle Messengers' Union: Complaints Are Rife in a Tough, Risky Job," *New York Times,* October 30, 1994. Just a few years before the push to unionize, Saskia Sassen and Robert Smith, studying changes in the New York labor market,

referred to bike messengering as part of "the massive increase in low-wage, dead-end service jobs" accompanying globalization. Saskia Sassen and Robert Smith, *Post-Industrial Employment and Third World Immigration: Casualization and the New Mexican Migration in New York,* Papers on Latin America 26 (New York: Columbia University, 1991), 2.

3. Michael Burawoy, *Manufacturing Consent: Changes in the Labor Process under Monopoly Capitalism* (Chicago: University of Chicago Press, 1979), 34.

4. This is one of the main reasons Burawoy's research is so compelling, and his emphasis on lived experience has had a strong influence on my argument. As a point of contrast we can think about prominent French Marxist Louis Althusser's "Ideology and Ideological State Apparatuses (Notes towards an Investigation)," in *Lenin and Philosophy and Other Essays* (New York: Monthly Review Press, 1972). For Althusser, the workers' consent to domination in capitalism *is* attributable to the permeation of bourgeois ideology throughout society.

5. These managerially beneficial aspects of the game described by Burawoy can be contrasted with the counterproductive games described by industrial sociologist Donald F. Roy in "Banana Time: Job Satisfaction and Informal Interaction," *Human Organization* 18 (1959): 158–68. Roy describes factory employees who are completely unmotivated to produce and spend their time playing games that slow down or even stop work.

6. See Herbert Marcuse, *One-Dimensional Man: Studies in the Ideology of Advanced Industrial Society* (Boston: Beacon Press, 1964).

7. Burawoy, 89.

8. See Steven Lukes, *Power: A Radical View* (New York: Macmillan, 1974); see also Anthony Giddens, *Central Problems in Social Theory: Action, Structure, and Contradiction in Social Analysis* (Berkeley: University of California Press, 1979).

9. Giddens, *Central Problems in Social Theory,* 149.

10. By contrast, the counterproductive games described by Roy presumably reduce exploitation by cutting into the surplus managers and owners extract from their workers.

11. Burawoy, 199.

12. See Michel de Certeau, *The Practice of Everyday Life,* trans. Steven Rendall (Berkeley: University of California Press, 1984), xvii. Strategies are practices that produce and reproduce differential power relationships. Those in structurally stronger positions utilize strategies to control those in structurally weaker positions. Contrasting with strategies are tactics. Try as they might, those in structurally powerful positions can never totally control those in weaker ones. Beneath proper and official practices there is always a panoply of alternative practices. These alternatives are tactics. They are practices that coexist with a strategy, but surreptitiously subvert it.

13. See Karl Marx, "Economic and Philosophic Manuscripts of 1844," in *The Marx-Engels Reader,* ed. Robert C. Tucker (New York: W. W. Norton, 1978), 66–125.

14. Following Marcuse's idea of repressive satisfaction, the more cynical reader may feel inclined to position messengers as alienated—so alienated they are unaware of it. Such a critique relies on the notion of false consciousness, but the existence of false consciousness (in anyone) and how such a concept can be operationalized is a debatable (and potentially unsolvable) matter. If nothing else, it is clearly a patronizing way for sociologists to analyze their subjects. Moreover, it is a mistake to write

off the creative control messengers exert in their labor simply because they supply surplus labor. I want to argue that alienation, and the ability to transcend it, is at the very heart of liberty.

15. See Saskia Sassen, *Cities in a World Economy* (Thousand Oaks, CA: Pine Forge Press, 2006).

16. Henri Lefebvre, *The Production of Space* (Oxford: Blackwell, 1991), 51; see also Andy Merrifield, *Henri Lefebvre: A Critical Introduction* (New York: Routledge, 2006).

17. Certeau, 98.

18. See, for example, Robert Blauner, *Alienation and Freedom: The Factory Worker and His Industry* (Chicago: University of Chicago Press, 1964); Richard Sennett, *The Corrosion of Character: The Personal Consequences of Work in the New Capitalism* (New York: W. W. Norton, 1998).

19. There is, of course, a contradiction here. Bike messengers are part of a postindustrial strategy for profit making. Their own interests, however, are removed from such matters. For an elaboration on this matter, see Jeffrey L. Kidder, "Mobility as Strategy, Mobility as Tactic: Post-Industrialism and Bike Messengers," in *The Cultures of Alternative Mobilities: Routes Less Travelled,* ed. Phillip Vannini (Aldershot, UK: Ashgate Publishing, 2009).

20. See André Gorz, *Farewell to the Working Class: An Essay on Post-Industrial Socialism,* trans. Michael Sonenscher (London: Pluto Press, 1982).

Appendix A

1. Arlie Russell Hochschild, "Emotion Work, Feeling Rules, and Social Structure," *American Journal of Sociology* 85 (1979): 553–54.

2. See James Averill, "A Constructivist View of Emotion," in *Emotion: Theory, Research, and Experience,* ed. Robert Plutchik and Henry Kellerman (New York: Academic Press, 1980); Kwai Hang Ng and Jeffrey L. Kidder, "Toward a Theory of Emotive Performance: With Lessons from How Politicians Do Anger," *Sociological Theory* 28 (2010): 193–214; Carl Ratner, "A Cultural-Psychological Analysis of Emotions," *Culture and Psychology* 6 (2000): 5–39.

3. Arlie Russell Hochschild, *The Managed Heart: Commercialization of Human Feeling* (Berkeley: University of California Press, 1983).

4. See Thomas J. Scheff, *Microsociology: Discourse, Emotions, and Social Structure* (Chicago: University of Chicago Press, 1990).

5. Jack Katz, *How Emotions Work* (Chicago: University of Chicago Press, 1999), 334.

6. Norman K. Denzin, *On Understanding Emotion* (San Francisco: Jossey-Bass Publishers, 1984), 85.

7. Katz, *How Emotions Work,* 332.

8. Denzin, 59.

9. Loïc Wacquant, *Body and Soul: Notebooks of an Apprentice Boxer* (New York: Oxford University Press, 2004), 7.

10. See Pierre Bourdieu, *Distinction: A Social Critique of the Judgment of Taste,* trans. Richard Nice (Cambridge, MA: Harvard University Press, 1984).

11. Pierre Bourdieu, *The Logic of Practice*, trans. Richard Nice (Stanford, CA: Stanford University Press, 1990), 68 and 73.

12. Émile Durkheim, *Division of Labor in Society*, trans. W. D. Hall (New York: Free Press, 1984), 61; see also Durkheim, "The Dualism of Human Nature and Its Social Conditions," in *On Morality and Society: Selected Writing*, ed. Robert N. Bellah (Chicago: University of Chicago Press, 1973).

13. George Herbert Mead, *Mind, Self, and Society: From the Standpoint of a Social Behaviourist* (Chicago: University of Chicago Press, 1962), 174.

14. Mead, 204.

15. See Jack Katz, *Seductions of Crime: Moral and Sensual Attractions in Doing Evil* (New York: Basic Books, 1988). Katz describes a "righteous slaughter" in which offended individuals become singularly focused on avenging their defamed sense of self.

16. This point is more thoroughly elaborated (in non-Meadian terms) in Anthony Giddens's theory of structuration in *The Constitution of Society: Outline of the Theory of Structuration* (Berkeley: University of California Press, 1984).

17. See Stephen Lyng, "Edgework: A Social Psychological Analysis of Voluntary Risk Taking," *American Journal of Sociology* 95 (1990): 851–86; Richard G. Mitchell, Jr., *Mountain Experience: The Psychology and Sociology of Adventure* (Chicago: University of Chicago Press, 1983).

18. Émile Durkheim, *The Elementary Forms of Religious Life*, trans. Karen E. Fields (New York: Free Press, 1995), 217.

19. See Jeffrey Alexander, "Cultural Pragmatics: Social Performance between Ritual and Strategy," *Sociological Theory* 22 (2004): 527–73.

20. See Roy Rappaport, *Ritual and Religion in the Making of Humanity* (New York: Cambridge University Press, 1999).

21. Durkheim, *Elementary Forms of Religious Life*, 213.

22. See Rappaport.

23. Herbert J. Gans, "Planning for People Not Buildings," *Environment and Planning* 1 (1969): 37–38 and 39; see also Gans, "The Sociology of Space: A Use-Centered View," *City and Community* 1 (2002): 329–39.

24. For example, see Roger Friedland and Deirdre Boden's introduction to *NowHere: Space, Time, and Modernity* (Berkeley: University of California Press, 1994); Allan Pred, *Place, Practice, and Structure: Social and Spatial Transformation in Southern Sweden, 1750–1850* (Cambridge, UK: Polity Press, 1986); Edward W. Soja, "Spatializations: A Critique of the Giddensian Version," in *Postmodern Geographies: The Reassertion of Space in Critical Social Theory* (New York: Verso, 1989), 138–56; Benno Werlen, *Society, Action, and Space: An Alternative Human Geography*, trans. Gayna Walls (New York: Routledge, 1993). Michel Foucault has also attracted the attention of social researchers to the importance of the built environment. As an example, see Michel Foucault, "Questions of Geography," in *Power/Knowledge: Selected Interviews and Other Writings, 1972–1977*, ed. Colin Gordon and trans. Colin Gordon, Leo Marshall, John Mepham, and Kate Soper (New York: Pantheon Books, 1980), 63–77. However, Foucault's genealogical approach—which removes the subjective from history, leaving only docile bodies subjected to power and knowledge—is antithetical to the hermeneutic approach of the argument developed here.

25. Giddens, *Constitution of Society*, 17.

26. Anthony Giddens, *New Rules of Sociological Method: A Positive Critique of Interpretative Sociologies* (New York: Basic Books, 1976), 119.

27. See William H. Sewell, Jr., "A Theory of Structure: Duality, Agency, and Transformation," *American Journal of Sociology* 98 (1992): 1–29.

28. Giddens, *Constitution of Society*, 33.

29. See Henri Lefebvre, *The Production of Space*, trans. Donald Nicholson-Smith (Oxford: Blackwell, 1991).

30. This point is detailed by Peter L. Berger and Thomas Luckmann in *The Social Construction of Reality: A Treatise in the Sociology of Knowledge* (New York: Anchor Books, 1966).

31. Pierre Bourdieu, "The Kabyle House or the World Reversed," in *Logic of Practice*, 271–83.

32. Lefebvre, *Production of Space*, 142.

33. For Western examples, see Dolores Hayden, *Redesigning the American Dream: The Future of Housing, Work, and Family Life* (New York: W. W. Norton, 1984); Daphne Spain, *Gendered Space* (Chapel Hill: University of North Carolina Press, 1992).

34. Lefebvre, *Production of Space*, 362.

35. On this issue of social capital and the built environment, see Mario Luis Small, *Villa Victoria: The Transformation of Social Capital in a Boston Barrio* (Chicago: University of Chicago Press, 2004).

36. Lefebvre, *Production of Space*, 404.

37. Thomas J. Gieryn, "A Space for Place in Sociology," *Annual Review of Sociology* 26 (2000): 466; see also Gieryn, "Give Place a Chance: Reply to Gans," *City and Community* 1 (2002): 341–43.

38. See Pred, *Place, Practice, and Structure*.

39. See Herbert J. Gans, *Urban Villagers: Group and Class in the Life of Italian-Americans* (New York: Free Press, 1962).

40. Edward W. Soja, "The Socio-Spatial Dialectic," in *Postmodern Geographies*, 81.

41. See David Harvey, *Social Justice and the City* (Baltimore: John Hopkins University Press, 1973); see also Derek Gregory, *Geographical Imaginations* (Cambridge, MA: Blackwell, 1994); Doreen Massey, *Spatial Divisions of Labor: Social Structures and the Geography of Production* (New York: Methuen, 1984).

42. See Pred, *Place, Practice, and Structure;* Edward W. Soja, "Taking Los Angeles Apart: Some Fragments of a Critical Human Geography," *Environment and Planning D* 4 (1986); David Harvey, *Paris, Capital of Modernity* (New York: Routledge, 2003).

43. Edward W. Soja, "Preface and Postscript," in *Postmodern Geographies*, 7.

44. See Michael Mayerfeld Bell, *Childerley: Nature and Morality in a Country Village* (Chicago: University of Chicago Press, 1994).

45. Caroline Fusco, "Spatializing the (Im)Proper Subject: The Geographies of Abjection in Sport and Physical Activity," *Journal of Sport and Social Issues* 30 (2005): 5–28. The same could also be said of John Manzo, "Social Control and the Management of 'Personal' Space in Shopping Malls," *Space and Culture* 8 (2005): 83–97; and of Christena Nippert-Eng, "Boundary Play," *Space and Culture* 8 (2005): 302–24.

46. See Michael Mayerfeld Bell, "The Ghost of Place," *Theory and Society* 26 (1997): 813–36.

47. Iain Borden, *Skateboarding, Space, and the City: Architecture and the Body* (New York: Berg, 2001), 101, 96, and 107.

Appendix B

1. See Bronislaw Malinowski, *Argonauts of the Western Pacific: An Account of Native Enterprise and Adventure in the Archipelagoes of Melanesian New Guinea* (New York: E. P. Dutton, 1950).

2. Nels Anderson, *The Hobo: The Sociology of the Homeless Man* (Chicago: University of Chicago Press, 1961); Edwin Sutherland, *The Professional Thief* (Chicago: University of Chicago Press, 1937); see also Robert Prus, *Symbolic Interaction and Ethnographic Research: Intersubjectivity and the Study of Human Lived Experience* (Albany, NY: State University of New York Press, 1996).

3. For more on detached involvement, see Dennison Nash, "The Ethnologist as Stranger: An Essay on the Sociology of Knowledge," *Southwest Journal of Anthropology* 19 (1963): 149–67.

4. The increased valuation of situated and subjective knowing comes from what Jean-François Lyotard describes as a crisis in verifying and validating objective, overarching knowledge claims. See Jean-François Lyotard, *The Postmodern Condition: A Report on Knowledge*, trans. Geoff Benninton and Brian Massumi (Minneapolis: University of Minnesota Press, 1984).

5. Richard K. Nelson, *Hunters of the Northern Ice* (Chicago: University of Chicago Press, 1969).

6. Daniel R. Wolf, *The Rebels: A Brotherhood of Outlaw Bikers* (Toronto: University of Toronto Press, 1991), 22 and 27.

7. Loïc Wacquant, *Body and Soul: Notebooks of an Apprentice Boxer* (New York: Oxford University Press, 2004), 11. Wacquant is borrowing the idea of "surrender" from Kurt Wolf, "Surrender and Community Study: The Study of Loma," in *Reflections on Community,* ed. Arthur J. Vidich and Joseph Bensman (New York: Wiley, 1964), 233–63.

8. Wacquant, *Body and Soul,* vi.

9. On this point, see Pierre Bourdieu, *Outline of a Theory of Practice,* trans. Richard Nice (New York: Cambridge University Press, 1977); see also Loïc Wacquant, "Towards a Social Praxology: The Structure and Logic of Bourdieu's Sociology," in *An Invitation to Reflexive Sociology,* ed. Pierre Bourdieu and Loïc J. D. Wacquant (Chicago: University of Chicago Press, 1992), 1–60.

10. Wacquant, *Body and Soul,* viii.

11. Bourdieu, *Outline of a Theory of Practice,* 1.

12. In New York, however, I was viewed as a rookie by other couriers. This distinction is no small matter. While I was accepted as an insider, I had not earned the rights and status of a veteran messenger. For example, around both rookies and outsiders, veteran messengers put on a facade of indifference toward poor weather, but they appear to have no problems bemoaning cold and wet conditions with other veterans. So I was an insider, but an insider with limits to certain categories of knowledge.

13. I am borrowing the phrase "interpretive gloss" from David Muggleton, *Inside Subculture: The Postmodern Meaning of Style* (New York: Berg, 2000), 7.

REFERENCES

Adkins, Lisa. "The New Economy, Property, and Personhood." *Theory, Culture, and Society* 22 (2002): 111–30.

Advertisement for Cycle Messenger World Championship. *Urban Death Maze* 7 (2000): 21.

Alexander, Jeffrey C. "Cultural Pragmatics: Social Performance between Ritual and Strategy." *Sociological Theory* 22 (2004): 527–73.

Allam, Hannah. "Messenger Chic Is Now a Fashion Statement / The Workplace: They Operate by the Seat of Their Bikes." *Minneapolis Star Tribune,* August 6, 1997.

Allan, Kenneth. *The Meaning of Culture: Moving the Postmodern Critique Forward.* Westport, CT: Praeger, 1998.

Althusser, Louis. "Ideology and Ideological State Apparatuses (Notes towards an Investigation)." In *Lenin and Philosophy and Other Essays,* translated by Ben Brewster, 127–86. New York: Monthly Review Press, 1972.

Anderson, Nels. *The Hobo: The Sociology of the Homeless Man.* Chicago: University of Chicago Press, 1961.

Aronowitz, Stanley. *False Promises: The Shaping of American Working Class Consciousness.* New York: McGraw-Hill, 1973.

Ashforth, Blake E., and Glen E. Kreiner. "How Can You Do It? Dirty Work and the Challenge of Constructing a Positive Identity." *Academy of Management Review* 24 (1999): 414–34.

"Assault by Bicycle." *New York Times,* November 21, 1997.

Averill, James. "A Constructivist View of Emotion." In *Emotion: Theory, Research, and Experience,* edited by Robert Plutchik and Henry Kellerman, 305–39. New York: Academic Press, 1980.

Bell, Michael Mayerfeld. *Childerley: Nature and Morality in a Country Village.* Chicago: University of Chicago Press, 1994.

———. "The Ghost of Place." *Theory and Society* 26 (1997): 813–36.

Berger, Peter L., and Thomas Luckmann. *The Social Construction of Reality: A Treatise in the Sociology of Knowledge.* New York: Anchor Books, 1996.

Berkman, Alex J. "Foot Power Gives Them a Leg Up: Shoe String Approach Has Some Messengers Pedaling to Success." *Daily News,* April 20, 2009.

Bialobos, Philippe. *Messengers Style.* New York: Assouline Publishing, 2000.

Biernacki, Richard. "Language and the Shift from Signs to Practice in Cultural Inquiry." *History and Theory* 39 (2000): 289–310.

"The Biker's Creed." *Urban Death Maze* 6 (2000): 11.

Blauner, Robert. *Alienation and Freedom: The Factory Worker and His Industry.* Chicago: University of Chicago Press, 1964.

Borden, Iain. *Skateboarding, Space, and the City: Architecture and the Body.* New York: Berg, 2001.

Bourdieu, Pierre. *Distinction: A Social Critique of the Judgment of Taste.* Translated by Richard Nice. Cambridge, MA: Harvard University Press, 1984.

———. "The Kabyle House or the World Reversed." In *The Logic of Practice,* translated by Richard Nice, 271–83. Stanford, CA: Stanford University Press, 1990.

———. *The Logic of Practice.* Translated by Richard Nice. Stanford, CA: Stanford University Press, 1990.

———. *Outline of a Theory of Practice.* Translated by Richard Nice. New York: Cambridge University Press, 1977.

Boyle, Andy. "St. Petersburg Police Ticket 16 Bicyclists as Safety Campaign Begins." *St. Petersburg Times,* August 28, 2010.

Bozzo, Philip A. "Law-Flouting Couriers: To the Editor." *New York Times,* December 16, 1983.

Brake, Mike. *Comparative Youth Culture: The Sociology of Youth Cultures and Youth Subcultures in America, Britain, and Canada.* Boston: Routledge and K. Paul, 1985.

Burawoy, Michael. *Manufacturing Consent: Changes in the Labor Process under Monopoly Capitalism.* Chicago: University of Chicago Press, 1979.

Caillois, Roger. *Man, Play, and Games.* Translated by Meyer Barash. New York: Free Press of Glencoe, 1961.

Cairncross, Frances. *The Death of Distance: How the Communications Revolution Will Change Our Lives.* Boston: Harvard Business School Press, 1997.

Castells, Manuel. 1989. *The Informational City: Information Technology, Economic Restructuring, and the Urban-Regional Process.* Malden, MA: Blackwell.

Certeau, Michel de. *The Practice of Everyday Life.* Translated by Steven Rendall. Berkeley: University of California Press, 1984.

Cheney, Peter. "Bicycle Couriers in Love with Life on Mean Streets." *Toronto Star,* March 27, 1993.

Chetkovich, Carol. *Real Heat: Gender and Race in Urban Fire Service.* New Brunswick, NJ: Rutgers University Press, 1998.

Clarke, John. "Style." In *Resistance through Rituals: Youth Subcultures in Post-War Britain,* edited by Stuart Hall and Tony Jefferson, 175–81. London: Hutchinson and Company, 1976.

Cohen, Stanley. "Symbols of Trouble: Introduction to the Second Edition." In *Folk Devils and Moral Panics: The Creation of Mods and Rockers,* xlvii–lxxiv. 3rd ed. New York: Routledge, 2002.

Collins, Randall. *Interaction Ritual Chains.* Princeton, NJ: Princeton University Press, 2004.

——. "On the Microfoundations of Macrosociology." *American Journal of Sociology* 86 (1981): 984–1014.

Cooper, Michael. "On Sidewalk, Fatal Collision with Bicyclist." *New York Times,* November 20, 1997.

Csikszentmihalyi, Mihaly. *Beyond Boredom and Anxiety: The Experience of Play in Work and Games.* San Francisco: Jossey-Bass Publishers, 1975.

Cuerdon, Don. "I Was a New York City Bike Messenger: Five Days as a Rough Rider in the Big Apple's Hard Corps." *Bicycle Magazine,* March 1990, 74–84.

Culley, Travis Hugh. *The Immortal Class: Bike Messengers and the Cult of Human Power.* New York: Villard, 2002.

Daley, Beth, and Jason Pring. "Outcry over Bicycle Couriers: Civic Leader Still in Coma after Being Struck." *Boston Globe,* November 7, 1997.

Dennerlein, Jack Tigh, and John D. Meeker. "Occupational Injuries among Boston Bicycle Messengers." *American Journal of Industrial Medicine* 42 (2002): 519–25.

Denzin, Norman K. *On Understanding Emotion.* San Francisco: Jossey-Bass Publishers, 1984.

Donnelly, Peter, and Kevin Young. "Reproduction and Transformation of Cultural Forms in Sport: A Contextual Analysis of Rugby." *International Review for the Sociology of Sport* 20 (1985): 19–38.

Dowd, James J. "Hard Jobs and Good Ambitions: U.S. Army Generals and the Rhetoric of Modesty." *Symbolic Interaction* 23 (2000): 183–205.

Dowdy, Zachary R. "Chamber Urges Firms to Use Licensed Bike Couriers Only." *Boston Globe,* November 14, 1997.

Downey, Gregory J. *Telegraph Messenger Boys: Labor, Technology, and Geography, 1850–1950.* New York: Routledge, 2002.

Doyle, John, Phillip Messing, and Clemente Cisi. "Door Crash Kills Bike Messenger." *New York Post,* November 19, 2004.

Dubin, Robert. *Central Life Interests: Creative Individualism in a Complex World.* New Brunswick, NJ: Transaction Publishers, 1992.

Durkheim, Émile. *Division of Labor in Society.* Translated by W. D. Hall. New York: The Free Press, 1984.

——. "The Dualism of Human Nature and Its Social Conditions." In *On Morality and Society: Selected Writing,* edited by Robert N. Bellah, 149–63. Chicago: University of Chicago Press, 1973.

——. *The Elementary Forms of Religious Life.* Translated by Karen E. Fields. New York: Free Press, 1995.

——. *Suicide: A Study in Sociology.* Translated by John A. Spaulding and George Simpson. New York: Free Press, 1951.

Duvall, William H., III. "Pedestrians May Swear at Bicycle Messengers, but Companies Swear by Them." *Chicago Tribune,* November 3, 1991.

Eco, Umberto. "Social Life as a Sign System." In *Structuralism: An Introduction,* edited by David Robey, 52–72. Oxford: Clarendon Press, 1973.

Eisenberg, Susan. *We'll Call You If We Need You: Experiences of Women Working Construction.* Ithaca, NY: ILR Press, 1997.

Epstein, Cynthia F. "Encountering the Male Establishment: Sex-Status Limits on Women's Careers in the Professions." *American Journal of Sociology* 75 (1970): 965–82.

Fincham, Ben. "Generally Speaking People Are in It for the Cycling and the Beer: Bicycle Couriers, Subculture, and Enjoyment." *The Sociological Review* 55 (2007): 189–202.

Finder, Alan. "New York to Ban Bicycles on 3 Major Avenues." *New York Times,* July 23, 1987.

Fine, Gary Alan. "In the Company of Men: Female Accommodation and the Folk Culture of Male Groups." In *Manly Traditions: The Folk Roots of American Masculinities,* edited by Simon J. Bonner, 61–76. Bloomington: Indiana University Press, 2005.

Foucault, Michel. "Questions of Geography." In *Power/Knowledge: Selected Interviews and Other Writings, 1972–1977,* edited by Colin Gordon and translated by Colin Gordon, Leo Marshall, John Mepham, and Kate Soper, 63–77. New York: Pantheon Books, 1980.

Friedland, Roger, and Deirdre Boden. Introduction to *NowHere: Space, Time, and Modernity,* edited by Roger Friedland and Deirdre Boden. Berkeley: University of California Press, 1994.

Friedmann, John. "The World City Hypothesis." *Development and Change* 17 (1986): 69–83.

Fusco, Caroline. "Spatializing the (Im)Proper Subject: The Geographies of Abjection in Sport and Physical Activity." *Journal of Sport and Social Issues* 30 (2005): 5–28.

Gans, Herbert J. "Planning for People Not Buildings." *Environment and Planning* 1 (1969): 33–46.

———. "The Sociology of Space: A Use-Centered View." *City and Community* 1 (2002): 329–39.

———. *Urban Villagers: Group and Class in the Life of Italian-Americans.* New York: Free Press, 1962.

Gecas, Viktor. "In Search of the Real Self: Problems of Authenticity in Modern Times." In *Self, Collective Behavior, and Society,* edited by Gerald M. Platt and Chad Gordon, 139–54. Greenwich, CT: JAI Press, 1994.

Geertz, Clifford. "Deep Play: Notes on the Balinese Cockfight." In *Interpretations of Culture: Selected Essays,* 412–53. New York: Basic Books, 1973.

———. "Religion as a Cultural System." In *Interpretation of Cultures: Selected Essays,* 87–125. New York: Basic Books, 1973.

———. "Thick Description: Toward an Interpretive Theory of Culture." In *Interpretation of Cultures: Selected Essays,* 3–30. New York: Basic Books, 1973.

Geist, William. "Fastest Is Best as Messengers Pedal in Pursuit of a $100 Day." *New York Times,* December 2, 1983.

Giddens, Anthony. *Central Problems in Social Theory: Action, Structure, and Contradiction in Social Analysis.* Berkeley: University of California Press, 1979.

——. *The Consequences of Modernity.* Stanford, CA: Stanford University Press, 1990.

——. *The Constitution of Society: Outline of the Theory of Structuration.* Berkeley: University of California Press, 1984.

——. *Modernity and Self-Identity: The Self and Society in the Late Modern Age.* Stanford, CA: Stanford University Press, 1991.

——. *New Rules of Sociological Method: A Positive Critique of Interpretative Sociologies.* New York: Basic Books, 1976.

Gieryn, Thomas J. "Give Place a Chance: Reply to Gans." *City and Community* 1 (2002): 341–43.

——. "A Space for Place in Sociology." *Annual Review of Sociology* 26 (2000): 463–96.

Goodman, Walter. "Screen: 'Quicksilver.'" *New York Times,* February 14, 1986.

Gorz, André. *Farewell to the Working Class: An Essay on Post-Industrial Socialism.* Translated by Michael Sonenscher. London: Pluto Press, 1982.

Graham, David. "Wide Eyed." *Toronto Star,* June 18, 1998.

Green, Frank. "Bike Messengers Roll with Changes: Six San Diego Companies Still Doing Business in Internet Age." *San Diego Union-Tribune,* February 16, 2006.

Gregory, Derek. *Geographical Imaginations.* Cambridge, MA: Blackwell, 1994.

Gregory, Derek, and John Urry. Introduction to *Social Relations and Spatial Structures,* edited by Derek Gregory and John Urry, 1–8. London: Macmillan, 1985.

Harvey, David. *The Conditions of Postmodernity: An Inquiry into the Origins of Cultural Change.* Cambridge, MA: Blackwell, 1990.

——. *Paris, Capital of Modernity.* New York: Routledge, 2003.

——. *Social Justice and the City.* Baltimore: John Hopkins University Press, 1973.

Hayden, Dolores. *Redesigning the American Dream: The Future of Housing, Work, and Family Life.* New York: W. W. Norton, 1984.

Hebdige, Dick. *Subculture: The Meaning of Style.* New York: Routledge, 1979.

Hendershot, Steve. "The Business of Speed: Racing against E-mail and Fax Machines." *Crain's Chicago Business,* July 9, 2007.

Ho, Vanessa. "The Plea of a Dying Breed: Don't Kill the Bike Messenger." *Seattle Post-Intelligencer,* February 26, 2008.

Hochschild, Arlie Russell. "Emotion Work, Feeling Rules, and Social Structure." *American Journal of Sociology* 85 (1979): 551–75.

——. *The Managed Heart: Commercialization of Human Feeling.* Berkeley: University of California Press, 1983.

Horton, Dave. "Fear of Cycling." In *Cycling and Society,* edited by Dave Horton, Paul Rosen, and Peter Cox, 133–52. Burlington, VT: Ashgate, 2007.

Hurst, Robert. *The Art of Urban Cycling: Lessons from the Street.* Guilford, CT: Falcon, 2004.

Jason. "The Line." *Urban Death Maze* 2 (1999): 9.

Johnson, Kirk. "Bicycle Ban on 3 Midtown Avenues Is Delayed for a Week by Judge." *New York Times,* September 1, 1987.

Katz, Jack. *How Emotions Work.* Chicago: University of Chicago Press, 1999.

——. *Seductions of Crime: Moral and Sensual Attractions in Doing Evil.* New York: Basic Books, 1988.

Kenway, Jane, Anna Kraack, and Anna Hickey-Moody. *Masculinity beyond the Metropolis.* New York: Palgrave Macmillan, 2006.

Kidder, Jeffrey L. "Mobility as Strategy, Mobility as Tactic: Post-Industrialism and Bike Messengers." In *The Cultures of Alternative Mobilities: Routes Less Travelled,* edited by Phillip Vannini. Aldershot, UK: Ashgate Publishing, 2009.

Kimmel, Michael S. *The History of Men: Essays in the History of American and British Masculinities.* Albany, NY: State University of New York Press, 2005.

Kugelmass, Jack M. "I'd Rather Be a Messenger." *Natural History* 90 (1981): 66–73.

Leander, Tom. "Backpedaling." *New York Times,* July 21, 1984.

Lee, Felicia R. "Coping: And You Think Crime Is Down?" *New York Times,* March 4, 2001.

Lefebvre, Henri. *Everyday Life in the Modern World.* Translated by Sacha Rabinovitch. London: Penguin Press, 1971.

——. *The Production of Space.* Translated by Donald Nicholson-Smith. Oxford: Blackwell, 1991.

Leidner, Robin. *Fast Food, Fast Talk: Service Work and the Routinization of Everyday Life.* Berkeley: University of California Press, 1993.

Levy, Bob. "Do Messengers Own Their Bikes?" *Washington Post,* September 4, 1987.

——. "Hope amid the Spokes and Wheels." *Washington Post,* February 17, 1989.

——. "The Squirrel That Got Biked to Death." *Washington Post,* November 2, 1991.

Light, Donald. *Becoming Psychiatrists: The Professional Transformation of Self.* New York: W. W. Norton, 1980.

Lipset, Seymour Martin, Martin A. Trow, and James S. Coleman. *Union Democracy: The Internal Politics of the International Typographical Union.* Glencoe, IL: Free Press, 1956.

Lipsyte, Robert. "Coping: Voices from the 'Sweatshop of the Streets.' " *New York Times,* May 14, 1995.

Lloyd, Richard. *Neo-Bohemia: Art and Commerce in the Postindustrial City.* New York: Routledge, 2006.

Lukes, Steven. *Power: A Radical View.* New York: Macmillan, 1974.

Lyall, Sarah. "For Manhattan Couriers, Brakeless Bikes Are the Way to Go." *New York Times,* June 14, 1987.

Lyng, Stephen G. "Edgework: A Social Psychological Analysis of Voluntary Risk Taking." *American Journal of Sociology* 95 (1990): 851–86.

Lyotard, Jean-François. *The Postmodern Condition: A Report on Knowledge.* Translated by Geoff Benninton and Brian Massumi. Minneapolis: University of Minnesota Press, 1984.

Malinowski, Bronislaw. *Argonauts of the Western Pacific: An Account of Native Enterprise and Adventure in the Archipelagoes of Melanesian New Guinea.* New York: E. P. Dutton, 1950.

Manzo, John. "Social Control and the Management of 'Personal' Space in Shopping Malls." *Space and Culture* 8 (2005): 83–97.

Marcuse, Herbert. *One-Dimensional Man: Studies in the Ideology of Advanced Industrial Society.* Boston: Beacon Press, 1964.

Marx, Karl. "Economic and Philosophic Manuscripts of 1844." In *The Marx-Engels Reader,* edited by Robert C. Tucker, translated by Martin Milligan, 66–125. New York: W. W. Norton, 1978.

Marx, Karl, and Friedrich Engels. "Manifesto of the Communist Party." In *The Marx-Engels Reader,* edited by Robert C. Tucker, translated by Martin Milligan, 469–500. New York: W. W. Norton, 1978.

Massey, Doreen. *Spatial Divisions of Labor: Social Structures and the Geography of Production.* New York: Methuen, 1984.

McKillop, Peter. "The Uneasiest Riders: Manhattan's Streets Are Aswarm with 'Bikers,' a Death-Defying New Breed of Urban Messenger." *Newsweek,* November 25, 1985, 28.

Mead, George Herbert. *Mind, Self, and Society: From the Standpoint of a Social Behaviourist.* Chicago: University of Chicago Press, 1962.

Merrifield, Andy. *Henri Lefebvre: A Critical Introduction.* New York: Routledge, 2006.

Mionske, Bob. *Bicycling and the Law: Your Rights as a Cyclist.* Boulder, CO: VeloPress, 2007.

Mitchell, Richard G., Jr. *Dancing at Armageddon: Survivalism and Chaos in Modern Times.* Chicago: University of Chicago Press, 2002.

——. *Mountain Experience: The Psychology and Sociology of Adventure.* Chicago: University of Chicago Press, 1983.

Mucha, Thomas, and Mark Scheffler. "Entrepreneurs in Action: The Need for Speed; Efficiency Theories and Occupational Hazards of a Bike Messenger." *Business Chicago Powered by Crain's,* July 9, 2007. http://link.brightcove.com/services/player/bcp id980748097.

Muggleton, David. *Inside Subculture: The Postmodern Meaning of Style.* New York: Berg, 2000.

Nash, Dennison. "The Ethnologist as Stranger: An Essay on the Sociology of Knowledge." *Southwest Journal of Anthropology* 19 (1963): 149–67.

Nelson, Richard K. *Hunters of the Northern Ice.* Chicago: University of Chicago Press, 1969.

Nesbit, Damien. "Motherfuckin' Monstertrack Race Report." *Urban Death Maze* 6 (2000): 19–21.

Ng, Kwai Hang, and Jeffrey L. Kidder. "Toward a Theory of Emotive Performance: With Lessons from How Politicians Do Anger." *Sociological Theory* 28 (2010): 193–214.

Nippert-Eng, Christena. "Boundary Play." *Space and Culture* 8 (2005): 302–24.

——. *Home and Work: Negotiating Boundaries through Everyday Life.* Chicago: University of Chicago Press, 1996.

Oberdorfer, Don. "62 Missile Crisis, via Western Union." *Washington Post,* November 18, 1989.

Padavic, Irene. "The Re-Creation of Gender in a Male Workplace." *Symbolic Interaction* 14 (1991): 279–94.

Park, Robert E. "The City: Suggestions for the Investigation of Human Behavior in the Urban Environment." In *The City,* edited by Robert E. Park, Ernest W. Burgess, and Roderick D. McKenzie, 1–46. Chicago: University of Chicago Press, 1967.

Perry, David B. *Bike Cult: The Ultimate Guide to Human-Powered Vehicles.* New York: Four Walls Eight Windows, 1995.

Pfeiffer, Sacha. "Suit Argues Couriers Are Not Contractors." *Boston Globe,* March 7, 2007.

Pred, Allan. *Making Histories and Constructing Human Geographies: The Local Trans-formations of Practice, Power Relations, and Consciousness.* San Francisco: Westview Press, 1990.

———. *Place, Practice, and Structure: Social and Spatial Transformation in Southern Sweden, 1750–1850.* Cambridge, UK: Polity Press, 1986.

Prus, Robert. *Symbolic Interaction and Ethnographic Research: Intersubjectivity and the Study of Human Lived Experience.* Albany, NY: State University of New York Press, 1996.

Purnick, Joyce. "Koch Approves Bill Regulating Bicycle Messengers." *New York Times,* July 7, 1984.

Raab, Selwyn. "Teamsters Seeking to Form Bicycle Messengers' Union: Complaints Are Rife in a Tough, Risky Job." *New York Times,* October 30, 1994.

Rappaport, Roy A. *Ritual and Religion in the Making of Humanity.* New York: Cambridge University Press, 1999.

Ratner, Carl. "A Cultural-Psychological Analysis of Emotions." *Culture and Psychology* 6 (2000): 5–39.

Reilly, Rebecca "Lambchop." *Nerves of Steel: Bike Messengers in the United States.* Buffalo: Spoke and Word, 2000.

Richardson, Miles. "Culture and the Urban Stage: The Nexus of Setting, Behavior, and Image in Uban Places." In *Human Behavior and Environment: Advances in Theory and Research,* vol. 4, edited by Irwin Altman, Amos Rapoport, and Joachim F. Wohl-will, 209–41. New York: Plenum Press, 1980.

Ritzer, George. *The McDonaldization of Society: An Investigation into the Changing Character of Contemporary Social Life.* Thousand Oaks, CA: Pine Forge Press, 1993.

Roane, Kit R. "Bicyclists Are Police Priority after a Fatal Crash." *New York Times,* November 30, 1997.

Roy, Donald F. "Banana Time: Job Satisfaction and Informal Interaction." *Human Organization* 18 (1959): 158–68.

———. "Work Satisfaction and Social Reward in Quota Achievement: An Analysis of Piecework Incentive." *American Sociological Review* 18 (1953): 507–14.

Salaman, Graeme. *Community and Occupation: An Exploration of Work/Leisure Relationships.* London: Cambridge University Press, 1974.

Sanders, Eli. "Keeping Downtown Rolling: Flouting the Systems and Serving It, Messengers Deliver." *Pacific Northwest: Seattle Times Magazine,* August 29, 2003, 2–4.

Sassen, Saskia. *Cities in a World Economy.* Thousand Oaks, CA: Pine Forge Press, 2006.

———. *The Global City: New York, London, Tokyo.* Princeton, NJ: Princeton University Press, 1991.

Sassen, Saskia, and Robert Smith. *Post-Industrial Employment and Third World Immigration: Casualization and the New Mexican Migration in New York.* Papers on Latin America 26. New York: Columbia University, 1991.

Scheff, Thomas J. *Microsociology: Discourse, Emotions, and Social Structure.* Chicago: University of Chicago Press, 1990.

Scott, Allen J., John Agnew, Edward W. Soja, and Michael Storper. "Global City-Regions." In *Global City-Regions: Trends, Theory, and Policy,* edited by Allen J. Scott, John Agnew, Edward W. Soja, and Michael Storper, 11–30. New York: Oxford University Press, 2001.

Sennett, Richard. *The Corrosion of Character: The Personal Consequences of Work in the New Capitalism.* New York: W. W. Norton, 1998.

Sewell, William H., Jr. "The Concept(s) of Culture." In *Beyond the Cultural Turn,* edited by Victoria E. Bonnell and Lynn Hunt, 35–61. Berkeley: University of California Press, 1999.

——. "A Theory of Structure: Duality, Agency, and Transformation." *American Journal of Sociology* 98 (1992): 1–29.

Shamblin, Don H. "Brotherhood of Rebels: An Exploratory Analysis of a Motorcycle Outlaw Contraculture." PhD diss., State University of New York at Buffalo, 1971.

Simmel, Georg. "The Stranger." In *On Individuality and Social Forms,* edited and translated by Donald N. Levine, 143–49. Chicago: University of Chicago Press, 1971.

Small, Mario Luis. *Villa Victoria: The Transformation of Social Capital in a Boston Barrio.* Chicago: University of Chicago Press, 2004.

Smith, Danitia. "Fast Company: Wheel Tales of Manhattan's Bike Messenger." *New York Magazine,* January 13, 1986, 38–43.

Soja, Edward W. "Economic Restructuring and the Internationalization of the Los Angeles Region." In *The Capitalist City: Global Restructuring and Community Politics,* edited by Michael Peter Smith and Joe R. Feagin, 178–98. New York: Blackwell, 1987.

——. "Preface and Postscript." In *Postmodern Geographies: The Reassertion of Space in Critical Social Theory,* 1–9. New York: Verso, 1989.

——. "The Socio-Spatial Dialectic." In *Postmodern Geographies: The Reassertion of Space in Critical Social Theory,* 76–93. New York: Verso, 1989.

——. "The Spatiality of Social Life: Towards a Transformative Retheorization." In *Social Relations and Spatial Structures,* edited by Derek Gregory and John Urry, 90–127. London: Macmillan, 1985.

——. "Spatializations: A Critique of the Giddensian Version." In *Postmodern Geographies: The Reassertion of Space in Critical Social Theory,* 138–56. New York: Verso, 1989.

——. "Taking Los Angeles Apart: Some Fragments of a Critical Human Geography." *Environment and Planning D* 4 (1986): 255–72.

Sonnenstuhl, William J., and Harrison M. Trice. "The Social Construction of Alcohol Problems in a Union's Peer Counseling Program." *Journal of Drug Issues* 17 (1987): 223–54.

Spain, Daphne. *Gendered Space.* Chapel Hill: University of North Carolina Press, 1992.

Steele, Valerie. Introduction to *Messengers Style,* by Philippe Bialobos, 1–3. New York: Assouline, 2000.

Sutherland, Edwin. *The Professional Thief.* Chicago: University of Chicago Press, 1937.

Sutherland, Peter. *Pedal.* New York: PowerHouse Books, 2006.

Suttles, Gerald. *The Social Order of the Slum: Ethnicity and Territory in the Inner City.* Chicago: University of Chicago Press, 1968.

Swidler, Ann. *Talk of Love: How Culture Matters.* Chicago: University of Chicago Press, 2001.

Thompson, William E. "Handling the Stigma of Handling the Dead: Morticians and Funeral Directors." *Deviant Behavior* 12 (1991): 403–29.

——. "Hanging Tongues: A Sociological Encounter with the Assembly Line." *Qualitative Sociology* 6 (1983): 215–37.

Thompson, William E., Jackie L. Harred, and Barbara E. Burks. "Managing the Stigma of Topless Dancing: A Decade Later." *Deviant Behavior* 24 (2003): 551–70.

Tommasson, Robert E. "Fax Displacing Manhattan Bike Couriers." *New York Times,* March 19, 1991.

Tönnies, Ferdinand. *Community and Association (Gemeinschaft und Gesellschaft).* Translated by Charles P. Loomis. London: Routledge and Paul, 1955.

Turner, Victor W. "Betwixt and Between: The Liminal Period in *Rites de Passage.*" In *The Forest of Symbols: Aspects of Ndembu Ritual,* 93–111. Ithaca, NY: Cornell University Press, 1967.

——. "Symbols in Ndembu Ritual." In *The Forest of Symbols: Aspects of Ndembu Ritual,* 19–47. Ithaca, NY: Cornell University Press, 1967.

Vanderbilt, Tom. *Traffic: Why We Drive the Way We Do (and What It Says about Us).* New York: Alfred A. Knopf, 2008.

Wacquant, Loïc. *Body and Soul: Notebooks of an Apprentice Boxer.* New York: Oxford University Press, 2004.

——. "Towards a Social Praxology: The Structure and Logic of Bourdieu's Sociology." In *An Invitation to Reflexive Sociology,* edited by Pierre Bourdieu and Loïc J. D. Wacquant, 1–60. Chicago: University of Chicago Press, 1992.

Walker, Rob. *Buying In: The Secret Dialogue between What We Buy and Who We Are.* New York: Random House, 2008.

Weber, Max. *The Protestant Ethic and the Spirit of Capitalism.* Translated by Talcott Parsons. Upper Saddle River, NJ: Prentice Hall, 1958.

——. "Religious Rejections of the World and Their Directions." In *From Max Weber: Essays in Sociology,* edited and translated by H. H. Gerth and C. Wright Mills, 323–59. New York: Oxford University Press, 1946.

Werlen, Benno. *Society, Action, and Space: An Alternative Human Geography.* Translated by Gayna Walls. New York: Routledge, 1993.

Williams, Eddie. *Bike Messengers Life: New York City.* Madrid: La Fabrica, 2006.

Willis, Paul E. *Profane Culture.* Boston: Routledge and K. Paul, 1978.

——. "Shop Floor Culture, Masculinity, and the Wage Form." In *Working-Class Culture: Studies in History and Theory,* edited by John Clarke, Chas Critcher, and Richard Johnson, 185–98. London: Hutchinson, 1979.

Wolf, Daniel R. *The Rebels: A Brotherhood of Outlaw Bikers.* Toronto: University of Toronto Press, 1991.

Wolf, Kurt. "Surrender and Community Study: The Study of Loma." In *Reflections on Community,* edited by Arthur J. Vidich and Joseph Bensman, 233–63. New York: Wiley, 1964.

Wood, Michael. "My Brilliant Courier: Scarred Knees, Bloody Palms." *The Independent,* August 16, 1994.

The Worm and the Apple. "Barreling Bikes and Blind Buses." *New York Times,* July 3, 1984.

——. "Red Light for Reckless Bikes." *New York Times,* December 9, 1983.

Zaloom, Caitlin. *Out of the Pits: Traders and Technology from Chicago to London.* Chicago: University of Chicago Press, 2006.

Zukin, Sharon. *Landscapes of Power: From Detroit to Disney World.* Berkeley: University of California Press, 1991.

INDEX

Page numbers in italics refer to photographs.